Charles Thomson
and the Making of a New Nation, 1729-1824

Charles Thomson
and the Making
of a New Nation,
1729–1824

J. Edwin Hendricks

Rutherford • *Madison* • *Teaneck*
Fairleigh Dickinson University Press
London: Associated University Presses

© 1979 by Associated University Presses, Inc.

Associated University Presses, Inc.
Cranbury, New Jersey 08512

Associated University Presses
Magdalen House
136-148 Tooley Street
London SE1 2TT, England

Library of Congress Cataloging in Publication Data

Hendricks, James Edwin, 1935-
    Charles Thomson and the making of a new nation,
1729-1824.

    Bibliography: p. 194
    Includes index.
    1. Thomson, Charles, 1729-1824. 2. United
States—Politics and government—Revolution,
1775-1783. 3. United States—Politics and
government—1783-1789. 4. Statesmen—United
States—Biography. 5. United States.
Continental Congress—Biography. I. Title.

E302.6.T48H4   1979   973.3'092'4 [B] 77-74392
ISBN 0-8386-2072-8

PRINTED IN THE UNITED STATES OF AMERICA

Contents

Acknowledgments

Charles Thomson has been barely remembered by the nation that he helped create. Thomson himself contributed to his lack of fame and recognition. Much of his work was done in secret, behind the scenes, and he left few records. Late in his life Thomson destroyed most of his private papers, leaving prospective biographers little material with which to work.

Dissipating the mists that surround the memory of Charles Thomson is possible only because many people have assisted in completing this biography. Professor Bernard Mayo of the University of Virginia made the suggestion that started the project, and although his insistence on high scholarly standards made the completion of the task more difficult, his encouragement kept it going even when the problems seemed insurmountable. The Administration of Wake Forest University provided not only a congenial place to work in which teaching and the pursuit of knowledge is permitted to inspire scholarship, but also an excellent staff of colleagues, who have encouraged me along the way.

Wake Forest also offered assistance through its Research and Publications Fund and through an R. J. Reynolds research leave. Additional financial support was obtained in the form of grants from the Harriton Association, the Piedmont University Center, and the American Philosophical Society. Without this assistance and without the aid of innumerable librarians and historical society staffs (whose number is so great that to attempt to name any is to invite the omission of many more), this book could never have been written. The same is true of that multitude of persons who provided editorial assistance, advice on style and content, typing, proofreading, encouragement, prodding, and that kind, understanding tolerance that all authors must have and with which I have been blessed.

Introduction

The making of a new nation is a complex task. Many threads must be skillfully interwoven to make a strong national fabric that will withstand the wear and tear of time. So it is also in the making of a successful life and so it was with the making of the life of Charles Thomson. The threads of his life were so woven as to create a man whose contributions were lasting and whose accomplishments would stand long after his death.

To a remarkable degree, the threads that wove Charles Thomson's life contributed also to the making of the American national fabric. Thomson's education and early training were well founded in the classical traditions of the Old World but were laced through with threads of pragmatism from the American experience. Thomson's religion was of that curious blend of Deism and devotion that shaped the lives of many of the leaders of the emerging nation. His dedication to truth, his compassion for his fellow beings, and his overall humanitarianism are striking, not in their uniqueness but in the fact that they mirror similar characteristics in many of those whom the United States honors as its founding heroes.

Charles Thomson combined the unlikely trades of schoolmaster and political propagandist. He turned his own mutual improvement group into the American Philosophical Society, which served to unite the cultural and scientific leaders of the British Colonies in North America. He invested in rum, iron, and wool manufacturing to advance his own wealth and urged his fellow colonists to do likewise, not only for their own benefit but also for the advancement of the American economy.

With the passage of the Stamp Act, Thomson continued his work as a propagandist and became an ardent and radical supporter of the American cause. At the age of nearly thirty, married, and an importer of British goods, he made a most unlikely rebel leader. But he proved to be so radical that the mechanics and artisans of Philadelphia at first refused to follow his lead. As the years passed and British infringements on American rights continued, Thomson's following grew until he became the recognized "life of the cause of liberty" in Philadelphia. His successful leadership brought Philadelphia's White Oaks and other groups of carpenters, seamen, and workers into the radical American camp. Thomson, an early advocate of American unity, an early worker for independence, and a successful radical leader, became indeed "the Sam Adams of Philadelphia."

But Thomson was more than the perpetual radical. He favored retention of the Pennsylvania Assembly and opposed the democratic Pennsylvania Constitution of 1776. The radical Whig had become a moderate Whig and was shortly to become a moderate Republican. He shifted his emphasis to the nascent national government and when the First Continental Congress convened in 1774, Thomson became the secretary. He continued as secretary to the national government during the entire Revolution, serving as secretary to all the congresses that met from 1774 until 1789.

As secretary to Congress, Thomson was far more than a passive recorder of events in that representative body. He kept the records, handled the correspondence, submitted reports and recommendations, filled vacant offices temporarily, presided over committees and even over Congress itself, was behind-the-scenes policymaker and mediator, and was the single unifying link between all the congresses. Thomson was so closely associated with the Declaration of Independence that the Northern Ireland Tourist Board in the publicity for his birthplace proclaims that "it was he who penned the American Declaration of Independence." His signature and that of John Hancock were the only names officially and publicly affixed to the Declaration for more than six months after it was adopted.

As the Revolution progressed, and as governmental stability was established, Charles Thomson aided the nation-making process in other ways. He supported its financial, commercial, and diplomatic development. He resumed his interest in science and the practical arts and corresponded with other national leaders who shared his interest. He contributed to the publications of Thomas Jefferson and others. Thomson published his own *Notes on Farming*, which bore a uniquely American flavor, and he applied a pragmatic agricultural science to his estate north of Philadelphia.

Pushed from high office with the change in government, Thomson retired to Pennsylvania but did not abandon public life altogether. He corresponded with his old friends and acquaintances and shared memories with them of the days of the Revolution. He participated, not always successfully, in the political life of his state. He refused to write a history of the Revolution and destroyed most of his private papers lest he "undeceive future generations" about the "supposed wisdom and valor of our great men." But most of all he devoted himself to the translation of the Old and New Testaments from the Greek and to the publication of this contribution to knowledge in an Americanized English. He then prepared a "Harmony of the Gospels" in the words of his own translation.

When he died in 1824, in his ninety-sixth year, Charles Thomson could rest secure in the knowledge that he had contributed significantly to the making of a nation.

1

The Making of the Man

Charles Thomson arrived in America in 1739 as a father-less ten-year-old. Driven by a desire to become a scholar and to make something of himself, he succeeded far beyond any reasonable expectations. At an early age he escaped the social and economic pitfalls of becoming no more than a local craftsman and began acquiring the classical education that would fit him for a better life. Independent of thought and daring in action even as a student, he must have troubled his mentors greatly as he rejected catechism, preferring to slip away to purchase a volume of the *Spectator* to use in his studies. Having chosen the scholar-teacher's role, he came to Philadelphia and interested himself in the life of the city and province. Within a short time he formed a circle of young friends who met regularly for their own self-improvement and would soon enter the political struggles of the province. He adopted the peaceful Quakers' concern for the treatment of the Indians, involved himself in negotiations between the colonial authorities and the neighboring Delaware Indians, and became a confidant and propagandist for their cause. He became friend and eager pupil of Benjamin Franklin and made a place for himself in the society, economy, and power structure of the colony. Thomson combined New World practicality and rationalism with the European intellectual currents present in the colonies into an American Enlighten-ment philosophy of life that spelled success for himself and promised to be equally applicable to the making of a nation.

Charles Thomson first stepped on American soil at New Castle, Deleware, in 1739. Here he and three older brothers, William, Alexander, and John, were put ashore by the captain of the vessel that had brought them and their father from their homeland to the New World. The father, John Thomson, had died of a shipboard illness, leaving his sons an inheritance of little more than the opportunities offered by their new land.[1]

The Thomsons had left Gorteade Cottage, a substantial home near Londonderry in Northern Ireland from which the family had conducted a prosperous linen trade. John Thomson was a widower and had left two children, Matthew and Mary, behind as he and his other sons (Charles, barely ten years old, was the youngest) came to America in search of a brighter future. They joined a multitude of fellow Scotch-Irish who came to America during this era and who contributed greatly to the formation of the freedom-loving land that became their home.

The story of American history both before and after the Revolution is filled with the names of these doubly transplanted Scotsmen who came to America in search of a better life. These Scots, living in Northern Ireland, an area Irish by heritage and English by ownership and control, found themselves in an increasingly difficult situation. Presbyterian by tradition and choice, they occupied a region controlled by London Anglicans and were excluded from political affairs unless they took the sacrament of the Lord's Supper according to the rites of the Irish Anglican Church. Landless people in a strange country, they faced the ever-present reality of increasing rents and other pressures from absentee landlords. Unable to support themselves in Ulster, thousands determined that a better life was available elsewhere and many of them came to America.[2]

John Tomson's body was lowered into the water before the ship made land at New Castle. The Thomson boys were put ashore and the captain presented them with the meager store of cash that he alleged was all that was due them from their father's estate. The Thomson sons were to insist throughout their lives that their father had deposited a substantial sum in the ship's safe at the beginning of the voyage, but, lacking proof, they could offer no effective protest. With no other alternative, the older boys, William, Alexander, and John, found work until they could accumulate enough money to acquire land on which to establish themselves. Other provisions had to be made for Charles.

The boy was placed with the family of a New Castle blacksmith where his quickness and dexterity almost consigned him to the obscure life of a small-town craftsman. After seeing one member of the family make a nail, Charles went to the forge and made a duplicate that was so well constructed that the family decided to have him apprenticed to them to be trained as a smith.[3] But Charles had other ideas. Somewhere in his background—perhaps from his father whose initiative had brought them to the New World, or perhaps from a mother about whom little is known—the youngster had acquired a desire for an education. Charles realized that if he became a blacksmith his hopes for an education would never be achieved, and he acted with the young man's bravado that was to characterize him during his early years. He packed his belongings on his back and left. As he walked along, unsure of his destination, a lady of the neighborhood met him and offered him a ride. Probably thinking him a runaway servant, she questioned him as they rode. The young boy impressed her with his responses and the lady asked him of his future plans. Charles replied that he would like to be a scholar. Pleased with his answer and apparently accepting his tale at face value, the unknown benefactress took him to her home and, with some help from his brothers, arranged for Charles to enter school.[4]

After a brief period of preparation, Thomson entered the academy of Dr. Francis Alison at New London, Pennsylvania. Dr. Alison was a classical scholar of note, educated at the University of Glasgow. As master of the school, he arranged the courses so that the first years were spent in the study of Greek and Latin. Alison's interests included more than the classical languages, however, and he insisted that his students delve into other subjects. English grammar was stressed and comparisons were made with Greek and Latin constructions. Students abstracted articles from the *Spectator* or the *Guardian*, English journals that upheld the best standards of the language. Dr. Alison, though weak in these areas himself, also required that his students do work in mathematics, science, and other fields of modern interest.[5]

Thomson began his training at a time when there was great diversity in educational methods. Various European intellectual movements had differing impacts on the process of learning as practiced in early eighteenth-century America. The Enlightenment and its emphasis on rationalism had already turned Harvard away from the path of its Puritan founders; according to more conservative elements, Yale and William and Mary were guilty of similar tendencies. Rationalism in the upper levels of colonial education was reflected on the secondary level by attention to "practical studies" involving such areas as double-entry or "Italian" bookkeeping, mathematics, surveying, geography, and astronomy. "English Schools" taught English, French, and German in modification of the older dependence on classical instruction.

Various attempts were made to provide schooling for girls and for those who could not afford to pay. In and around Philadelphia at least, those interested in acquiring an education could get rudimentary training if they were willing to accept the charity of the Quakers and other groups. Those who were beyond the charity school and not quite up to the social, financial, and educational levels of the colleges might turn to the numerous "academies" of this period. Many ministers such as Dr. Alison kept a few students in their homes and trained them in many branches of learning. Alison's academy differed from the others largely in the number of students and in the excellence of instruction. The other academies all taught primarily the classics with diversions into English, mathematics, and practical science, varying in emphasis according to the taste of the schoolmaster.

Most of the schools that Thomson might have attended would have shown effects of the Great Awakening in one manner or another. The "log colleges" of the "new light" Presbyterians emphasized repentance and emotional conversion as the means of spreading Christianity, and their instruction was designed to prepare ministers for the revival fields. Formal study, whether classical, modern, or practical, suffered from a lack of attention. Dr. Alison was an "Old Side" Presbyterian and was devoted to scholarship. He reflected the latest in Scottish educational developments in the British

Isles. Alison regarded the log colleges as anti-intellectual and considered it his duty to rescue the American colonies from their influence.[6]

Thomson was fortunate to obtain a room in the Alison home, and during his stay there he was treated as one of the family. Dr. Alison imparted to him a further devotion to learning as well as a love of liberty. Alison was a dour person, and Thomson later reported that during the four or five years he lived at the Alison home, Dr. Alison never smiled or appeared in good humor. Charles failed to embrace the strict Presbyterian leanings of Dr. Alison. He once horrified the minister-teacher by proclaiming rebelliously that he did not know his catechism and had no intention of learning it, but would develop his own beliefs from a study of the scriptures.[7] Even so, from time to time during his life, Thomson displayed a religious orthodoxy that seemed out of context with his rationalistic leanings. Perhaps Dr. Alison's influence prevailed more than the young Thomson showed.

While at Dr. Alison's school Thomson showed a devotion to his studies as well as a spirit of adventure and daring. Readings in the *Spectator* were assigned as a guide to better English usage, but copies of the journal were scarce among the students. When he learned that a volume of the journal was available in Philadelphia, Thomson took his small store of money and walked forty-five miles to buy it. His purchase was so valuable that he was praised, not punished, for his unauthorized trip.[8]

For a time in the late 1740s, after leaving the New London Academy, Thomson operated a school on John Chambers' farm near the Pennsylvania-Delaware boundary. In a converted cooper's shop he organized a subscription school for the neighborhood children and continued there with much local fame until 1750, when he moved to Philadelphia.[9]

Philadelphia in 1750 was the cultural and commercial center of the British settlements in the new world. Growing rapidly, it was the second largest city in the British Empire by the time of the American Revolution. Mercantile interests extended trade in all directions across the seas and within the colonies. Ships at the Philadelphia docks engaged primarily in coastwise trade with the other colonies but many came from

England, Europe, and the West Indies. Trade went to New Jersey and Delaware, reached into the western frontier of the Penn province, branched down into the Shenandoah Valley of Virginia, and up the Susquehanna River into the lower regions of Pennsylvania's Wyoming Valley. The paths of commerce made communication with all these regions easier and helped establish cultural as well as commercial bonds.

The city itself had lost the well-ordered appearance given to it by its Quaker designers. Ten years after Thomson's arrival in Philadelphia, he saw an influential citizen of the city break his leg when his horse floundered in the mud on one of the main streets. Thomson and others immediately collected a fund and had the street paved—the first paved street in the city. Walkways, publicly lighted streets, and other conveniences did not appear in Philadelphia for years.[10]

Despite the lack of many things that are considered necessities in a city of today, Philadelphia was greatly advanced in the social, educational, and cultural fields. An aristocracy of wealth was developing among the more prosperous merchants and landowners. The most successful had country estates along with lavish town houses. Those of moderate wealth resided in the suburban areas and the more exclusive districts of the city. The many "tradesmen" and "mechanics" of the middle class, though showing signs of desiring status and power, took little part in the conduct of affairs, social or otherwise, in the Philadelphia of this mid-eighteenth-century era. Their ideals and standards were, as a rule, set by the classes above them and they emulated such standards rather than originating new ones. This often led to good things. Thomson, as a Latin and Greek instructor, found that many children from the lower levels of society sought classical as well as practical knowledge so that they might conduct themselves with ease in polite society. Perhaps they were merely seeking upper-class status, but they were gaining a rich background that would later enable them to enjoy a fuller life.[11]

Another traditional means for personal advancement was the acquiring of influential friends. Thomson as a boy had instinctively used this method when he obtained the assistance of the New Castle lady in his search for an education. Upon his arrival in Philadelphia Thomson appears to have consciously sought out Benjamin Franklin and asked his assistance and advice. Thomson's early meeting with Franklin and his friendship with this great Philadelphian served Thomson well. It was at Franklin's suggestion that Thomson applied to the trustees of the Academy of Philadelphia, the forerunner of the University of Pennsylvania, for a position as tutor in Latin and Greek. The academy was a newly established institution that had developed from a plan published by Franklin in 1749. The trustees considered Thomson's application on December 17, 1750, and upon the recommendation of David Martin, its rector, the academy employed Thomson at a salary of sixty pounds a year.[12]

The program of the academy had a uniquely American cast. Classical languages made up a large part in the curriculum, but modern languages, drawing, accounting, and an emphasis on clear, concise writing were also included in the studies. Mechanics, the development of inventions, natural history, and other useful knowledge were stressed along with the usual study of the classics.[13]

In December 1751, only a year after Thomson began his duties, David Martin, the first rector of the Academy, died. Martin had also served as head of the Latin and Greek School, so this position had to be filled. Through Thomson the trustees learned of Dr. Francis Alison, who was offered the position so that Thomson and his former instructor were reunited. The two men devoted much work to the teaching of the classical languages and actively supported the other aspects of the liberal program of the academy.[14]

During Thomson's years at the academy, Benjamin Franklin and Thomson developed a friendship that endured until Franklin's death in 1790. Franklin, after retiring from the printing business, was a man of some leisure and agreed to advise Thomson's further study and reading. With Franklin's aid Thomson devoted himself to some areas of study that were neglected in his earlier training. Franklin's widespread interests covered many fields, and his advice was invaluable to a young man vitally interested in improving himself.[15] With Franklin's scope of interests leading an already active, well-trained mind, Thomson developed a sense of inquiry that would involve him in most of the intellectual movements of his day. Thomson continued as a tutor in the Latin and Greek School until March 1755, when he resigned. The trustees expressed their satisfaction with Thomson's performance of his duties and directed Dr. Alison to secure a replacement.[16]

Thomson's resignation from the academy marked an increasingly active involvement in the public affairs of the colony and, as has been the case with many academicians entering public life, it resulted in a considerable improvement in his own fortune. Benjamin Franklin seems to have directed young Thomson in his pursuit of a richer life, and Thomson followed some of the same techniques that Franklin had used when he was younger. In 1727, Franklin, newly arrived in Philadelphia, gathered a few congenial and ingenious persons together and formed a "Junto," which met in a tavern every Friday night. These men devoted themselves to the discussion of self-improvement and topics of timely concern. Matters of morals and reputation, business opportunities, possibilities of making influential acquaintances, reports of new medicines and remedies, and other similar topics were considered over friendly glasses of wine. The "Junto" continued its existence long after its members rose to prominence in the city and similar groups were organized by other interested men.[17]

When Thomson arrived in Philadelphia in 1750, Franklin helped him obtain a teaching position and make a place for himself in the city. On Franklin's advice, Thomson and some of his newly made friends founded a mutual improvement society with aims similar to those of Franklin's old "Junto." Twelve members, all near Thomson's own age of twenty-one, joined the new group. All were interested in advancing themselves in social, business, and intellectual circles in Philadelphia. Thomson and William Franklin, son of the founder of the old "Junto," were the two leading members of the group and were responsible for maintaining interest in the group's activities. Contacts that Thomson made through the society helped him enter many influential Philadelphia circles and become a part of that city's life and culture.[18]

During this period of his life Thomson kept a notebook in which he abstracted books that he read and made notes on things that seemed pertinent to society as a whole or to his own advancement. This notebook, portions of which date from 1754, contained a list of "Questions asked by a Society meeting weekly in Philadelphia for their mutual Improvement in Knowledge." Included in the list of inquiries were requests for suggestions about new books, stories "agreeable for telling in conversation," and other devices for making one's way in society. Questions dealing specifically with prospering economically included "have you lately heard of any Citizen's thriving well, and by what means?" and "Have you lately heard how any present rich man here, or elsewhere, got his Estate?" A bit more altruistic but still self-interested question was "Do you think of any thing at present in which the Junto may be of service to mankind, to their Country, to their Friends or to themselves?"[19] In this group of young men concerned for their world and their role in it, Thomson led the way.

Thomson had chosen an exciting and complex time and place in which to make his way in the world. The American colonies were on the verge of a maturity that was to lead to conflict and separation from the mother country, and Thomson and men of his generation would direct the emergence of the new nation. Philadelphia and Pennsylvania were to play crucial roles in the process of nation making. Thomson's part in that process demonstrates that devotion to principles, the application of reason, and astute analysis of the situation mixed well in the life of the Pennsylvania colony in the middle of the eighteenth century.

The 1750s was a decade of political, social, and intellectual turmoil for Philadelphia. John Kinsey, longtime leader of the Pennsylvania Quakers, died in 1750 and was succeeded by Isaac Norris II as speaker of the Pennsylvania Assembly and by Israel Pemberton as clerk of the Pennsylvania and New Jersey yearly Quaker meeting. Not only was the political and religious control of the Quakers divided between two men of differing views, but these two elements of Quaker life were shortly to split Quaker influence into schismatic camps. The conflict between Quaker pacifism and Quaker politics would bring Quakers and the Quaker colony much grief in the coming years, and Charles Thomson was involved in the events that precipitated the division.[20]

As Quaker forces lapsed into divided weakness, proprietary and royal forces tried to wrest some powers from the provincial assembly. The assembly had gained control during a period of proprietary neglect and Quaker unity and, as long as John Kinsey lived, this unity and control had not been threatened. Now increasing Indian attacks along the frontier served as a catalyst for the ensuing struggle, and Benjamin Franklin stood as a dominant figure against all the turmoil—mediating, negotiating, leading here, pushing there, and always working for the good of Philadelphia, Pennsylvania, the British Colonies of North America, the British Empire, humanity as a whole, and himself, in something approximating that order.

Into the midst of this turbulent society Charles Thomson injected himself as a scholar, teacher, and generally ambitious young man. At the same time Thomson faced a dilemma as to the nature of life and its meaning. In his notebook, dated April 3, 1754, is the following:

> Is my life and conduct such as it ought to be? How came I into being? Certainly not by chance. For chance never could produce such a regular well ordered machine, in which appears so much design, so much harmony, and such a nice adjustment of the several parts. I must then be the work of some intelligent Being. If so, there must have been some design in bringing me into existence. All these powers of soul & body which I find myself endowed with, plainly indicate that I was formed for some end. That end must be worthy the divine author.[21]

Such sentiments bespeak much of Thomson's religious background and training. His grandfather had been a Presbyterian minister in Northern Ireland, and Thomson is believed to have read the Bible through by the age of six. His family training was reinforced by the strict Presbyterianism of Dr. Francis Alison while Thomson lived in the Alison home during his stay at the New London School. Although Thomson rejected the strict sectarianism of his training, he retained the moralistic doctrines throughout his life.

The selection from Thomson's notebook also illustrates another trend prominent in the thoughts of the young man. The rationalism of the Enlightenment was an ever-present part of the intellectual life of America and Europe at this age. Alison was himself a reflection of the Scottish Enlightenment and manifested many of its rationalistic tendencies. Although Alison was the minister of the First Presbyterian Church during the 1750s and Thomson was one of his more active members, Thomson at the same time showed the enlightened influences of Deist Benjamin Franklin—perhaps the archetype of the American Enlightenment.

Thomson's enlightened and rationalistic interests led him in many directions, some of which are discussed at length in the next chapter. As for his religious attitudes, the evidence indicates that he preferred to worship God in the way which he, with characteristic independence and confidence in his own intellectual ability, conceived proper. Several of the members of Thomson's mutual improvement society were Quakers who held that the proper way to discover the true character of God was to study and contemplate within oneself. So from his own inclination, and from the spirit of the times, Thomson evolved an individualistic and inquiring faith.[22]

One of the tenets of this faith, and the rationalism from which it came, was a concern for the condition of one's fellow man. This humanitarianism, closely associated with Quakerism, included many reforms in the laws and practices of the eighteenth century. Most especially included was a general feeling of respect for all men without regard for their status and condition.[23] William Penn had demonstrated this theory in practice by his treatment of the Indian inhabitants of Pennsylvania as he worked to establish his colony. Penn had respected Indian rights; he paid for their lands that he wished to use and he generally treated them as fellow human beings. Such treatment gained the friendship of the area's Indians and gave the early Pennsylvania settlers a time of peace. After Penn's death his proprietorship passed to his sons who abandoned their father's humane treatment of the Indians. An influx of squatters along the frontiers and increasing conflict with the French over the frontier lands also contributed to rising Indian difficulties.[24]

Continuing Indian unrest was accompanied by political unrest in Philadelphia and London. During the 1750s the proprietors and their supporters in Pennsylvania gradually developed into a unified faction that consistently opposed the "Quaker Party" led initially by Isaac Norris and ultimately by Benjamin Franklin. At the same time a group of pacifist Quakers, under the leadership of Israel Pemberton, began to question not only the actions of the proprietors but also the very participation of Quakers in government—especially a government that was under increasing pressure to use force to defend the colony from Indian and French attacks. To give voice to this pacifist attitude, Israel Pemberton organized the Friendly Association in 1756.[25]

The Friendly Association consisted largely of Quaker businessmen and political leaders. They opposed any measure of warfare against the Indians, and insisted that most Indian troubles had been brought on by the misconduct of the proprietors or their representatives in America. One of their strongest opponents in Pennsylvania politics was Benjamin Franklin, who urged the province to provide an active defense system against possible Indian attacks.

Charles Thomson entered this political arena—young, idealistic, and ambitious. Thomson's initial contacts ran the entire range of the Pennsylvania political spectrum. He was indebted to Franklin for his appointment to the Philadelphia Academy. He had developed friendships with Norris, Pemberton, and a host of lesser lights in both Quaker camps. Through the administration of the academy he had contact with the proprietary group in Philadelphia (although it appears that these contacts produced no friendships).

Thomson's day-to-day life during the early 1750s left few records but events were happening around him that would shape the life of the colony for years to come. Within months after Thomson's employment at the academy, Benjamin Franklin yielded to pressures from the Quakers and was elected to the Pennsylvania Assembly. The Assembly ordered a bell from England and Thomson may have been on hand when the bell was uncrated, tried, and cracked. In the same year, 1752, Franklin continued his work with electricity and performed his famous kite experiment. In 1753, Franklin was named deputy postmaster general for the colonies and persuaded the proprietors to contribute 15,000 pounds to the academy. In 1755, the academy received a charter as the College, Academy, and Charitable School of Philadelphia.[26]

As these things happened, Thomson was doubtlessly aware of events occurring outside the colony that posed a threat to its well-being. In October 1753, George Washington went into the Ohio region to demand the withdrawal of the French from that area. The French refused and within a short time a full-fledged war faced the American colonies. Meeting at Albany, New York, in July 1754, representatives from the colonies could not agree on a suitable program to provide for their common defense despite an ingenious plan prepared by Franklin. Indian attacks increased along the colonial frontier, and the Pennsylvania Indians proved more and more restless. When the Pennsylvania Assembly was convened to provide for the defense of the colony, conflict erupted between proprietors and Quakers, pacifist and nonpacifist Quakers, Quakers and non-Quakers, and frontiersmen and city dwellers. Complicated by Quaker determination to tax the proprietors' lands, this conflict would continue for years and would contribute to the rise of revolutionary sentiments in Pennsylvania.[27]

As Thomson actively entered the political life of the colony, it was on the side of Israel Pemberton and the Friendly Association—a choice that temporarily placed him at odds with Franklin, his benefactor and friend. Although Franklin was working avidly to provide for the defense of the colony, the Friendly Association seemed to be working primarily to embarrass the proprietors. The association repeatedly demanded fair treatment for the Indians and redress for earlier misdeeds by representatives of the proprietors and by whites who encroached on Indian lands. Israel Pemberton and his friends, including Thomson, appeared convinced that, if treated fairly, the Indians would resume their friendship with the English and restrain their attacks on the frontier, and peace would return to Pennsylvania.[28]

As the early months of 1755 passed, Thomson found it increasingly difficult to continue his association with the Philadelphia Academy. Shortly after Thomson submitted his resignation in March, Provost William Smith placed himself squarely in the camp of the proprietors by the publication of his *Brief State of the Province of Pennsylvania*, which blamed the Quakers for the poor defense of the colony. That July the possibility of invasion grew even more imminent as General Braddock was defeated by the French at Fort Duquesne despite much effort in his behalf by Franklin and other Pennsylvanians.

In September 1755, Thomson was employed as master of the Friends' Public School of Philadelphia. His salary was 150 pounds a year—a rather high salary indicating that perhaps his Quaker employers were paying him for more than merely running the school. The fact that Thomson spent much of his time for the next several months attending Indian treaties and propagandizing the Quaker view of what went on there may well be some indication of what Thomson was being paid to do.[29]

But Thomson was also hired to run a school. The Friends' School was in the heart of Philadelphia, only a block from the State House, where the Assembly convened. Supported by voluntary contributions and controlled by the Quakers, the school excluded no one because of religious beliefs and had limited arrangements for paying the tuition of poor scholars. Thomson, well on the way up the ladder of success himself, was in a position to assist other poor children in acquiring an education. Thomson, as master, ran the school, taught those courses he was qualified to teach, and employed and supervised the other teachers. His breadth of interests assured a proper balance between classical, scientific, and practical knowledge.[30]

At the same time he was preparing for the fall school session, Thomson apparently spent much time in the colonial archives familiarizing himself with the Indian affairs of Pennsylvania, including a thorough study of all the treaties on record between the Penns and the neighboring Indian tribes. In the records Thomson found an account of good relations between Indians and white men that had gradually gone sour. William Penn's favorable treatment of the Indians had established an early friendship that was destroyed as Indian lands were more and more threatened by white settlement. Vague treaties, an imperfect understanding of land ownership on the part of the Indians, and the inability of the proprietors to prevent unauthorized settlements all contributed to further misunderstanding. The Delaware and Shawnee Indians, Pennsylvania's nearest neighbors, had special grievances. They were being driven from their Susquehanna River homes by what they considered to be dishonest measures. When the English were defeated by the French at Fort Duquesne in 1755, the Indians grew even more ready to quarrel with their former English allies.[31]

Concerned about the threats to their lands and supported by the French, the Indians began a general revolt. The spark that set off the frontier warfare came from a Jersey Indian known as Teedyuscung. This well-meaning but frequently drunken and untrustworthy native succeeded in uniting the Susquehanna Delawares, the Shawnees, the Mohicans, and some local stragglers from various other tribes into one large fighting tribe. In October, only a month after Thomson went to work for the Quakers, Indian warfare broke out on the frontiers of Pennsylvania. During the winter of 1755-1756 forts were constructed along the Pennsylvania frontier from Fort Hamilton in the Blue Mountains to the Maryland border. But the Indian raids continued. Finally, in April 1756, Governor Robert Hunter Morris declared war against the Delawares and attacked their towns.[32]

Open warfare between the Indians and the province was the last thing the Friendly Association wanted. Thomson and the Quaker leaders immediately proposed an attempt to restore peace. From May through August 1756, the Quakers tried to negotiate with Teddyuscung and his warring tribesmen. Scattered Indian raids continued until November, when a new conference was held at Easton between Teedyuscung and the new provincial governor, William Denny. Charles Thomson and Israel Pemberton, leader of the Friendly Association, were present to advise the Indians. Thomson was present because of his knowledge of the Indian treaties and took shorthand notes during the conference as he had done at some earlier meetings with the Indians.

When Governor Denny asked the Indians the cause of their unrest and their attacks against the Pennsylvania settlements, Teddyuscung began to complain about the unfair land purchases of the proprietors. The governor's secretary, Richard Peters, threw down his pen and said that the Quakers had encouraged these claims and that he refused to record them. Teedyuscung heard this and inquired if Thomson, the unofficial secretary, had recorded his complaints. Thomson had taken down the entire speech, and the Indian seemed pleased that someone had noted his words. Governor Denny then asked the Delaware chief how much money would be required to satisfy all the Indians concerned in the unfair purchases. Teedyuscung surprised eveyone by replying that he had no authority to speak for the other Indians, but that he would bring them all down to meet with the governor and settle the matter. The conference then broke up with little accomplished.[33]

The Delawares were pleased to find that Charles Thomson's unofficial minutes supported their claims and they immediately resolved to adopt him as a member of the tribe. In a solemn ceremony he was named "Wegh-wu-law-mo-end,"—"the man who talks the truth." Years later, during the rumors and uncertainties of the Revolutionary War, Thomson helped the Continental Congress retain the faith and support of the people by insisting that full and honest reports be issued, under his signature, concerning all battles and engagements whether won or lost. His reputation was such that his reports were in great demand. The reports were welcomed with such remarks as, "Here comes the truth; here is Charles Thomson!"[34] Thomson's devotion to truth as he saw it remained a characteristic throughout his life.

While Teedyuscung and the governor were negotiating at Easton in November 1756, a party of Indians surprised one of the forts on the Pennsylvania frontier. The inhabitants of the post were captured, killed, or driven away and the fort was burned. Despite renewed warfare the Assembly and the governor continued to quarrel over money matters. On January 28, 1757, the Assembly sent Franklin to London to force the proprietors to allow taxation to their estates in Pennsylvania. Before leaving, Franklin persuaded the Assembly to pass an appropriation omitting, for the time being, the tax on the Penn lands. The governor signed the bill and the defense of the colony was provided for—but the Assembly members insisted that they had yielded only to necessity. In April, Franklin sailed for London to press their cause.[35]

In Philadelphia, meanwhile, the Friendly Association requested permission to look at the proprietors' copies of all the treaties with the Delaware Indians. Many of the treaties were not registered and were available only in the minutes of the governor and his council. The governor refused to allow an examination of these records and Charles Thomson, who had been copying and making extracts of the treaties for the association, was forced to be content with those records already public.[36]

In July 1757, Thomson attended another conference at Easton between Governor Denny and Teedyuscung. Accompanying Teedyuscung were representatives for the four nations of which he was chieftain, as well as representatives of the Six Nation Confederation. Governor Denny arrived on July 20, and deliberations began the next day. Teedyuscung addressed the governor and voiced the hope that the mistakes of past meetings might not hinder the making of peace. He then requested that he be allowed to appoint a secretary to take minutes of the proceedings along with the secretary of the province. Governor Denny first refused. Teedyuscung was resolute in demanding this right, and for four days he refused to discuss any business. Seeing that the determined Indian would wreck the conference rather than relinquish his demand for a secretary, George Croghan and some other members of the governor's party persuaded Denny to give his assent. The Indian appointed his friend from the last Easton conference, Charles Thomson, as secretary, and the negotiations began on the twenty-sixth.[37]

Thomson's charges of proprietary misconduct at this treaty are typical of the accusations levied throughout his accounts of Indian affairs. According to Thomson the proprietary interests kept Teedyuscung and the other Indians so drunk that they could not negotiate in order to prevent their examining the land purchase records, which would reveal proprietary wrongdoing. When the deeds and records were at last presented for the Indians to examine, Thomson found that a treaty of 1718, which outlined more specifically the boundaries of several previous purchases, was not included. Thomson and the Quakers believed this was done knowingly so that the vague boundaries of the other treaties might work to the advantage of the proprietors. Knowing that a revelation of this fact would irritate the Indians and perhaps lead to renewed hostilities, they refrained from bringing the omission to Teedyuscung's notice. But Thomson informed the governor by letter that he had discovered the 1718 deed to be missing and protested this violation of the "Honor of his Majesty, King George, and the real interest of the province. . . ."[38]

Teedyuscung still refused to make a settlement with the governor or with Sir William Johnson, superintendent of Indian affairs. Instead he insisted that the treaties and documents be sent to London and the matter settled by the king of England. Governor Denny and his party strongly suspected that Thomson and the Quakers were behind this move. Pemberton and his group appeared as interested in embarrassing the proprietors in London over the land purchases as in seeing justice done to the Indians. The Delaware chief finally won his point; the matter of the disputed land purchases was submitted to the king of England for settlement. Before the conference adjourned, Teedyuscung requested supplies from the proprietors to defend himself against the French and their Indian allies. He had returned completely to the English camp.[39].

Thomson continued his friendship with Teedyuscung during 1757 and 1758. The Delawares had resettled in the Wyoming Valley (along the Susquehanna River) and were short of food and provisions. The Friendly Association sent one of their members, John Hughes, to finish the job of building log cabins for the Indians, a task that had been started the year before. In spite of gifts of food and provisions and the log huts, the Delawares and their neighbors were restless. In

June 1758, Thomson and Frederick Post, a Moravian missionary who had married a Delaware convert, were sent out by Governor Denny to deliver messages of peace and reassurance. Perhaps the governor, who was seeking friends wherever he could find them, sent Thomson on the mission in hopes that he might be swayed to the proprietary position. Since he was not a Quaker, his close association with the Friends seemed a little unusual, and Denny was interested in gaining the friendship of as many as possible of those who opposed his superiors. Denny would have been less sanguine about Thomson's conversion to the proprietary cause had he known that Thomson was the author of articles advocating a "soft" Indian policy, which were published in the *Pennsylvania Journal* just prior to his departure.[40]

When Thomson and Post reached Indian territory, they found that some marauding Seneca braves were passing through. Friendly Indians accompanying the party advised them not to venture all the way to Teedyuscung's village for fear of attack. Teedyuscung was informed of their coming and met them at the edge of the Indian lands. He reported that many of the neighboring Indians were still dissatisfied with the treatment they were receiving from the English and favored an alliance with the French. The young men of the Seneca tribes were especially friendly to the French and were striving to place the entire Seneca nation under French control. Teedyuscung agreed to bring all the dissatisfied tribes together for a conference with the Pennsylvania governor.[41]

Immediately upon their return to Philadelphia, Thomson and Post reported the results of the meeting to the governor and the Assembly. Thomson's report was very favorable to Teedyuscung, and Governor Denny realized that under no conditions could Thomson be brought to support the proprietary party. A few weeks later, when Post was sent on a similar mission, the governor refused to appoint Thomson as his colleague.[42]

Thomson was eager to return to Indian territory to assist in freeing some whites who were still held captive. He believed that Governor Denny kept him from going for fear that he would provoke the Indians by more talk of their land controversies. Isaac Norris, however, blamed the proprietary council rather than Denny for refusing to let Thomson accompany Post again. Norris also commented that Thomson's not going was "kinder to him as he had at that Time the Great Affair of Matrimony in his Head which he has since reduced to practice and permanency."[43]

Thomson's marriage to Ruth, daughter of James Mather, of Chester, Pennsylvania, probably took place in 1758. Thomson met the Mather family through Ruth's brother, Joseph, who entered the Philadelphia Academy as a student in the same year that Thomson became an instructor. Joseph was an active member of the "Young Junto" until he left Philadelphia in the late 1750s. The young married couple took up residence at 324 Market Street in a house owned by Dr. Francis Alison, just across the street from the Benjamin Franklin home. Ruth Mather seems to have brought much property to Thomson's household, and the marriage may be seen as yet another step in Thomson's social and economic growth. The marriage was reportedly a very happy one until it was marred by the death of newborn twin boys and the resultant declining health of Ruth Mather Thomson, which ultimately led to her death in about 1770.[44]

Meanwhile Teedyuscung's claims to the land on the Susquehanna River were being considered across the Atlantic. As he had agreed, Governor Denny forwarded the Indian claims to London where he expected the claims to have little chance against the proprietary position. Then the antiproprietary party in the Pennsylvania Assembly discovered that Charles Thomson's minutes of July 1756 disagreed in several places with those of the governor's secretary. They immediately sent Thomson's minutes to Benjamin Franklin, their representative in London. Israel Pemberton, at odds with the politically oriented Quakers who were behind Franklin's presence in England, had sent a copy of Thomson's accounts of the negotiations to his agents in London as early as January 1758, but Franklin did not receive his copy until late May or early June. Franklin made use of the information in many ways, including circulating the manuscript minutes to influential friends. Finally he obtained promise of a hearing before the Board of Trade in May 1759.[45]

As time for the hearing on the Deleware claims neared, Franklin arranged for Thomson's account of proprietary mistreatments of the Indians to be published. The anonymous *An Enquiry into the Causes of the Alienation of the Delaware and Shawanese Indians from the British Interest, and into Measures taken for Recovering their Friendship* was a scathing attack on the Penn proprietors and their handling of Indian affairs. It served as an effective counterweight to William Smith's *A Brief State of the Province of Pennsylvania* (1755) and *A Brief View of the Conduct of Pennsylvania* (1756), which had praised the Penns and blamed the Quakers for the colony's troubles.[46]

The main portion of the *Enquiry* was Thomson's discussion of Indian affairs. Recognizing that Thomson's closely reasoned analysis of the numerous Indian treaties and the conflicting claims would not attract readers, Franklin added "The Journal of Christian Frederick Post ... among the Ohio Indians in 1758." This vivid record of the Moravian missionary's successful efforts to regain the friendship of the Ohio Indians during the campaign against Fort Duquesne supplied a popular appeal that ensured wider circulation. Two letters, one by Thomson and one by Israel Pemberton of the Friendly Association, made the publication more complete. The work was published in early March 1759, almost two months prior to the hearing before the Board of Trade.[47]

Franklin was delighted with the reception accorded the *Enquiry*. In April 1759, he reported to Joseph Galloway, rising leader of the antiproprietary faction in Pennsylvania that the book was "more read than I expected." On April 12 Franklin wrote to his wife: "Tell Mr. Thomson that I have just heard the proprietor is writing an answer to his book and will pay off him and the Quakers."[48]

The *Enquiry* condemned the proprietary dealings with the Indians. From his studies of Indian treaties for the Friendly Association and the information gained as secretary to Teedyuscung, Thomson had gathered impressive evidence of fraudulent land purchases. He especially condemned the Walking Purchase of 1737 in which Thomson claimed the proprietors had employed professional "walkers" who virtually ran rather than walked and who by various devices more than doubled the size of the purchase. The extent of this and other proprietary land grabs was detailed in a map drawn by Thomas Jeffreys. After recounting the series of Easton Conferences as seen through the Friendly Association eyes, Thomson concluded his appeal for justice for the Indians:

> Here then, the Affair rests. If the proper Papers, and true State of the Case be laid before the King and Council for a just Determination; if the Indians be assisted in making this Settlement, secured in their Property, and instructed in Religion and the civil Arts, agreeable to their Request, and the Trade with them regulated and set on such a Footing that they may be secure from Abuse, there is not the least Doubt but the Alliance and Friendship of the Indians may be forever secured to the British Interest; but, should these Things be neglected the Arms of the French are open to receive them.
>
> We have already experienced the Cruelties of an Indian War, and there are more Instances than one to show they are capable of being our most useful Friends or most dangerous Enemies. And whether, for the future, they are to be the one or the other, seems now to be in our own Power. How long Matters will rest so, or whether, if the present Opportunity be neglected, such another will ever return, is altogether uncertain. It becomes Men of Wisdom and Prudence to leave nothing to Chance where Reason can decide.[49]

The publication of Thomson's *Enquiry* was followed by a meeting of the Board of Trade at which Franklin exhibited copies of all the disputed treaties and deeds. Evidence was presented that the proprietors were depriving the Indians of their lands by unjust methods. The proprietary influence was strong in London, however, and the Board of Trade did not rule directly against the Penns. Instead they referred the case to Sir William Johnson of New York, the crown's representative to the Six Nations, who, although he did not grant the Delawares the lands they claimed, did allow the Delawares to remain in their homes in the Wyoming Valley.

Thomson's *Enquiry*, though polemical in form and incendiary in content, was instrumental in obtaining a peaceful settlement of the dispute and it brought him into the front ranks of the opponents of the proprietary government. He advocated measures of gaining local control of the province. The Quakers, who had controlled Pennsylvania policies for decades, were losing their power and Franklin and a group of middle-class merchants were assuming command. As their power developed, Thomson emerged as a prominent figure. In return for his services with the Indians and in recognition of his importance in provincial politics, Thomson received one of the few political sinecures of the time. Between 1756 and 1760 Thomson was named in six or seven money bills to countersign the paper currency issued by the Assembly.[50]

Thomson's role in this entire affair has never been fully evaluated. At the time of the publication of the *Enquiry*, partisans of both sides attacked or defended him according to their own political leanings. At least two of the participants in the events left detailed notes denying the validity of Thomson's charges. Thomas Penn apparently never made use of his notations; neither did Conrad Weiser, the Penns' primary Indian agent, who felt that many of Thomson's charges were pointed at him. The editor of the influential London *Monthly Review*, Ralph Griffiths, was persuaded by Thomson's account that "the best method of ending all disputes ... will be for the government of the mother-country to take that of this province into its own hands, and to settle it upon the same footing with the rest of our most flourishing colonies."[51]

Thomson's activities as a secretary to Teedyuscung and as a propagandist apparently pleased his Quaker employers. In March 1759 his salary was increased from one-hundred fifty to two hundred pounds per year. Two months earlier the overseers had paid usher Samuel Eldridge "seven pounds, as a present" for an increased work load since "for some time past Charles Thomson's Marriage & other Engagements have frequently Prevented his attendance on his School."[52]

Thomson's rather good salary and the fact that his Quaker employers seemed to approve his frequent absences from his duties as master of the Friends' Public School might lead to questions regarding his motivations and his sincerity. But statements in his letters of the same period counter any such charges. From Easton on July 28, 1759, Thomson wrote "I need not mention the importance of the business we are come about. The welfare of the Province, and the lives of thousands depend upon it." He then proceeded to condemn the governor and those about him for their attempts to keep Teedyuscung too drunk to negotiate.[53]

The squabble between Franklin and the antiproprietary party on one side and the Penns on the other continued long after the Indian troubles had subsided and the development of an antigovernmental attitude certainly helped pave the way for the coming of the Revolution in Pennsylvania. Franklin, Thomson, and their associates went largely to the Revolutionary side and emerged victorious. Their view became the accepted version of the events prior to the Revolution, and the *Enquiry* went unquestioned until well into this century. In 1867, it was even reprinted in an apparent effort to call for more humane treatment of the Indians of the western United States, despite it's one-sided presentation of the Indian problems of the 1750s. But the book had served Thomson's and Franklin's purposes well. The causes of the Indians, of peace, and of the colony of Pennsylvania had all been advanced. And Thomson had gained skill and recognition as a propagandist.[54]

It appears that in writing the *Enquiry* and in his entire involvement with the Friendly Association and with Benjamin Franklin and provincial politics, Thomson was acting out of a sincere desire to do justice to the Indians, bring peace to the province, wrest political power from the Penns, and establish it within Pennsylvania. That Thomson was able to combine these goals and at the same time advance himself professionally, socially, and economically is evidence that he had indeed become, to a degree, the master of his fate. Astute analysis revealed an occasion to be of service to society to himself and Thomson proceeded to seize the opportunity.

This fortuitous combination of service to self and to community and colony was shortly to be extended beyond the boundary of Pennsylvania. As Thomson's interests became intercolonial in nature he found other men like himself—alert and interested in advancing themselves and their native land. Thomson's role in linking some of these men into an intercolonial network of interested and involved minds would be his greatest contribution over the next few years. And such activities would play a major part in the making of the American nation.

NOTES

1. Accounts of Thomson's arrival in America are found in John F. Watson, *Annals of Philadelphia and Pennsylvania in the Olden Time* (Philadelphia, 1850), 1: 567-68; "American Biography," *American Quarterly Review* 1 (1827): 28-30; and Lewis R. Harley, *Life of Charles Thomson* (Philadelphia, 1900), pp. 15-20. See also the notice of Matthew's death in the *Richmond* (Va.) *Enquirer*, April 19, 1822. Matthew, who with the boys' only sister, Mary, probably arrived a few years later, settled in Augusta County, Virginia. Mary, who never married, spent her life with Alexander and his son John near New Castle on an estate presented to them by Charles some years later. William traveled to South Carolina, where he too was an avid supporter of the Revolutionary cause.

2. Gorteade Cottage, Thomson's birthplace, still stands and is recognized by the Northern Ireland Tourist Board as a historic site. For the Scotch-Irish immigration see Lawrence H. Gipson, *The British Empire before the American Revolution* (Caldwell, Idaho and New York, 1936-1970), 1: 255-63; Wayland S. Dunaway, *The Scotch-Irish of Colonial Pennsylvania* (Chapel Hill, 1944), pp. 3-22, passim; James S. Leyburn, *The Scotch-Irish, A Social History* (Chapel Hill, 1962), pp. 296-316.

3. Watson, *Annals of Philadelphia*, 1: 568.

4. Ibid., 1: 568; Deborah Logan, Philadelphia contemporary of Thomson, records that in later life Thomson indicated that during these days "his greatest anxiety was to procure the advantages of education." And that, "one of his brothers kindly furnished him with money from time to time, to pay for his schooling, which he afterwards gratefully repaid." Miscellaneous Manuscripts, Historical Society of Pennsylvania.

5. Dr. Francis Alison, like Thomson an immigrant from Ulster, came to America in 1735. In 1737, Alison was assigned as a minister to the Presbyterian congregation at New London, Pennsylvania. The following year he began a school at his home at Thunder Hill, two miles southwest of New London. In November 1743 he moved the school into New London, and in 1744 the Philadelphia Synod assumed control of the school, and named Dr. Alison as rector. He continued in this position until early 1752 when he became Latin master of the College and Academy of Philadelphia. Thomas Clinton Pears, "Francis Alison, Colonial Educator," *Delaware Notes*, Seventeenth Series (1944), pp. 9-22; George Morgan, "The Colonial Origin of Newark Academy," *Delaware Notes*, Eighth Series (1943), pp. 7-30. The best sketch of Alison and his work is in Douglas Sloan, *The Scottish Enlightenment and the American College Ideal* (New York, 1971); Alison and other representatives

of the Scottish educational philosophy are portrayed as having a greatly formative influence on American academies and colleges.

6. Harvey Wish, *Society and Thought in America* (New York, 1950), 1: 152-53; Edward Potts Cheyney, *History of the University of Pennsylvania* (Philadelphia, 1940), pp. 11-16.

7. So relates a contemporary, Benjamin Rush, in his *Autobiography of Benjamin Rush*, ed. George W. Corner (Princeton, 1948), p. 294.

8. Ibid., p. 289.

9. Harley, *Thomson*, p. 33.

10. Watson, *Annals of Philadelphia*, 1: 212, records the paving of the first street; Carl and Jessica Bridenbaugh, *Rebles and Gentlemen* (New York, 1942), pp. 1-28, present an excellent discussion of prerevolutionary Philadelphia. An excellent, concise, and readable account of the history of Pennsylvania is Philip S. Klein and Ari Hoogenboom, *A History of Pennsylvania* (New York, 1973).

11. Merle Curti, *The Growth of American Thought* (New York, 1943), pp. 144 ff.

12. Thomas H. Montgomery, *A History of the University of Pennsylvania to A.D. 1770* (Philadelphia, 1900), p. 142; Cheyney, *History of the University of Pennsylvania*, pp. 73-74.

13. Richard M. Gummere, *The American Colonial Mind and the Classical Tradition* (Cambridge, Mass., 1963), pp. 44-75, indicates that a knowledge of the classics was still the test of the most rudimentary education and points out that most of the leaders of the Revolution had thorough backgrounds in Greek and Latin studies. On the other hand, Curti, *Growth of American Thought*, pp. 175-76, emphasizes the declining importance of classical knowledge. The Academy of Philadelphia is described in Carl Van Doren, *Benjamin Franklin* (New York, 1938), pp. 189-94, and Montgomery, *University of Pennsylvania*, pp. 35-40.

14. Montgomery, *University of Pennsylvania*, pp. 162-66.

15. "American Biography," *American Quarterly Review*, 1: 30.

16. Montgomery, *University of Pennsylvania*, p. 148.

17. Van Doren, *Benjamin Franklin*, pp. 74-79.

18. "American Biography," *American Quarterly Review* 1 (1827): 30.

19. Charles Thomson, Notebook, Thomson Papers, Historical Society of Pennsylvania. The "Young Junto," a forerunner of the American Philosophical Society, is discussed in Chapter 2.

20. A good analysis of the crisis faced by the Quakers is given in Richard Bauman, *For the Reputation of Truth, Politics, Religion, and Conflict among the Pennsylvania Quakers, 1750-1800* (Baltimore, 1972). Bauman attempts a historical-anthropological survey of the dilemma faced by the Quakers. James H. Hutson, "Benjamin Franklin and Pennsylvania Politics, 1751-1755: A Reappraisal," *PMHB* 93 (1969): 303-71 not only provides detailed documentary evidence that Franklin acted from principle during this period but also offers astute analysis of the recent literature on the period including William S. Hanna, *Benjamin Franklin and Pennsylvania Politics* (Stanford, 1964); Gary B. Nash, *Quakers and Politics—Pennsylvania, 1681-1726* (Princeton, 1968); Ralph H. Ketcham, "Conscience, War, and Politics in Pennsylvania, 1755-1757," *WMQ* 20 (1963): 416-39.

21. Thomson notebook, Historical Society of Pennsylvania.

22. Benjamin Rush, *Autobiography*, p. 294.

23. Sidney V. James, *A People among Peoples; Quaker Benevolence in Eighteenth-Century America* (Cambridge, Mass., 1963), concludes that the Enlightenment brought a widening of an already existent humanitarianism among Quakers. Thomson's general humanitarianism and his ready inclusion in Quaker groups buttresses this theory. See also Thomson, "An Essay on Indian Affairs," *Collections of the Historical Society of Pennsylvania* 1 (1853): 80-85.

24. As is indicated in note no. 20, the history of this period and especially the matter of the treatment accorded the Indians by the proprietors is open to various interpretations. What follows is an effort to present the situation as clearly as possible and to relate the role of Charles Thomson in the developing events. cf. Hutson, "Benjamin Franklin and Pennsylvania Politics, 1751-1755: A Reappraisal," pp. 312-59.

25. Theodore Thayer, "The Friendly Association," *PMHB* 67 (1943): 356-59.

26. Bridenbaugh, *Rebels and Gentlemen*, pp. 7-28, 47-48.

27. Robert L. Davidson, *War Comes to Quaker Pennsylvania, 1682-1756* (New York, 1957), pp. 21-69.

28. Thayer, "Friendly Association," pp. 358-62.

29. The Friends' Public School, or the Penn Charter School as it was later known, was founded in 1689 by the Philadelphia Quakers to provide a place to educate their children. It was chartered by William Penn in 1707 and has continued in operation until the present time. Thomas Woody, *Early Quaker Education in Pennsylvania* (New York, 1920), pp. 45, 202-20; Jean S. Straub, "Teaching in the Friends' Latin School of Philadelphia in the Eighteenth Century," *PMHB* 95 (1967): 434-56 contains an excellent account of the curriculum.

30. The "Overssers' Minutes" contain much evidence that Thomson's conduct of the school met with their approval. Straub, "Teaching in the Friends' Latin School," pp. 437-43; Woody, *Early Quaker Education*, pp. 180-81.

31. Paul A. W. Wallace, *Indians in Pennsylvania* (Harrisburg, 1961), pp. 16-25, 140-45.

32. Anthony F. C. Wallace, *King of the Delawares—Teedyuscung, 1700-1763* (Philadelphia, 1949), pp. 136-58; Ketcham, "Conscience, War, and Politics in Pennsylvania, 1755-1757," pp. 418-30.

33. Ketcham, "Conscience, War, and Politics in Pennsylvania, 1755-1757," pp. 431-32; Theodore Thayer, *Israel Pemberton, King of the Quakers* (Philadelphia, 1943), pp. 81-131, discusses the Quaker role in detail. At best Teedyuscung was acting erratically and irresponsibly by injecting the land issue into the conference at this time. He later admitted as much himself. The failure of the conference, and indeed the whole problem brought about by the reairing of the twenty-year-old land controversy, can be blamed on Israel Pemberton and the Quakers. Locked in a power struggle in the Assembly and in a dispute with the proprietors over their policies of taxation and control, the Friendly Association endangered the Pennsylvania frontier by encouraging the Indians in their grievances against the British. Thomson, concerned over real injustices to the Indians, was in reality involving himself in a larger, much more danger-ridden struggle. See Nicholas B. Wainwright, *George Croghan, Wilderness Diplomat* (Chapel Hill, 1959), pp. 118-34.

34. Watson, *Annals of Philadelphia*, 1: 570.

35. Ketcham, "Conscience, War, and Politics in Pennsylvania, 1755-1757," pp. 432-35.

36. Thomson to Governor Denny, August 4, 1757, *Pennsylvania Archives*, 1st ser., ed. Samuel Hazard (Philadelphia, 1852-1856), 3: 256.

37. The records of the conference are in *Pennsylvania Archives*, Colonial Records (Harrisburg, 1840-1853), 8: 649-712.

38. Thomson to Governor Denny, August 4, 1757, *Pennsylvania Archives*, 1st ser. 3: 256.

39. *Pennsylvania Archives*, Colonial Records, 8: 702.

40. Denny sought support from everyone during his first months in Philadelphia but soon accepted the old divisions as inviolate. Nicholas B. Wainwright, "Governor William Denny in Pennsylvania," *PMHB* 81 (1957): 170-98. *Pennsylvania Journal*, June 15, 22, and 29, 1758; Benjamin Franklin, *The Papers of Benjamin Franklin*, ed. Leonard W. Labaree et al. (New Haven and London 1959-), 8: 77 n.

41. Thomson's and Post's report of their journey is in *Pennsylvania Archives*, 1st ser., 3: 412-22.

42. *Pennsylvania Archives*, Colonial Records, 8: 132-47; Thomson to Susannah Wright, July 20, 1758, Miscellaneous Collection, American Philosophical Society Library.

43. Isaac Norris to Benjamin Franklin, January 15, 1759, Franklin *Papers*, 8: 230.

44. Hannah Benner Roach, "Benjamin Franklin Slept Here," *PMHB* 84 (1960): 165; "Junto Minutes," American Philosophical Society; Harley, *Thomson*, pp. 187-88; Straub, "Teaching in the Friends' Latin School," pp. 439, 442.

45. "Votes and Proceedings of the Assembly" (September 29, 1757), *Pennsylvania Archives*, 8th ser., 6: 4649; Franklin to Joseph Galloway, February 17, 1758, Franklin *Papers*, 7: 376-377.

46. For publication of the *Enquiry*, see Franklin *Papers*, 7: 376 n, 377 n, and 8: 99 n, 100 n; and Lawrence C. Wroth, *An American Bookshelf, 1755* (Philadelphia, 1934), pp. 17-18.

47. Franklin to Israel Pemberton, March 19, 1759, Franklin *Papers*, 8: 297-300.

48. Benjamin Franklin to Joseph Galloway, April 7, 1759, Franklin *Papers*, 8: 313; Benjamin Franklin to Deborah Franklin, April 12, 1759, ibid., 8: 324. The Thomas Penn copy of the *Enquiry* with extensive "exasperated" notations is in the John Carter Brown Library, but Penn apparently never responded publicly.

49. Thomson, *Enquiry*, pp. 111-12. Thomson's account, read without an understanding of the involved political quarrels that engendered its publication, has misled many an unwary scholar. Cf. Van Doren, *Franklin*, pp. 257-59. Good accounts of the Walking Purchase are in John A. Lucas' unpublished "Sport and Politics: The Infamous Pennsylvania Walking Purchase of 1737," and William A. Hunter, "The Walking Purchase," Historic Pennsylvania Leaflet No. 24. Pennsylvania Historical and Museum Commission, Harrisburg, Pa.

50. John J. Zimmerman, "Charles Thomson, 'The Sam Adams of Philadelphia,'" *Mississippi Valley Historical Review* 45 (1958): 467.

51. *Monthly Review*, June, 1759, pp. 545-48. A discussion of the entire affair from the view of Conrad Weiser is in Paul A. W. Wallace, *Conrad Weiser, 1696-1760* (Philadelphia, 1945). See especially pp. 72, 358, 360, 583, and 602. Weiser's "Observations, made on the Pamphlet, intitled, 'An Inquiry into the Causes of the Alienation of the Delaware and Shawano-Indians from the British Interest,'" is in the Moravian Archives, Bethlehem, Pennsylvania.

52. Straub, "Teaching in the Friends' Latin School," pp. 439, 442. Woody, *Early Quaker Education*, pp. 180-81.

53. Thomson to Samuel Rhodes, *PMHB* 20 (1896): 421-22. Similar sentiments appear in Thomson to William Franklin, June, 1757, January 2, 1758, and March 12-16, 1758, American Philosophical Society Library.

54. The 1867 facsimile edition bore the title *Causes of the Alienation of the Delaware and Shawanese Indians from the British Interest.* It was reprinted by John Campbell, a Philadelphia bookseller and publisher who frequently took on unpopular causes. The 1759 *Enquiry* was reissued in 1970 by the Scholarly Press, Inc., St. Clair Shores, Michigan.

2

Promoting Useful Knowledge

*W*hile Charles Thomson was developing his educational
and political involvement in Pennsylvania, he was also
engaged in other activities that made a significant contribution
to the intellectual and political unification of the British
colonies in North America. In order for any area, no matter
how homogeneous, to become truly unified as a nation, its
leaders must have common interests and an awareness of the
mutual nature of their concerns. Once such an awareness is
established, the basis for an exchange of ideas and attitudes is
created. Then, when a threat appears, there is a foundation
for a reasoned, unified reaction within the leadership community. Charles Thomson played a major part in creating
two such areas of communal interests in prerevolutionary
America—the joining of mercantile and political interests
that led to the Committees of Correspondence and the Continental Association and the assembling of those interested in
the pursuit of science, or "useful knowledge," into the
American Philosophical Society. Thomson's work with the
merchants and politicians is discussed in succeeding chapters.

Thomson's enlightened Americanism in promoting useful
knowledge made him the driving force behind the formation
of the American Philosophical Society, held at Philadelphia,
for Promoting Useful Knowledge. Benjamin Franklin is
rightly acclaimed as the intellectual father of the society—the
original idea came from his 1743 proposals, and it was according to the outline of these suggestions that the final
organization was formed. But the efforts of Franklin and
others failed to create a permanent society in the 1740s and it
remained for Charles Thomson to give the idea a rebirth in

the 1760s. Thomson reintroduced the idea to Philadelphians; got the society off to a faltering start; brought in members from outside Philadelphia and Pennsylvania; and finally it was Thomson who wrested a strengthened society from a struggle between classes and parties that had threatened to kill organized scientific inquiry in Philadelphia.[1]

Soon after Thomson's arrival in Philadelphia in 1750 he organized a self-improvement club patterned after Benjamin Franklin's Junto. Twelve young men, two of them sons of members of Franklin's old society, met weekly to discuss matters of mutual interest. Both membership and meetings were secret. Political, scientific, and personal interests vied with other topics, and little of lasting importance came from the club during its first years. The group kept no minutes until 1758, and its activities were not mentioned in the newspapers of the day. Therefore, only the personal correspondence of its members provides any information about the group. It influenced the lives of its members but had little other significance until after 1758. In that year, and again in 1766, Charles Thomson introduced changes that significantly altered the group along the lines of "promoting useful knowledge."[2]

In 1758, Thomson directed the metamorphosis of his informal group of friends into a fully organized society with a goal of self-improvement for its members. It was called the "Young Junto" to distinguish it from the similar group that Franklin had organized in his early years in Philadelphia, and included young workers, teachers, merchants, and professional men. They met on Friday evenings in a rented room and fined absent members six-pence unless they were out of town or ill. Officers served four weeks in a system of alphabetical rotation with the exception of the treasurer who was elected twice yearly. At each meeting a member, again chosen by a system of rotation, proposed two questions concerning politics, sciences, and a number of other subjects. The questions were considered for a week and then discussed at the next meeting. The meetings were not publicized, no visitors were admitted, and new members were accepted only by unanimous vote.[3]

The weekly questions touched numerous and varied subjects. The Junto minutes for the years 1758-1762 show that forty-three topics were discussed. These ranged from the scientific to the speculative realms and included such subjects as death, history, the problems of empire, the construction of scales and barometers, agriculture, tides, inoculation, chimneys, and the phenomena of sound and gasses. Each member contributed his knowledge on the subject being debated and a summation was made. They conducted no scientific experiments during the early years, and there is no evidence that the members resorted to authorities in search of answers. In a few instances, speculative discussion gave way to practical advice, as when Charles Thomson asked for instructions on the best time to transplant tulips and strawberries, but this happened only occasionally. The forty-three questions discussed in the period under consideration reveal eleven topics concerning earth sciences; seven relating to the biological sciences; five relating to international politics; and three or less relating to law and government, individual improvement, agriculture, and technics.[4]

Attendance at the weekly meetings was fairly regular from September 1758 to February 1761. Few meetings were missed during the first eleven months but then occasional ones were skipped during the summer season. As time passed, members moved or died, and by 1761 only five active members remained in Philadelphia. Two members were added in an expansion effort but one of those soon left for England. The Junto missed several meetings in 1761, and Charles Thomson and Edmund Physick attempted a revival in August. The two men found that the laws of the original group were missing and they rewrote them from memory. Meetings of the revived group were held for only three months when another lapse occurred. In September 1762 the group met again for a few weeks. Attendance was worse than before, and Thomson abandoned all attempts at revival for more than three years.[5]

The "Young Junto" did not meet from October 1762 until April 1766. It had been organized as a self-improvement club, and as its members advanced their careers they found less and less time to meet together. Some of the members left the city and as others grew disinterested in the purpose of the club the meetings ceased. But circumstances were changing to favor the revival of the society on an larger, more grandiose scale.

In the aftermath of the French and Indian War, Philadelphia settled down to a period of relative economic and political calm. Thomson, who had embroiled himself with the problems of the Indians and the proprietors, left teaching, put aside his political activities, and concentrated on business and the problems of starting a family. He lived across Market Street from Benjamin Franklin and, while Franklin was in London, frequently assisted Deborah Franklin as she attended to her husband's Philadelphia business concerns.[6]

Meanwhile in London, events were occurring that would change all this not only for Thomson but for Philadelphia and the colonies as a whole. In 1764 a changed attitude on the part of the British toward their colonies led to the passage of the Stamp Act in 1765, and colonial protests mounted.[7]

Charles Thomson headed Philadelphia agitation against the acts and supported nonimportation agreements to bring economic pressure on the British merchant classes who controlled Parliament. Rebels of the time encouraged the exclusive use of American-made goods. As the nonimportation agreements went into effect, British goods were not available and patriotic colonists produced, sold, and used only local goods. Hoping to foster this atmosphere of emergent American nationalism, Thomson spoke to his friends about reviving the "Young Junto." Only three members remained from the group that had ceased meeting in 1762—Thomson, Isaac Paschall, and Edmund Physick. Thomson was the most active in the attempts at revival, but Paschall and Physick eagerly sought new members and aroused interest in the club.[8]

The first meeting of the revived Junto was held on April 25, 1766. The members were exuberant because of rumors of the repeal of the hated Stamp Act. In addition to Thomson, Paschall, and Physick, the society had six new members. Two, Isaac and Moses Bartram, were druggists; Joseph Paschall, like his brother, was a merchant; Owen Biddle was a clockmaker; James Pearson was a hatter; and Isaac Zane, Jr., was an iron master. All but two, Thomson and Physick, were Quakers though of the more liberal faction of this sect. They were an intellectually curious group although not all had had formal educations that were as impressive as Thomson's.[9]

The aims of the club remained similar to those of earlier years but with one significant difference. The revised bylaws referred to the members as meeting "for their mutual improvement in useful knowledge." Events that had just taken place in the province directed the interests of the members toward "useful" matters—a slight difference, perhaps, but one that pointed toward an expanded view of the society that would be publicly expressed by the end of the year.[10]

The reanimated Junto discussed an interesting list of questions at its first meetings. They considered four topics dealing with problems of the empire brought to prominence during the Stamp Act controversy; a proposal for providing a paper currency for the colonies; and methods by which the colonies could provide funds for the crown should this be required of them. Other questions dealt with scientific interests including electricity, botany, and optics. Frequent mention was made of "liberty," and the advancement of liberty formed the basis for the support or rejection of proposals.

The members were better qualified to discuss problems relating to government, trade, and empire than they were to deal with questions of a scientific nature. Their excursions into the sciences show alert minds capable of making exact observations even though they were not acquainted with the most advanced theories explaining the phenomena observed.

Charles Thomson was devoted to useful and practical matters. He wondered why one felt cooler after drinking tea and which were the best remedies for burns. In a memo book kept during this period Thomson recorded a series of herb cures that may have come from these discussions. He made observations on historical artifacts preserved with cedar oil and then proposed a "query whether an Oil extracted from them [American red and white varieties of cedar] would preserve other wood or guard it from worms." He read a paper on agriculture that met the approval of the society and resulted in further discussion of agricultural matters. Apparently the discussions were interesting and valuable because attendance at the meetings was regularly good. Seven new members joined in the autumn of 1766 and Isaac Zane, Jr., was dropped for failure to attend the meetings. Of a total membership of fifteen, more than half were normally on hand for meetings. Such regular attendance gave evidence of enjoyable and interesting meetings.[11]

Still the group was hesitant to stray out of the path set by Franklin in 1743. Their inquiries and their membership were limited and the rules by which they operated stayed much the same. But Franklin was in London and the American temper had changed considerably. And Thomson, the man who corrected Franklin's misjudgment of the American resistance to the Stamp Act, was behind the scene shaping the nature of the society and its activities.

In December 1766, under Thomson's urging, the members named themselves "The American Society for promoting and propagating useful knowledge, Held in Philadelphia." In the same month they decided to add corresponding members from the other colonies and from Europe. The choice of the name and the widened vision of the "American Society" show what Thomson had in mind. The group had developed from a studentlike attitude that sought improvement for its own benefit into an organization for "promoting and propagating useful knowledge." The members were interested, thanks to Charles Thomson's broadening perspective, in the development of useful knowledge and its spread among their fellow citizens.[12]

Perhaps a more important change was indicated by their naming the group the "American Society." Not only were they no longer interested solely in self-improvement but their expanded ideas envisioned an organization that was to extend to all the British colonies in North America. Charles Thomson was the man behind this extended vision. He had seen attempts at colonial unity at the Stamp Act Congress of 1765 in New York defeated by the lack of real ties between the colonies. Evaluating the problem he resolved to find a solution. If the public-spirited gentlemen of all the colonies could be bound together and frequent communication achieved among them, a successful colonial union would not be at all difficult to accomplish.[13]

The society soon began electing "foreign" or corresponding members. The selection of Dr. John Morgan, F.R.S. and Professor of "Physick," fostered this action since he proposed many of his European acquaintances for membership, several of whom accepted. The first corresponding members chosen were largely colonial and were confined to the Pennsylvania-New York region. William Henry, revolutionary munitions manufacturer of Pennsylvania, William Johnson, profession unknown, Dr. Samuel Bard of New York, David Rittenhouse, the astronomer, and Charles Mason, the surveyor, were all acquaintances of one or more of the local members and preserved the liberal-Quaker cast of the organization.[14]

During 1767 the society went into a decline although none of the weekly meetings was canceled. No discussions were held during most of the year and business was largely confined to fining absent members. In mid-1767, however, the Townshend Acts were passed by Parliament and the calm that had followed the repeal of the Stamp Act was replaced by renewed interest and agitation against the oppressive measures of the mother country. In September, Charles Thomson, one of the leading agitators against imperial authority over the colonies, proposed that the American Society study the situation of American agriculture with a view to advancing that branch of American economy. In following meetings members discussed the state of manufacturing in America as well as some proposals for altering the society.

Charles Thomson led in the movement to change the organization but his ideas of uniting the colonies within the society met with opposition. The members favored improving the status and increasing the output of agriculture and the promotion of manufacturing in Pennsylvania, but they failed to understand the broader purpose behind Thomson's proposals. At the first meeting of 1768, Thomson addressed the group and presented a detailed plan for the improvement of the society. The majority of the group agreed with Thomson's proposals and officially adopted his "Proposals For Enlarging the Plan of the American Society, ... that it may the better answer the Ends for which it was instituted." In March the *Pennsylvania Journal* carried the complete recommendations of the body "published in order to explain the design of the institution, and increase the number of correspondents."[15]

Thomson's proposals were circulated for many years as a statement of aims by the American Society and were then used by the combined American Philosophical Society as a preface to the first volume of the *Transactions*. The prospectus began by declaring the intention of the American Society "to confine their disquisitions, principally, to such subjects as tend to the improvement of their country, and the advancement of its interest and prosperity." Thomson expounded the many advantages of the country occupied by the English in North America, noting that the climate and soil of the region should be suitable for the growth of plants in use in China, Japan, and the East Indies. He urged Americans to become more familiar with native plants and their many uses as illustrated by the medicines, dyes, and other products known to the Indians. "Each one, according to his opportunities and ability, should explore the virtues of our native plants, &c. and search out the treasures which nature has concealed in the bowels of the earth." He also proposed that the Society "make it a principal part of their business to inquire, and try to find out, what our country is capable of producing." These and other practical designs for improving the country would be discovered, "But it is not proposed to confine the views of the society wholly, to these things, so as to exclude other useful subjects, either in physics, mechanics, astronomy, Mathematics, &c."[16]

Thomson then went on to explain how favorable conditions were for the success of the project. "The means of conveying Knowledge are now become easy," he said. Numerous printing houses were in existence and regular posts carried letters and papers from one colony to another and made for the rapid spread of knowledge and ideas. "Besides, Hints thrown out in our public circulating Papers are not lost, as in this country almost every man is fond of reading, and seems to have a thirst for knowledge." Interested members of all professions were urged to aid the society in promoting and propagating useful knowledge. The society claimed only the merit of "encouraging and directing Inquiries and experiments, of receiving, collecting, and digesting Discoveries, Inventions, and Improvements, of communicating them to the Public, and distinguishing the Authors; and of thus uniting the labors of many, to attain one end, namely tha advancement of useful knowledge and improvement of our country."

Men like Thomson believed that it was absolutely necessary that the benefits of increased learning be applied for the good of America. Though most had not yet reached the point where the growth of the colonial economy was seen as a step in obtaining independence from the mother country, the men involved in such movements realized that, if their local economies were to prosper, advances in distributing useful knowledge were necessary. Thomson proposed that the American Society become a body for "receiving, collecting, and digesting Discoveries, Inventions, and Improvements" to communicate them to the public in order to advance knowledge and improve the country. In so doing Thomson indicated the advanced position he occupied among the enlightened Americans of his day in both intellectual and patriotic fields. Thomson was a leader in the opposition to the Stamp and Townshend acts and combined his radical American position in politics with his efforts for the advancement of knowledge.

Thomson not only provided a program for the American Society, but he also assumed the task of organizing the group to better carry out his aims. The society asked him to draw up a new set of rules and the following week he presented an outline that he later completed. When he was absent from one meeting, the secretary noted an apology in the minutes to the effect that only the necessity of the business caused the society to act in his absence. In line with the proposals, seven new members were nominated and the society began its expansion.[17]

Frequent articles were transmitted to the *Pennsylvania Chronicle*. The *Pennsylvania Journal* and *Gazette* were used to a lesser extent, and through the three newspapers the aim and purpose of the society were transmitted to all the colonies. Contributions were sought from scientists in the West Indian Islands and on the continent as well as in America.

Soon scientific articles from South Carolina, Connecticut, and other colonies were appearing in the Philadelphia papers.

Desires for expansion of the American Society intensified when a rival organization became active within the city of Philadelphia. The majority of the members of Thomson's American Society belonged to the Quaker or Assembly party and were noted for their antiproprietary views. The conservative and proprietary faction of Pennsylvania politics therefore looked with disfavor on the cultural and scientific activities of their political opponents. They were particularly disturbed by the prominent positions occupied in the new society by Thomson and Dr. John Morgan. Thomson's part in attacking the proprietary treatment of the Indians had gained him few friends among proprietary ranks, and Dr. Morgan had created antagonism in 1765 when he founded a medical society—an action viewed as eagerness to place himself ahead of the old established physicians in the city.[18]

In November 1767, this conservative group consisting of Thomas Bond, M.D., Dr. William Smith, Provost of the College of Philadelphia, Dr. Francis Alison, Thomson's former teacher, and Drs. William Shippen and William Shippen, Jr., revived the American Philosophical Society, which had been founded by the members of Franklin's old Junto in 1743. This society had not been active since 1745, and Franklin was greatly disappointed when its members ceased to meet. The "revival" appeared to the members of the American Society as an attempt to gain prestige from Franklin's name. They also resented the formation of a rival group by their political opponents and the obvious attempt to extend political and social quarrels to the fields of science and colonial unity.

The minutes of the revived Philosophical Society began with January 19, 1768, and from this time on the competition between it and the American Society increased. The two groups disagreed on many points, not among the least of which were the social and political differences. The Philosophical Society elected Governor John Penn, former Governor James Hamilton, Chief Justice William Allen, and about twenty other members of Philadelphia's upper classes to membership. Members of Thomson's group easily recognized that competition between social classes would hurt both societies.

Soon after the Philosophical Society began its meetings, Thomson's associate Dr. John Morgan approached Dr. Thomas Bond with a suggestion for a union between the two societies. Morgan, Bond, and others in both organizations recognized that the cause of science and learning was being harmed by the existence of the two quarreling bodies. The two physicians agreed to work for union on terms that would be equally acceptable to both societies. But the members of the Philosophical Society preferred not to admit that the older American Society was of equal or greater status than their own. In February 1768, all of the members of the American Society received notice that they had been elected to membership in the Philosophical Society. Thomson's group refused, for its association would have been merely absorbed and its identity lost.[19]

The members of the two rival societies then began an extensive campaign for new members. The Philosophical Society made use of David Hall's *Pennsylvania Gazette* to attract attention by the publication of scientific reports from various contributors. Thomson and the American Society confined their publicity largely to the columns of William Goddard's *Pennsylvania Chronicle*. This antiproprietary paper had such an intercolonial circulation that the American Society soon achieved notice among men of science and practical knowledge throughout North America. The non-Pennsylvania members gained by the American Society in this manner raised the number of colonial and foreign members to sixty-seven by December 1768. Thomson's contacts among merchants in London and Bristol as well as those in the colonial cities enabled him to reach many men of note and to persuade them to join the organization.[20]

In February 1768 the American Society elected Benjamin Franklin to membership. Although Franklin was in London, his son, William, was instructed to inform his father of his election. Franklin's becoming a member of the society gave added stature to the organization, and in November of that year, Franklin was elected president of the society. Thomson was again elected as secretary, and Samuel Powell was elected vice-president. At the same time Dr. John Morgan's Medical Society was incorporated into membership giving the society even more prestige. In a letter to Franklin informing him of his election, Thomson told Franklin of the condition of the society. He reminded Franklin that the society had prospered under his watchfulness and told him of the enlarged plan to make the society useful to the public. Thomson informed Franklin that "we have brought the Society to some degree of Perfection. We have established a Correspondence in most of the Colonies on the Continent and in some of the Islands [of the West Indies]." He concluded by telling Franklin of the promising future of the society and the hopes that it had for continuing to serve the public with the added prestige of his patronage and assistance.[21]

While the two organizations continued their contest for membership and influence the differences between the two bodies grew much less noticeable. Once the two societies had vastly different aims as well as social and political differences. The American Society was a liberal Quaker group seeking to advance scientific understanding and the development of the American colonies. The Philosophical Society was dominated by gentlemen and professional men and was devoted to the advancement of knowledge by investigation and publication in the manner of the Royal Society of London. As the groups developed their programs and expanded their numbers the differences lessened. Men of higher social classes and provincial leaders became members of the American Society and that society turned its interest to projects that were abstract and "philosophical" as well as useful and practical. The Philosophical Society, in turn, gave much attention to utilitarian projects and at the same time broadened its membership base. Soon then, the two bodies presented almost the same face to the interested public.[22]

Many came to tire of the continuing struggle of groups that had been established for similar purposes. Thomson initiated the movement that finally resulted in union. On November 18, 1768, he reported to the American Society that a committee had been appointed by the Philosophical Society to consider uniting the two groups. Thomson did not mention that he had earlier informed the Philosophical Society that such a union would be agreeable to the American Society. As a result of his report, the American Society instructed its officers to meet with the committee from the other body and arrange for the unification. The committees met, completed their work, and a formal union was made on December 20, 1768. The name selected for the newly formed body was the American Philosophical Society, Held at Philadelphia, for Promoting Useful Knowledge.[23]

On January 2, 1769, the combined body met at the College of Philadelphia to elect officers. Franklin, although still in London, was elected president and Dr. Thomas Bond, who had worked from the beginning to convince his own group that a union was to be desired, was elected vice-president. Dr. William Smith, Thomas Mifflin, an early member of the American Society, and Charles Thomson were elected secretaries. This deliberate balancing of the society's officers with members from both of the old groups paid good dividends. Political and social differences were pushed into the background and the society concentrated its efforts on developing scientific interest in the colonies.

The society continued to expand its influence over scientific activities in the colonies after 1769. The officers worked to communicate with all colonial scientists of any note and to gain their interest and support. Not only were important men of science and invention contacted but public figures in all the colonies were also induced to become members. The inclusion of prominent colonial and European figures furnished a method of keeping the society in the public eye whereas the election of men of wealth and leisure gave social prestige and assured adequate financial support. Thus, the program outlined in Charles Thomson's 1768 plan was carried to fruition, and the society became the coordinating center of colonial scientific and practical knowledge. Thomson had succeeded in obtaining a union of the most influential men in all the British-American colonies.

The contest between the two original organizations furthered the advance of the united society. In appealing for membership to the many levels of Pennsylvania social classes, the groups had aroused much interest. The newspaper articles concerning the work of the two bodies had spread knowledge of the societies throughout much of the colonial region and had attracted the attention of many who otherwise would have remained ignorant of their existence.

The intellectual atmosphere that fostered the founding of the American Philosophical Society also produced the political and governmental developments of the American Revolution. In addition to their emphasis on the useful aspect of knowledge, the other common interests of such enlightened Americans as Franklin, Jefferson, and Thomson are most impressive. Thomson was hardly in a financial class to compete with Franklin or Jefferson in the acquisition of books, yet an inventory of his library in 1760 shows a collection covering many fields. Thomson possessed books far greater in number than the average well-educated individual of his time.[24] His books covered the gamut of knowledge and included the classical, philosophical, theological, political, mathematical, literary, and practical works of his day. Thomson was no sophisticated scholar though; inserted between two volume works on Greek Antiquities and the orations of Socrates was a book entitled *Good Wines*. Accounts of the Netherlands and Denmark and four volumes of "Modern Travels" and seven volumes of "Modern Voyages" showed Thomson's desire to know the rest of the world.

Near the head of Thomson's list of books came works that were initimately linked with the Enlightenment. A three-volume collection of the works of Francis Bacon gave him insight into the science of the preceeding century and the scientific method it had produced. A copy of Sir Isaac Newton's *Principia* and other mathematical works testified to Thomson's advanced knowledge of mathematics, and made it possible for him to study in detail Newton's discoveries concerning a rational description of the universe. This dependence on reason firmly characterized the European Enlightenment. Since Newton demonstrated that the basic forces of nature—motion and gravity—could be described by rational men, why then could not all the workings of nature be so explained? Thomson immersed himself in this line of inquiry. His books included William H. Wollaston's *Religion of Nature Delineated* (1724), which viewed the "natural" life based on reason as providing the ultimate happiness.[25] In the same memo book that contained Thomson's inventory, Wollaston's work was carefully outlined along with the ideas of Francis Hutcheson on rationally describing such subjects as the "Idea of Beauty and Virtue," "On the Passions," and "Moral Philosophy." But Thomson, like Jefferson and most American products of the Enlightenment, rejected such attempts to impose a completely rational view on the universe.[26] Great literary works both ancient and modern filled out his list of books. Volumes on education, law, and philosophy evidenced a concern for man and his development that carried far beyond the simple paths of reason. Books of sermons, volumes on religion, and a four-volume edition of the Greek Septuagint testified to Thomson's devotion to religious matters that a total rationalist would reject.

Naturally Thomson's library included the classical works that were a part of his education and early livelihood. Editions of Virgil, Homer, Livy, Tacitus, Ovid, and others filled his shelves. Also, he had acquired eight volumes of *Spectators* (Remnants of his student days), an edition of Addison's poems, and volumes of Milton and Shakespeare. Books such as Montesquieu's *Spirit of the Laws*, and Algernon Sidney's *Discourses on Government*, show the impact of both the Enlightenment and English political developments on Thomson and the American scene.

Conspicuous by their absence from Thomson's library were the works of John Locke. But on the front cover of the memo book is a quotation from Locke concerning the difference between wit and judgment, which showed that Thomson sought knowledge not only from his own books but also from those of friends and from the growing collections of the Library Company of Philadelphia, the first circulating library in America. Seeking in another way to promote the expansion of knowledge, Thomson served as treasurer, secretary, librarian, and director of the Library Company during the years 1762-1771.[27]

Thomson's list of books and his notes on some of them present a rather confused, multifarious picture. The devotion to reason of the European Enlightenment combined with the practical simplicity of the new environment of America to provide an interesting intermixture. The reason of the American Enlightenment was unsophisticated—a reason tempered by experience, practicality, and the ultimate test of usefulness.[28]

A few years later Thomson took time out from his studies and organizational attempts on both scientific and political levels to draw up a "Plan of an American University," which further mirrored some of the complexities of promoting useful knowledge. The plan begins with a statement that is illustrative of American thought at this time: "Learning should be connected with Life and qualify its possessor for Action, else it is just so much lumber, serving at best an idle Amusement."[29] Thomson's preliminary statement concerning an American seat of learning continued along the same lines:

> As all habits especially the active ought to be early acquired, along with their studies at home youth should be taught to look much abroad; not plunge into the gaieties & fopperies of the idle but to view towns, fields, forts, harbours, & magazines, & to converse with men of all characters, professions, & trades & to inform themselves of their lives manners & connections. To this end they should learn address & agility of Body & even to wield the weapons & handle the tools of the several callings they are inspecting. Why should letters disqualify a man to take up a foile, mount in the great saddle or rein in the hunting horses. The ingenious mechanics the workers in stores & metals and improvers in trade, navigation & agriculture ought to be searched out and conversed with, no less than the professors of speculative science. Thus blending the active & contemplative life would enliven & polish both and produce models of men as Xenophon or Sir Walter Raleigh.

Much of the American Enlightenment was exemplified in this plan. The ideal of the English gentleman was transferred to America and combined with the interest in useful and practical things that were so necessary on the frontier. Learning was to be "connected with Life and qualify its possessor for Action." The young man should avoid the "gaieties &

fopperies of the idle" and spend his time viewing towns, fields, and forts, and conversing with the men who dwell there. "Address & agility of Body" were to be sought after and the company of mechanics and workers was to be valued with that of "the professors of speculative science." This blending of "the active & contemplative life" produced the models of men sought after on the new shores.

To further support his plan Thomson continued:

> For want of such a plan of Education many a man miscalled great is less useful to Society than the meanest peasant & many a gentleman of family of less consequence to it than the little boy in his kitchen.
>
> Not such the worthies that adorned Queen Elizabeth's court, nor the race of private Gentlemen who were the supports of British Liberty from her age down to the Revolution. Cards, dress & ruffling did not then engross their time; expensive diversions and amusements did not drain their Estates. They thought themselves obliged to be good for something. They thought, they studied, they exercised, they entered on life with a resolution to excell & thereby acquired great knowledge of affairs as well as letters.
>
> Youth wholesomely educated, under a sober manly discipline would supersede the cobweb penalties of laws; & vices acquired by mean habits & an effeminate Education that now occupy our tribunals would then disappear.

For the acquisition of such a worthwhile education Thomson's plan did not call for the establishment of a great university on the European style. No such seat of exalted learning could provide the great men and leaders that young America needed. Thomson's solution was idealistic and simple and yet could produce men of great character and ability. Thomson made "a proposal,"

> To prepare youth for the public, inspire them with a love of virtue & make them early acquainted with the necessity of forming & preserving a public character. Let every County be divided into districts. Once every year on a certain day & at a certain place let all the males above 15 or 16 be solemnly assembled. A particular place may be assigned

for such females as chuse to attend. Let the assembly be opened by a discourse or oration on public virtue, the duties of youth and the connexion we stand in to Society & the services we owe to the public. After this let all the youth of 15 or 16 be brought forward one by one & presented by their parent guardian or nearest relation to the president & assembly, & as each is brought up let an enquiry be made concerning his modesty, filial obedience & regular deportment since he passed the age of 12; & if in these he stands approved let him be admitted into the assembly under this restriction that he shall not be allowed to speak in any public assembly until he is 21, & as a mark of admission let him be invested with a belt or some other ensign which he is to wear in all public assemblys. Such as are disapproved to be put on probation until the next assembly, & some persons appointed to have an eye to their conduct. At 21 or 22 let the young men pass under examination. In this let a strict enquiry be made into their moral conduct & public deportment & according as they are approved let them either be received into the class of men or continued under probation in the class of youth. For gross misbehavior to be excluded from the assembly.

This was not an adaptation of European ideas—not even those of the most advanced and enlightened thinkers of England and France. Young men were to be educated in the best fashion by a combination of active and theoretical training. They were to become acquainted with all aspects of life and the abilities of the men who filled all productive positions. Their character and training were at all times to be supervised by the adults of the community and only after approval in formal session were they to be admitted into the ranks of adulthood. Even then "gross misbehavior" would exclude young men from full association with their fellows.

Thomson's proposal may have been idealistic and not practical in effect, but when viewed without the formal assemblies and the examination and insignia of admission, this was basically what happened in almost all American communities as young American men grew into manhood in the late eighteenth and early nineteenth centuries. This was a basic part of Jefferson's beloved agrarian republic, and such a system, however informal its operation might have been, did produce the great leaders that blessed America in her early years.

One of the places in which a young man could acquire such training in the practical, active, and theoretical knowledge of his day was in the recently formed American Philosophical Society, Held at Philadelphia, for Promoting Useful Knowledge. One of the first projects the society undertook in Philadelphia was the observation of the "transit of Venus across the Sun" on June 3, 1769. Three places near Philadelphia were designated as observation sites. Owen Biddle was to view the eclipse from a lighthouse on the Capes of Delaware, and David Rittenhouse, who had demonstrated his scientific ability by building a model of the planetary system, was to view the eclipse from his own conservatory at his home outside Philadelphia. The third site was to be the Public Observatory on the State House Square, and there on Saturday, June 3, 1769, Thomson and five others gathered to make their observations. The weather was favorable, and successful observances were reported at all three sites. The calculations of the records of these and other observations in the colonies furnished not only new scientific data but also the first cooperation of American scientific men on a project of this nature.[30]

Such cooperation was necessary if American science was to advance beyond the colonial—almost primitive—state in which each man worked alone and had contact with others only through a limited correspondence with European scholars. By joining with other Americans, the scientist could share individual research, communicate problems and solutions, share facilities and equipment that were still scarce, and generally enable himself to produce better work. Even today, men work for years seeking solutions to problems that have already been solved elsewhere, but through lack of communication such solutions are not known. So in Philadelphia, even before the American Revolution, the American Philosophical Society, following the lead of Charles Thomson, was taking steps to remedy the lack of cooperation and communication.

Even before the cooperation among those interested in science led to the merger of the two competing societies, both groups had turned to the newspapers as a means of solving the communication problem. In the 1768 "Proposals" for enlarging the American Society, Thomson had emphasized that "Hints thrown out in our public circulating papers are not lost, as in this Country, almost every man is fond of reading." With the *Pennsylvania Gazette* serving as the primary voice of the Philosophical Society and the *Pennsylvania Chronicle* and the *Journal* serving as the initial voices of the American Society, the papers not only expressed the competition among the societies but also stirred interest in their activities. After the merger the papers continued printing the activities of the Society as they were communicated to them, and Thomson, as secretary, was responsible for the publication of numerous items.[31]

A more orderly scheme of publication was desired, however, and shortly an ingenious plan was devised to print the activities of the society in such a form that they might be bound into a single volume. Lewis Nicola, an Irishman introduced into the American Society by Charles Thomson, began a new journal, *The American Magazine, or General Repository*. As an appendix to each monthly issue Nicola published a paper entitled "the Transactions of the American Philosophical Society, &c." Separately and continuously paged, the twenty "Transactions" were designed to be bound as a single volume. None of the papers was by Thomson, but he, as secretary to the society, had elicited several papers from members living outside Philadelphia and it was Thomson who provided these articles for publication. But even when these articles were bound into a single volume, they did not provide a satisfactory answer to the problem of communicating the findings of the society to the public. So Thomson proposed, and in September 1769 the society announced, a plan to publish a volume of its transactions. With this announcement Nicola ceased publication of the papers in the *American Magazine*. Thomson had found a better way to disseminate the "useful knowledge" of the society.[32]

Thomson modified his "Proposals" of 1768 to serve as an introductory preface to the first volume of the *Transactions of the American Philosophical Society* (Philadelphia, 1771). Thus, the purpose of the society and the intent of the *Trans-*

actions were made clear. The volume consisted of four sections. Section one was devoted to the recent observations of the "Transit of Venus"; the other sections dealt with agriculture, medicine, and new inventions. Many of the papers were those transmitted to the society by Thomson in his role as secretary and he apparently had much to do with the choice of which papers were to be included in the volume. Thomson and his coeditors chose well as is indicated by the praise the *Transactions* received both in this country and abroad. Even leading European scientists were impressed with what their Philadelphia colleagues had accomplished. The propagation of useful knowledge thus served to further the American cause.[33]

One of the important parts of Thomson's original plan for the society had been the improvement of American agriculture, manufacture, and trade. Members of the society were to report the discovery of any new crops or new methods of cultivating crops that would improve the state of agriculture. In May 1769, Thomson read an essay by Judge Edward Anthil on the cultivation of grapes and the making of wine in North American climates. Thomson, who became a rum distiller in the autumn of 1769, probably inquired into this matter for his own benefit. The essay was well received and was published in the first volume of the society's *Transactions.*

Thomson and many other disciples of the American Enlightenment constantly strove to apply practically the knowledge that they had gained. Europeans, with their more settled society and static institutions, were able to put greater effort into abstract theories and the development of valuable, though not immediately practical, principles, whereas Americans were facing the multiplicity of problems that arose from bringing order and progress to a developing society and culture. New approaches were needed in the new land, and men of culture and knowledge naturally utilized their foundation in the spirit of the era in their search. Native remedies were sought for local illness whether these illnesses were of the body or of society. If products were lacking, means for their acquisition were sought. If products were expensive when imported, cheaper local substitutes were desired. If native products were inferior, then methods for their improvement were found.

Thomson's ideas concerning the promotion of American-made products were put to good use when he bought a rum distillery in 1769. Throughout the next two years Thomson operated his distillery in Kensington (then on the outskirts of the city but now a part of Philadelphia) and a cordial store on Second Street, a few blocks above Market Street. His advertisements for rum showed how Thomson was putting into private use the ideas he was urging publicly for the American Philosophical Society. "This RUM, by a new Process, is freed from the disagreeable Tang which usually accompanies Continent Rum, and is so much improved in Smell and Flavour, as to be little inferior to, and scarce distinguishable from, that made in the West-Indies." In one of his memorandum books Thomson described the "new Process,"

To Meliorate Rum Spirits,—
for a hhd [hogshead]. Take 1 lb bohea tea, boil it in 6 quarts River or soft water till the strength is extracted then put the leaves into a long bag of thin linen & having poured the liquor into the hhd, hang the bag with the leaves in the cask. Next take about 2 lb flour made with water only into a paste & roll it out into small Rolls about the bigness of your finger; bake these very brown, but not burnt, pound or break them into crumbs & put them into the hhd.
4 oz sp: nit. dulcis [*Spiritus Nitritis Dulcis*—Sweet Spirits of Niter] will greatly mend home made Rum.[34]

Thomson did not confine the application of useful knowledge in his own behalf to his rum distilling operations and his cordial store. He also purchased land and invested in basic American industries such as the Batso Furnace on Little Egg Harbor in New Jersey. This bog iron furnace was built around 1766 and furnished cannon balls, shot, kettles, and spikes and nails to the American armies during the Revolutionary War. Although Thomson, along with Israel Pemberton, was part owner of the foundry during the period in which he was operating the distillery and cordial store, he remained a resident of Philadelphia and continued to be active in provincial affairs.[35]

Thomson's activities during the decade 1760-1770 were many and varied. In addition to his work in opposition to the Stamp Act, Townshend Acts, and other attempts by Parliament to tax the colonies, he was active in other colonial affairs. Seeing the advantageous position occupied by the English colonies with respect to natural resources, climate, and other natural blessings, Thomson perceived that if the area were to advance as it should, united efforts from the interested men in all of the colonies were a necessity. He then proceeded to put his ideas into effect. In order to facilitate colonial improvements and cultural union, Thomson aided materially in establishing the American Philosophical Society. While promoting his personal interests and those of the antiproprietary party, he worked to improve the state of agriculture and manufacturing in the colonies. Active as an amateur in the field of scientific investigation, he showed his concern for his country by investigating new agricultural methods and new crops for North America.

Dramatic aspects of the period are well known while quieter activities are often ignored. Thomson was active in the opposition to the British measures of taxation and deprivation of liberties, but he also spent much time and effort improving the conditions of colonial industry and agriculture. He worked unceasingly to bring scientific and cultural union to the colonies, and this unity was as necessary as political unity in bringing about the Revolution. The nation that was to come was made greater by the attitude that Thomson helped foster—private and public interests alike required the utmost in "promoting useful knowledge."

NOTES

1. The best account of the creation of the American Philosophical Society and the important role that Thomson played is Brooke Hindle, "The Rise of the American Philosophical Society, 1766 to 1787" (Ph.D. diss., University of Pennsylvania, 1949). A brief version is in Hindle, *The Pursuit of Science in Revolutionary America, 1735-1789* (Chapel Hill, 1956), pp. 121-41.

2. Charles Thomson to Benjamin Franklin, November 6, 1768, Thomson Papers, Library of Congress. Lewis R. Harley, *Life of Charles Thomson* (Philadel-

phia; 1900), pp. 35-38, 61-65; Hindle, "Rise of the American Philosophical Society," pp. 31-42.

3. "Junto Minutes," American Philosophical Society Library. On the first pages of the volume in which the minutes of each meeting were kept are rental receipts signed by Samuel Carruthers, tavern keeper. Thomson's leadership is evident in the records of the meetings. It was he, for example, who proposed fines for late and absent members; it was he who forced a favorable resolution of the question of whether or not to keep a minute book. See minutes for meetings of September 22, 1758, and December 1, 1758, January 5, 1759, January 12, 1759.

4. "Junto Minutes," 1758-1762, Hindle, "Rise of the American Philosophical Society," pp. 35-40. In June 1757 the society agreed to purchase "an electrical Apparatus" and an "optical Apparatus." Although there is no record of such activities in the minutes, it seems logical to assume that experiments were conducted with the equipment. Charles Thomson to William Franklin, June __, 1757 (no date given), American Philosophical Society manuscript collection.

5. "Junto Minutes," September 3, 10, 17, 24, and October 1, 7, 15, and 22, 1762.

6. Deborah Franklin to Benjamin Franklin, May 16, 1767, Benjamin Franklin, *The Papers of Benjamin Franklin*, ed. Leonard Labree et al. (New Haven and London, 1959—), 14: 158. *Pennsylvania Gazette*, October 2 and November 20, 1760.

7. This is discussed fully in succeeding chapters.

8. Charles Thomson to Benjamin Franklin, November 6, 1768, Franklin *Papers*, 15: 261-62. Hindle, "Rise of the American Philosophical Society," pp. 51-52.

9. Hindle, *Science in Revolutionary America*, pp. 122-23.

10. "Questions asked by a Society meeting weekly in Philadelphia for their mutual Improvement in Knowledge," Thomson Notebook, Historical Society of Pennsylvania.

11. "American Society Minutes," June-October, 1766. The American Society Minutes are in the same volume but separately paged from the "Junto Minutes" and separated by several blank pages. Hindle, "Rise of the American Philosophical Society," 56-63.

12. "American Society Minutes," November 28, December 5, and December 13, 1766.

13. Francis X. Dercum, "The Origin and Activities of the American Philosophical Society," American Philosophical Society *Proceedings* 66 (1927): 21.

14. "American Society Minutes," November and December 1766 meetings.

15. *Pennsylvania Journal*, March 10, 1768. Carl Bridenbaugh, *The Spirit of '76* (New York, 1975), p. 136.

16. Ibid. See also "Propagating Useful Knowledge from Philadelphia, 1768-1771 (Commemorative Essay by a Member of the Society)," in *Early Transactions of the American Philosophical Society* (American Philosophical Society *Memoirs*, vol. 77, Philadelphia, 1969), pp. 121-25.

17. "American Society Minutes," January 15, 1768, January 22, 1768.

18. The American Philosophical Society, *An Historical Account of the Origin and Formation of the American Philosophical Society* (Philadelphia, 1914), p. 122; Whitfield J. Bell, Jr., *John Morgan, Continental Doctor* (Philadelphia, 1965), pp. 139-40.

19. Dercum, "Origins of the American Philosophical Society," p. 23; Bell, *John Morgan*, pp. 168-71.

20. Carl and Jessica Bridenbaugh, *Rebels and Gentlemen* (New York: 1942), p. 337.

21. "American Society Minutes," February 14, 1768; Thomson to Franklin, November 6, 1768, Thomson Papers, Library of Congress.

22. Hindle, *Science in Revolutionary America*, pp. 132-34.

23. "American Society Minutes," November 18, 1768, "American Philosophical Society Minutes," November and December, 1768; The official record of the proceedings for union have been printed in "Early Proceedings of the American Philosophical Society," compiled from the manuscript minutes by Henry Phillips, Jr. (American Philosophical Society *Proceedings* 22, Philadelphia, 1885): 20-21.

24. The inventory of Thomson's library, 110 titles valued at more than sixty-five pounds, is in Thomson Notebook, Historical Society of Pennsylvania.

25. For a brief discussion of Wollaston's effect on another product of the American Enlightenment see Adrienne Koch, *The Philosophy of Thomas Jefferson* (Chicago, 1964), pp. 5-6.

26. Ibid., pp. 15-17. Thomson Notebook.

27. Minute books, 1762-1771. The Library Company of Philadelphia.

28. Two excellent discussions of the Enlightenment in America are: Henry F. May, *The Enlightenment in America* (New York, 1978) and Henry Steele Commager, *The Empire of Reason, How Europe Imagined and America Realized the Enlightenment* (Garden City, New York, 1977). Commager shows a greater understanding and appreciation of the work of Thomson and others like him.

29. Thomson Notebook. The "Plan" is undated but the date 1766 occurs a few pages later in an entry which appears to have been written about the same time. Many proposals for an American university appear in the post-revolutionary period. Bernard Bailyn, *Education in the Forming of American Society* (Chapel Hill, 1960), p. 113.

30. *Pennsylvania Gazette*, June 8, 1769; Harry Wolf, *The Transits of Venus: A Study of Eighteenth Century Science* (Princeton, 1956), pp. 191 ff.

31. "Propagating Useful Knowledge from Philadelphia, 1768-1771," pp. 125-31.

32. The twenty articles published by Nicola have been reprinted in *Early Transactions of the American Philosophical Society*.

33. Hindle, *Science in Revolutionary America*, pp. 141-45, 158-59.

34. *Pennsylvania Gazette*, November 2, 1769; Thomson Notebook; "Charles Thomson's Philadelphia Rum," *PMHB* 89 (1965): 151.

35. In 1768, Thomson owned 150 acres in Strabane township, York County. In 1770 he owned 120 acres in the older, more settled county of Cumberland. *Pennsylvania Archives*, 3d ser., 2: 439; 24: 772. Watson, *Annals of Philadelphia and Pennsylvania in the Olden Time* (Philadelphia, 1850), 1:568; Charles S. Boyer, *Early Forges and Furnaces in New Jersey* (Philadelphia, 1931; reprinted 1963), pp. 174-90.

3

The Young Merchant
and the Stamp Act

Until about 1760 Charles Thomson gave every evidence of being a careful, meticulous young man who was circumspectly working to advance himself socially and economically. As a student he had concentrated on the classical studies—the traditional measure of a man's education. As a young teacher in the Philadelphia Academy he was so concerned with his reputation that he obtained a certificate of good character before he left the lodgings of a gossipy landlord. When on occasion he showed streaks of brashness, it was of a type to win approval from his elders—escaping from the blacksmith to pursue an education, or slipping off to Philadelphia to obtain a volume of the *Spectator*. While he was master of the Friends' School he boldly condemned the proprietors for their treatment of the Indians—but in so doing he obviously pleased his employers. Rapid economic advance and the accompanying possibility of the loss of his newly acquired financial status made Thomson a likely prospect to lead the radical cause. It took only the threat of the Stamp Act to turn Thomson, the prosperous young merchant, into Thomson, the radical leader.[1]

Approximately a year after his marriage, Thomson found that teaching at the Friends' Public School was not advancing him, either socially or financially, as rapidly as he desired. In January 1760 he notified the Board of Overseers of the Friends' School that he intended to resign and enter business. In October he appeared before the board and gave final notice and settled his accounts for the past year. The board expressed regret at his resignation and seemed to have difficulty securing a replacement.[2]

On October 2, four days before his resignation became final, Thomson advertised the opening of his mercantile shop "in Market Street, nearly opposite to the King of Prussia tavern, and a few doors below the Indian Queen." "Imported in the last vessels from London and Bristol, and to be sold by CHARLES THOMSON," was a wide variety of merchandise including broadcloths, poplins, blankets, silk hankerchiefs, tablecloths, pins, needles, gloves, paper, pewter plates, tea, spices, and a long list of other necessities and luxuries of colonial life.³

Thomson's entrance into business came at an eventful time for both the British Empire and her American colonies. Four weeks earlier, on September 8, 1760, the French had capitulated at Montreal and surrendered all their remaining holdings in Canada to the British. The war was going well for the English in Europe and India and the conflict was nearing an end. Three weeks after Thomson opened his mercantile establishment, King George II of England died suddenly of a heart attack and young George III became king. Thomson's customers had many great events to discuss while purchasing items from the "Neat assortment of goods" on display.⁴

Within a few years Thomson would find his activities severely restricted by the tightening of controls from London. In 1760, however, the colonial regulations laid few restrictions on the dry goods store "nearly opposite to the King of Prussia tavern." Business was booming in Philadelphia. A population of almost nineteen thousand made the city the largest in British America—an honor only recently acquired from Boston. Wealthy merchant families such as the Whartons, Shippens, and Morrises thrived in an economy that left much trade and profit for a newcomer such as Thomson.⁵ The bonds of the trade in which Thomson engaged stretched across the Atlantic and brought English and American merchants together in a common interest. Goods coming from London and Bristol meant that dealers in those cities knew the name of Charles Thomson even though his orders were small. These contacts proved useful later in furthering the cause of American science and in resisting Parliamentary taxation. Thomson's participation in American business life gave him a firm base of action in the coming years. He had never been one of the inarticulate poor from which revolutions sometimes are said to come, and by 1760 Thomson was moving into a position to become a leader of the masses.

There is little evidence of Thomson's life during the early 1760s. He apparently continued his close contacts with the great Philadelphian and neighbor Benjamin Franklin. Thomson occasionally witnessed legal documents for Franklin, and one can imagine "Poor Richard" and other friends stopping by Thomson's store to transact business or discuss current topics. Although he was no longer an educator, Thomson nevertheless continued his interest in books and learning. In August 1761 he bought some books from an estate that Isaac Norris was trying to settle. As a member of the Library Company of Philadelphia, Thomson, along with Dr. Francis Alison, Samuel Rhodes, and Franklin, constituted a committee to prepare a set of rules for the conduct of the Library. That same November Thomson was reported as "fighting for his life with a powerful Consumption. . . . He appears like a skeleton in an old tapestry." His recovery may have been hastened by word that the long war between France and England was ended, and the hopes of continued prosperity that such news brought with it.[6] In July 1764, Thomson gave proof not only of his solvency but also of his hope for future wealth when he subscribed 250 pounds along with Franklin, Norris, and several others to establish a "Linen Manufactory" in or near Philadelphia. The Philadelphians hoped to capitalize on increased linen prices caused by one of the provisions of the Sugar Act just passed by Parliament. Pennsylvania exported much flax to Ireland and possessed a growing number of poor who had no opportunities for employment. So, by 1764, Charles Thomson, son of a linen bleacher, had become a prospective linen manufacturer.[7]

Thomson's well-being was not matched by the Pennsylvania colony. The Assembly was at odds with the proprietors and old political alignments within the colony were in a state of flux. The Quakers were determined to tax the Penns' estates, and the Indians were attacking the frontier. From the frontier the Paxton Boys marched toward Philadelphia in early 1764 to demand that the Quaker-dominated assembly cease its bickering with proprietary representatives and provide for defense against Indian attacks. No record exists of Thomson's activities at this point, but his later actions place him in league of those who were critical of the Quakers and who supported Franklin's hastily raised militia that defended the city from the threatened attack by the Paxtons. Certainly the split between Quakers and Presbyterians that occurred here foreshadowed the rise of the Presbyterian (or Liberty) party that Thomson headed at a later time.[8]

Late in 1764 Thomson's neighbor Franklin sailed for London on a second mission to secure the removal of the Penns as proprietors and the establishment of Pennsylvania as a royal colony. A party of some 300 friends accompanied Franklin to Chester to see him off. Thomson missed the sailing and wrote on December 18 to explain that "the urgency of my business which called me another way deprived me of the pleasure of waiting on you to Chester."[9] In recounting his trip Thomson reported that in traveling thirty-two miles up the Lancaster Road he encountered nineteen taverns. He then launched into an attack on the proprietary governor, repeating a longstanding charge that an excessive number of tavern licenses were granted in order to enrich the governor who received the fees. In providing Franklin with more information to use as ammunition in his fight to end the proprietary government, Thomson proceeded to elaborate on an account from Herodotus: "You remember the Story of Cyrus, the Way he took to break the Spirit and soften the War-like Disposition of the Lydians and render them more abject Slaves by erecting Bagnios and public Inns." The editors of the *Franklin Papers* comment that Herodotus' account is "somewhat less luridly presented than Thomson suggests." Thomson concluded:

I will not say that this is the design of our great Ones. But certain it is that almost in every tavern keeper the Proprietors have a warm advocate and that the more effeminate and debauched a people are, the more they are fitted for an absolute and tyranical Government.

Franklin noted on the back of the letter, "Mr. Thomson. 19 Inns in 30 miles." Not only were Thomson's propagandistic talents flowering, but Franklin and others were aware of them and eager to put them to use. Thomson's next propaganda blasts would be directed toward Parliament and its efforts to tax the colonies.

Parliament, faced with a vastly expanded empire at the end of the French and Indian War, began to make real efforts to regulate the colonies effectively at just the time that the colonies were becoming aware of their own importance. To the British the conduct of the war in the colonies had revealed the inability of the loosely confederated empire to unite and act in a coordinated manner in times of necessity. The British government saw that stronger ties between Great Britain and her colonies were needed if the empire was to survive. To this was added a crushing debt owed by Britain as a result of her expenditures during the war with France and a rising demand from the British public that the colonies assume at least part of the cost of defending and garrisoning North America.

Parliamentary leaders moved first to strengthen the bonds of the empire by issuing orders for stricter enforcement of the existing navigation acts. They placed more American products on the list of goods enumerated by Parliament for shipment only to Great Britain or the other English colonies. The Revenue Act of 1764 (Sugar Act) halved the duties on foreign molasses imported to the colonies but provided for more effective collection of the lower duties. New duties were laid on silk, lawn, and calico, and unfavorable rates were placed on all wines not imported by way of England. Much opposition to the new duties developed in the colonies. Although these aroused no determined protests such as would come with the passage of the Stamp Act the next year, the merchants of Boston, New York, and Philadelphia petitioned their legislatures for relief while rumbles of opposition and discontent were heard from businessmen from all the colonies. No record exists of Philadelphia merchant Charles Thomson's response to these new regulations, but it is certain that he chafed under the restrictions and the increased prices resulting from Parliament's action.[10]

In March 1764, George Grenville, the English prime minister since the peace with France and Spain in the preceding year, announced his intention of introducing a stamp act for the coloines during the next session of Parliament. When the colonists learned of Grenville's proposals, their assemblies began framing protests. The legislators sent petitions to England remonstrating this levying of an internal tax for revenue by a Parliament in which they were in no manner represented. The petitions reached London in February 1765 but Parliament refused to hear the petitions on the grounds that they questioned the supremacy and authority of that body. Thus, early in 1765, the colonies and the London government had already begun to dispute the fundamental issues that later led to ten years of struggle and resulted in the end of British domination over the thirteen American colonies.[11]

In Pennsylvania the dominant Quaker party was already divided over opposition to the Currency Act and over the struggle to depose the Penn proprietorship and replace it with a government under royal control. Ironically, since he would ultimately emerge as a leader in the Presbyterian, or splinter group, it was Benjamin Franklin's continuing delusion over the likelihood of a shift to royal government for the province that kept the Quakers supporting this policy long after it ceased to be feasible. Franklin in London and Joseph Galloway in Philadelphia led the Quaker faction throughout the early 1760s. They operated consistently with a view to pleasing whichever British ministry might be in power at the time in order to obtain their assistance in securing a royal charter. So great was the illusion that a royal grant would solve all the political troubles for Pennsylvania that Franklin was induced to accept the Stamp Act and to attempt to minimize the colonial protests until Thomson and others revealed to Franklin the strength of colonial opposition. Galloway, on the other side of the Atlantic, opposed Thomson and those who were fighting for the repeal of the Stamp Act because their actions might alienate the ministry in whose hands lay all hope for Pennsylvania's becoming a royal colony.[12]

This placed the two old opponents of Pennsylvania politics—the Quaker and the proprietary factions—in the same camp. Neither could afford to openly demand an end to the Stamp Act for fear of creating powerful enemies in London. Thus, Dickinson and Thomson and others of the Presbyterian faction (so called from the fact that most of its leaders and its members were members of that denomination) became the leading proponents of civil liberties in Pennsylvania.[13]

In spite of the petitions from America and the protests of the London agents of some of the colonies, the Stamp Act passed in March 1765, providing for taxes on newspapers and on legal and other business documents. News of the passage of the act was received in Philadelphia in mid-June. On June 19, the day before the news of the act was made public in the *Pennsylvania Gazette*, Thomson sent a lengthy letter to Franklin setting forth his arguments not only against the Stamp Act but also against the other restrictive legislation that Parliament had imposed upon the colonists. "The Act of Parliament, imposing a Stamp duty on the American Colonies, is just published among us, and occasions very great uneasiness." Thomson objected to "being deprived of those rights, those distinguishing and invaluable rights of Britons, of being governed by laws of their own making; and at the same time being subjected to arbitrary unconstitutional courts." He rejected the argument that the colonies were virtually represented in Parliament and opposed the levying of a tax at a time when the colonies were already in debt as a result of their efforts in the French and Indian War. Then, in the methodical manner that typifies much of his propagandistic writing, Thomson enumerated the restrictions imposed on the colonies by the Woolen Act, the Hat Act, the Iron Act, the Staple Act, the Sugar Act, the Currency Act, and other legislation passed by Parliament.[14]

Franklin, in London on behalf of the antiproprietary party in Pennsylvania, had opposed the passage of the Stamp Act but had not anticipated the strong reaction that would take place in the colonies. Some days before Thomson's letter was written, Franklin had written from London:

Depend upon it, my Good Friend, every possible step was taken to prevent the passing of the Stamp Act. But the tide was too strong against us. The nation was provok'd by American claims of independence, and all parties join'd in resolving by this act to settle the point. We might as well have hindered the sun's setting. But since it is down, my Friend, and it may be long ere it rises again, let us make as good a night of it as we can. We may still light candles. Frugality and Industry will go a great way towards indemnifying us. Idleness and Pride tax with a heavier hand than Kings and Parliaments. If we can get rid of the former, we may easily bear the latter.[15]

Upon receipt of Thomson's letter of July 19, Franklin edited it slightly and had it printed in the *London Chronicle* and the *Lloyd's Evening Post* as the first of a series of letters expressing American sentiments against the acts. Thomson's letter so cogently opposed the act on the basis of violations of essential British liberties that Franklin believed his arguments would find support among the readers of London papers.

As Thomson predicted, when news of the Stamp Act spread through the colonies, a storm of protest arose. Daniel Dulany of Maryland and John Dickinson of Pennsylvania, a Quaker soon to break with the pacifist element of his party and a close friend to Thomson, prepared pamphlets denying the idea that the colonists were virtually represented in Parliament since they were all English subjects, and claiming that a tax on the colonies levied by Parliament for revenue only was unconstitutional. Prodded by the oratory of Patrick Henry, the Virginia House of Burgesses condemned the Stamp Tax as a violation of the rights of Englishmen. Several versions of the Virginia Resolutions existed—along with his July 19 letter Thomson apparently sent Franklin a copy of one of the more radical forms that included the strongest denunciations of the Stamp Act.[16]

Everywhere in the colonies men protested about the harm the Stamp Act would do to trade and business. Massachusetts proposed a meeting of the colonies to consider action to secure repeal of the act and nine colonies sent representatives. The Pennsylvania Assembly chose John Dickinson, John Morton, and George Bryan to attend the Stamp Act Congress in New York. By the time the congress met in October 1765, antistamp feeling was beginning to reach such heights that it appeared that the act would never be enforced in the colonies.

Charles Thomson was a leader among those taking a determined stand against the execution of the Stamp Act. As a merchant in Philadelphia he would be only slightly affected by a tax on legal documents and luxury goods, but he opposed this deprivation of the liberty and privileges that were most dear to the colonists. He was disappointed when he discovered that his friend and neighbor Benjamin Franklin had urged that the colonies employ "frugality and industry" to compensate for the losses suffered because of the new revenue act. On September 24, Thomson answered Franklin's July letter and quickly corrected Franklin's illusion that the colonists of British North America were willing to accept the tax and continue their loyalty to England. Thomson argued clearly and effectively for the repeal of the Stamp Act by stating the American causes as he saw them. In his 1765 arguments against the act Thomson foreshadowed the reasons advanced ten years later for the Declaration of Independence and the revolt against England.

Yes, my friend, I grant that 'Idleness and Pride tax with a heavier hand than Kings and Parliaments,' and 'that frugality and industry will go a great way towards indemnifying us.' But the misfortune is, the very thing that renders industry necessary cuts the sinews of it. With industry and frugality the subjects of eastern tyrants might be wealthier than those of England or Holland. But who will labour or save who has not a security in his property? When people are taxed by their own representatives, though the tax is high they pay it cheerfully, from a confidence that no more than enough is required, and that a due regard is had to the ability of the giver. But when taxes are laid merely to 'settle the point of independence,' and when the quantity of the tax depends on the caprice of those who have the superiority, and who will doubtless lay it heavier in order to bring down the spirits or weaken the power of those who claim independence, what encouragement is there to labour or save? The wealth we thereby acquire will be a new motive, which fear of avarice will suggest, to tax us anew. No wonder then if people will chuse to live poor and lazy rather than labour to enrich their tax-masters, or furnish colonies aiming at independence, till the ministry began to abridge them of their liberties. I will venture to affirm, and to you I can appeal for the truth of what I say, that History cannot shew a people so numerous, so far removed from the seat of Royalty, who were so loyal, so attached to their King, and who at the same time had such true sentiments of liberty, as the British American Colonies. How long this will continue God knows.

The sun of Liberty is indeed fast setting, if not down already, in the American colonies: But I much fear instead of the candles you mention being lighted, you will hear of the works of darkness. They are in general alarmed to the last degree. The colonies expect, and with reason expect, that some regard shall be had to their liberties and privileges, as well as trade. They cannot bring themselves to believe, nor can they see how England with reason or justice could expect, that they should have encountered the horrors of a desert, borne the attacks of barbarous savages, and, at the expence of their blood and treasure, settled this country to the great emolument of England, and after all quietly submit to be deprived of every thing an Englishman has been taught to hold dear. It is not property only we contend for. Our Liberty and most essential privileges are struck at: Arbitrary courts are set over us, and trials by juries taken away: The Press is so restricted that we cannot complain: An Army of mercenaries threatened to be billeted on us: The sources of our trade stopped; and, to compleat our ruin, the little property we had acquired, taken from us, without even allowing us the merit of giving it; I really dread the consequence. The parliament insist on a power over all the liberties and privileges claimed by the colonies, and hence require a blind obedience and acquiescence in whatever they do: Should the behavior of the colonies happen not to square with these sovereign notions, (as I much fear it will not) what remains but violence to compel them to obedience. Violence will beget resentment and provoke to acts never dreamt of: But I will not anticipate evil: I pray God avert it.

I congratulate you on the change in the ministry: We hope for much good from it. For such seems the state of the British constitution at present, that from them we are to look for good or ill. Heretofore we have been taught to look for redress from another quarter. I am,

Dear Sir, Your affectionate Friend, &c.[17]

Thomson's letter convinced Franklin that the Americans would not accept the Stamp Act. He began to send numerous articles and essays to those London papers that were friendly to the colonial cause in an attempt to influence Parliament to repeal the duties. Franklin gave Thomson's letter and an abstract from his own letter that had evoked Thomson's reply to William Strahan, the London printer who had published Thomson's *Enquiry*. Strahan printed both letters, omitting the names of Franklin and Thomson, in the London *Chronicle* as being the sentiments of a "North American in London" and "his Friend in America." Franklin realized that if men of Thomson's nature were so firmly opposed to the Stamp Act and if the colonists believed that they were deprived of their liberties and their property, the repeal of the act was necessary to preserve the British Empire.[18]

Meanwhile, as early as September 1765, Thomson and the other foes of the Stamp Act were making plans to prevent the enforcement of the bill in Philadelphia. They realized that if the stamps were available in the province they would be put to use by the timid and by those not in opposition to the duties. This would place those refusing to use the stamps in a treasonable position. To prevent this they decided that the stamps should never be distributed throughout the colony. In order to accomplish this the stamp distributors must either be forced to resign or be coerced into refusing to carry out their duties.

With these ends in mind, Thomson and his fellow opponents of the act instituted an extensive campaign of propaganda in the newspapers of the province. William and Thomas Bradford, publishers of the *Pennsylvania Journal*, were especially active in the campaign and printed letters and articles from local sources as well as from newspapers in other colonies. The London Coffee House, opened by William Bradford in 1754, became a meetingplace for those working for repeal of the duties. Here they brought the latest papers for discussion and argument, wrote new articles, and replied to those who favored accepting the bill. Some of the more determined opponents of the act began taking active measures to prevent its execution. A delegation of the more eager Coffee House group visited John Hughes who had been appointed chief distributor of stamps in Pennsylvania and Delaware on Franklin's recommendation. They demanded that Hughes resign his position, but he successfully put them off by pointing out that as yet he had received no official word of his appointment from London.[19]

On September 16 a mob of Philadelphians gathered and threatened to destroy Hughes' house if he continued his refusal to resign. Apparently it was little more than a device to scare Hughes for several of his friends were informed of the action early enough in advance to defend his home. Thomson and the Quaker leaders had no intention of weakening their position by resorting to violence. The mob roamed the streets until after midnight, and Hughes was so disturbed that he spent the entire night expecting their assault, but the group made no attempt to attack the residence and no damage was done. Hughes remained adamant in his refusal to resign, and further complicated the matter when he fell ill and was confined to his bed for the next three weeks. During his illness those who had directed the mob on the night of September 16 prepared for a large public demonstration to take place when the stamps arrived from England. They continued the newspaper campaign but created no more disturbances until they heard that the ship bringing the stamps and stamped papers was on its way up the Delaware River to Philadelphia.[20]

On October 5 this news reached the London Coffee House and orders went out for muffled drums to be beaten through the streets of Philadelphia and for the bells of the churches and the State House to be tolled as though it were a day of public mourning. At this signal a crowd of over a thousand residents of Philadelphia collected in front of the State House. While William Bradford and Charles Thomson urged the crowd to take action to assure that the stamps would not enter the city, news came that Hughes' commission as stamp distributor for Pennsylvania and Delaware had arrived. After a hurried conference Thomson, Bradford, and those other agitators who had summoned the mob decided that the moment had come to force Hughes to resign. They maneuvered the gathering into choosing Charles Thomson, Archibald McCall, Robert Morris, merchants, along with James Tilghman, attorney, and printer William Bradford as emissaries to ask Hughes to surrender his commission.[21]

Although the stamp distributor was still weak and bedridden, he received the deputation from the State House gathering. Hughes was a courageous man and immediately informed his visitors that he was determined not to resign. Thomson knew of Hughes' fortitude and courage. Hughes had led a party to the Wyoming Valley in 1757 to build houses for the Delaware Indians and had remained there, in spite of raiding parties from some of the neighboring tribes, until one of the workmen was killed and the others refused to stay longer. Thomson advised his fellows that a man of Hughes' determination was not likely to yield unless it was absolutely necessary for him to do so. After arguing with Hughes for an hour, the delegates realized that Thomson was correct. They compromised to the extent of allowing Hughes to sign a written promise not to put the Stamp Act into effect until the king's further pleasure was known or the act was enforced in the neighboring colonies. Because Hughes was exhausted from his session with the deputies, they allowed him until Monday (it was then six o'clock on Saturday) to deliver his promise to the Coffee House.

On Sunday morning Charles Thomson received a message requesting that he return to Hughes' residence. There Thomson found that Hughes had read the document left to be signed and discovered that it was a more positive statement than he had agreed to the day before. Hughes then asked if Thomson and the delegation were sincere in opposing the Stamp Act or whether they would be satisfied with such cooperation as they could obtain easily. Thomson replied that he was sincere himself but that he could not answer for the others. Hughes attempted to weaken his determination by reminding him that he was opposing the execution of a legal act of Parliament. Thomson answered "I do not know, but I hope it will not be deemed rebellion." When Hughes retorted that he knew no other name for it, Thomson continued, "I know not how it may end, for we have not yet determined whether we will ever suffer the act to take place here or not."[22] He then departed and on Monday the entire delegation returned to Hughes' home. After more dispute they devised a statement that satisfied both parties. Hughes signed the agreement, which was soon afterward displayed in a prominent position at the Coffee House.[23]

On Monday, November 7, the same day that the Hughes agreement was signed, the Philadelphia merchants met at the Court House and adopted resolutions not to import any more goods from Great Britain until the Stamp Act was repealed. Each merchant agreed to countermand all orders for goods then resting in the hands of English merchants, and a strongly worded printed order was drawn up to ensure that no goods would be shipped. Thomson suggested that such a maneuver would secure the support of the English merchants in the effort to repeal the Stamp Act. In an endeavor to gain the support of the London companies with which he did business, Thomson included with the notice countermanding his orders accounts of the agitated state of affairs in the colonies. For example, on the same day the merchants agreed to the boycott, Thomson wrote the London firm of Welsh, Wilkinson, & comp., "you must look out for other markets to vend your wares. ... It would be unsafe for any man to import while the Stamp Act continues unrepealed."[24]

Thomson set forth his views at length two days later in a note countermanding his orders for goods from the firm of Cook, Lawrence & Co., of London. Thomson pointed out that the English merchants had an interest in the welfare of the colonies and the effect of the regulations imposed by Parliament, "because what distresses us will in the end affect you." Tracing the history of Parliamentary treatment of the colonies during the years since the end of the French and Indian War, he showed how the English government had subordinated the welfare of the colonies to the welfare of British merchants and industrialists by prohibiting manufacturing, restricting trade by not allowing a paper currency, and confining trade to the British Empire. The Stamp Act had aroused opposition not only by its revenue feature but also by the arbitrary manner in which violators were to be judged before Admiralty Courts without juries. This state of affairs had caused the colonies to stop their trade with England. "The Stamp officers have every where ... been obliged to resign ... and the whole Continent have submitted to a suspension of Law with regard to Civil matters rather than submit to take the stamps." The Stamp Act Congress that had met in New York in October petitioned "to have the stamp act repealed, some of the restrictions on our trade abated and some other grievances redressed. ... In order to restore the former prosperous trade with England we expect that all who have any Interest or Connexion here will use their utmost endeavours to obtain for us a redress of our Greivance and a full and free enjoyment of our natural and inherent Rights."[25]

For a few days after the Stamp Act went into effect on November 1, 1765, Philadelphians conducted little or no business. They held legal matters in abeyance and did not print newspapers or printed them on unstamped paper without the name of the publisher. Merchants spent more time discussing the unjustness of the act than in transacting business. At the November 7 meeting, which resulted in the merchants' boycott of British goods, Thomson spoke for the radicals in demanding that John Hughes "totally and fully resign his Office," and endeavored to compel public officials to do business on unstamped paper.[26]

At this point Thomson's radicalism either had outstripped his supporters or he was utilizing a device that he used later—appearing to push for an extreme measure in order to secure the adoption of a more moderate one. At any rate, Thomson's demands were blocked by hisses of opposition from the White Oaks, a group of "inarticulate ship carpenters." The White Oaks also conferred with Hughes and Joseph Galloway at a tavern and afterward pledged to prevent any damage to Hughes' home or person. Thomson, the radical, had indeed exceeded the tenor of the "mob."[27]

Slowly things returned to their normal state and business was resumed without the use of the stamps. Thomson's suggestion that they ignore the Parliamentary Act was ultimately adopted by the merchants, and by December even the lawyers resolved to conduct legal affairs without stamped documents. Thomson and others claimed that the act was unconstitutional and that nothing bound them to obey it.

By February 1766 the combined efforts of the nonimporting merchants and colonial agents in London had convinced the English merchants and public that the act should be repealed. Franklin appeared before the House of Commons and clearly presented the case for the colonies. On February 27 he wrote to Thomson, "We at length after a long and hard struggle, have gained so much ground that there is little Doubt the Stamp Act will be repealed."²⁸ Within a few weeks the king granted his grudging assent to the repeal of the act and the first major colonial dispute with Parliament ended. By appealing to the business interests of English merchants, men like Thomson had successfully overthrown a measure that would have deprived them of property and liberty. And Thomson had firmly established himself as a leader among those men who were determined that no power would take away their rights.

Parliament had temporarily restored the ties of the Empire and if it had acted wisely the Stamp Act unpleasantness would have disappeared. The colonies still adhered firmly to the mother country and rejoiced when they learned of the removal of their principal subject of contention. Philadelphia held a noisy and boisterous celebration upon the receipt of news that the Stamp Act was repealed. The leading agitators held a large banquet at the State House and voiced their joy over the re-establishment of harmony and goodwill with Great Britain. Thomson wrote to Franklin concerning the manner in which the news of the repeal was received.

> Joy there was to be sure ...; a Joy not expressed in triumph but with the warmest sentiments of Loyalty to our King and a grateful acknowledgement of the Justice and tenderness of the mother Country—and what man who had the feelings of humanity (not to mention more) but rejoices that an affair which might have had such terrible Consequences is thus happily accommodated. May there never arise a like occasion!²⁹

"Like Occasions" would come and they would come soon. Charles Thomson, the radical merchant, would lead the resistance to them. But in 1766 it was Charles Thomson, the merchant, who rejoiced in the triumph of the American cause.

It is difficult to assess the impact of Thomson's role as a leader in the resistance to the Stamp Act. It certainly marked him as a radical—one whom the mechanics of Philadelphia were not yet willing to follow. It also made him one of Benjamin Franklin's most trusted informants concerning events and attitudes in the American colonies. Franklin, in turn, used Thomson's insights to the American temper as propaganda to sway the English public and Parliament. Their relationship continued in other areas as well. Thomson on occasion assisted Franklin's wife in some of the more complex affairs of Franklin's Pennsylvania business dealings. He kept Franklin informed of the debates between the American Society and the Philosophical Society and their ultimate merger into the American Philosophical Society. His known associations with Franklin and his radical reputation would assist Thomson's political leadership in the years to come, but for the moment there was hope of peace between England and America.

NOTES

1. The nature of revolutionary leadership, particularly the nature of leadership in the American Revolution, has not been adequately explored. In Thomson's case opportunities for personal advancement and the advancement of his colony and adopted country coincided remarkably. The making of the man and the making of the nation required the same talents and even the same responses to English threats and oppression.

2. Thomas Woody, *Early Quaker Education in Pennsylvania* (New York, 1920), p. 221.

3. *Pennsylvania Gazette*, October 2, 1760; and November 20, 1760.

4. Bernhard Knollenberg, *Origin of the American Revolution: 1759-1766* (New York, 1960), pp. 17-18 discusses the events of September and October 1760.

5. Arthur M. Schlesinger, *The Colonial Merchants and the American Revolution, 1763-1776* (New York, 1918), pp. 15-31, portrays the generally prosperous conditions in the American colonies at this time and supports Knollenberg as to the lack of effectiveness of British colonial regulations in 1760.

6. Benjamin Franklin *The Papers of Benjamin Franklin*, ed. Leonard Labree et al. (New Haven and London, 1959-   ), 9;336; 10:187, 386-88; 11:442. 521.

7. The project never prospered and was abandoned by 1767. Whether Thomson

and the other promoters lost the entire 250 pounds that they each invested is difficult to determine, but the fact that Thomson had this kind of money to invest is indicative of his improved status. Charles Thomson Stock Certificate, American Philosophical Society. Printed along with additional information in Franklin *Papers*, 11: 315-16.

8. James H. Hutson, *Pennsylvania Politics, 1746-1770: The Movement for Royal Government and Its Consequences* (Princeton, 1972), pp. 84-121.

9. Thomson was apparently expanding his business interests at a great rate. In addition to dealing in property adjacent to the Philadelphia area, he had land holdings in Virginia and elsewhere. His trip may have been in conjunction with some of these properties. In September he and John Foxcroft advertised land for sale or lease near Winchester, Virginia, and were looking for a sawmill operator and a blacksmith. *Pennsylvania Journal*, September 12, 1765. Franklin *Papers*, 11:521 n, 522 n.

10. For a more complete discussion, see Edmund S. and Helen M. Morgan, *The Stamp Act Crisis* (Chapel Hill, 1953), pp. 21-39; and Merrill Jensen, *The Founding of a Nation* (New York, 1968), pp. 3-69. Joseph A. Ernst, *Money and Politics in America, 1755-1775* (Chapel Hill, 1973), deals with the Currency Act of 1764 and delineates "the political economy of revolution."

11. Morgan, *Stamp Act*, pp. 60-69. The protest petitions from the colonial legislatures and their consideration and rejection in London are discussed at length in Knollenberg, *Origin of the American Revolution*, pp. 196-227.

12. Hutson, *Pennsylvania Politics*, pp. 210-11. Ernst, *Money and Politics in America*, pp. 89-133. Benjamin H. Newcomb, *Franklin and Galloway: A Political Partnership* (New Haven, 1972), treats extensively the relationship between Franklin and Joseph Galloway. Thomson and Galloway had worked together with Israel Pemberton on behalf of the Delaware Indians but had differing responses when faced with the Stamp Act. Galloway chose to remain loyal to the mother country and established authority at whatever cost; Thomson would soon emerge as a leader of the radicals. Franklin seems to have tried to keep the two old associates together for as long as possible.

13. The term *party* is somewhat inaccurate for the politics of this period. *Faction* perhaps more accurately defines the loose political alliances that existed at the time, but the word carries implications of harsh dissension that are not necessarily present. As used here the two terms are interchangeable and refer to the political groupings from which parties would emerge.

14. Franklin *Papers*, 12:183-88.

15. Franklin to Thomson, July 11, 1765, Franklin *Papers*, 12:206-08.

16. Franklin *Papers*, 12:213 n.

17. [Thomson to Franklin], September 24, 1765, from the *London Chronicle*, November 16, 1765; included in Verner W. Crane, *Benjamin Franklin's Letters to the Press, 1758-1775.* (Chapel Hill, 1950), pp. 36-38; Franklin *Papers*, 12:278-80.

18. Franklin to Thomson, February 27, 1766, Franklin *Papers*, 13:178-79.

19. John Hughes to Benjamin Franklin, September 8, 1765, printed along with other letters from Hughes and Joseph Galloway in the *Pennsylvania Journal*, September 4, 1766; Franklin *Papers*, 12:263-66.

20. Morgan, *Stamp Act*, p. 249.

The Young Merchant and the Stamp Act   73

21. Hughes to the Commissioners of the Stamps, October 12, 1765, *Pennsylvania Journal*, September 4, 1766.

22. Pauline Maier, *From Resistance to Revolution* (New York, 1972), pp. 52-53, interprets this to mean a reluctance to resist the act. Although her overall account of the making of revolutionaries out of radicals is excellent, Miss Maier has wrongly interpreted some of Thomson's letters and portrays him as only "ambiguously involved" with the Stamp Act opposition, pp. 221-22. A closer reading of the evidence in Philadelphia and London indicates otherwise.

23. *Pennsylvania Journal*, September 4, 1766. By his determined refusal to resign as distributor of the stamps, Hughes completely lost favor in Pennsylvania. His obstinancy undoubtedly assisted Thomson in winning away the support of the White Oaks and other artisans who backed Hughes at this point. Thomson's presence in Philadelphia on November 6 and 7 is cited by John J. Zimmerman as evidence that Thomson was not the secretary to the Stamp Act Congress that convened in New York on Monday, November 7. Thomson was so credited by several nineteenth-century historians—probably because of a copy of the actions of the Congress in Thomson's handwriting that survived in his papers in the Library of Congress. "Charles Thomson, 'The Sam Adams of Philadelphia,' " *Mississippi Valley Historical Review* 45 (1958): 471 n.

24. Thomson to Messers, Welsh, Wilkinson & comp., November 7, 1765, "Thomson Papers," New York Historical Society *Collections*, 11 (1878): 6.

25. Thomson to Messers. Cook, Lawrence & Co., November 9, 1765, Thomson Papers, N.Y.H.S. *Collections*, 11:7-12.

26. Joseph Galloway to William Franklin, November 14, 1765, Franklin *Papers*, 12:372-73.

27. James H. Hutson, "An Investigation of the Inarticulate: Philadelphia's White Oaks," *William and Mary Quarterly*, 3d ser. 29 (1972): 109-42.

28. Franklin to Thomson, February 27, 1766, Franklin *Papers*, 13:178-79.

29. Thomson to Franklin, May 20, 1766, Franklin *Papers*, 13: 277-79.

4

Thomson and the Townshend Acts

The immediate effect of the repeal of the Stamp Act was the return of peaceful relations between the colonies and the mother country. A long-range effect was the emergence of a new group of colonial leaders. Men like Charles Thomson had for the first time led their fellow colonists into active political participation and they had achieved their goals. This new cadre of radical activists possessed not only leadership experience and a following, they had developed successful tools in dealing with the British attempts at regulating the colonies—mass meetings and economic boycotts made powerful weapons.[1]

Thomson's growing stature in Pennsylvania politics came primarily from his activities in opposition to the Stamp Act but was enhanced by his earlier involvement in the life of the colony. His work with the Friendly Association and their dealings with the Delaware Indians, his association with colonial authorities in this and in his capacity as an educator, and his work with the American Philosophical Society, along with his connections with Benjamin Franklin and his activities as a merchant and as a public-minded citizen all contributed to his rapid rise to a place of prominence. The pieces of his life were now fitting together nicely.

Thomson and the other colonial radical leaders would probably not have been able to put their newly found political strength to use had it not been for events then taking place in England. The cause of American liberties was to experience a new threat and the Presbyterian (Liberty) party would again respond to Thomson's guidance. When the new crisis had passed and the Townshend Duties were repealed,

Thomson's position of leadership would be even stronger than before.

In early 1767, the new chancellor of the exchequer, Charles Townshend, in an effort to relieve debt-ridden England of some of the costs of administering her colonies, proposed a series of acts that were to strengthen the enforcement of British trade regulations, raise a revenue for defending and governing the colonies, and provide a surplus that would be used to make royal officials in America independent of the colonial legislatures.[2]

The colonists were in a dilemma of their own making. In opposing the Stamp Act many Americans had stressed that, although Parliament had an undoubted right to regulate trade, they had no right to lay a direct tax on the colonists. Parliament had responded with the Duty Act, which laid new taxes on the importation of tea, paint, paper, glass, and lead. The new duties, although designed to raise revenue, were in the guise of trade regulations. The Quaker and proprietary interests in Pennsylvania were faced with another test of the politics of ingratiation which they had been practicing—how could American rights be defended without alienating important British friends? The Presbyterians had no such problem. Thomson, Dickinson, and others began a propaganda campaign against the Townshend Acts. The best known part of the campaign was a series of letters by Dickinson signed "A Pennsylvania Farmer." These "Farmers Letters" reflect the tone of the opposition and rank among the most important documents of the coming of the American Revolution. Beginning in early December 1767, the "Letters" were printed in all the Philadelphia newspapers and were reprinted throughout the colonies. In March 1768, as soon as they were completed, the "Letters" were published in pamphlet form. Dickinson stressed that the Townshend Acts were unconstitutional because the duties had been laid for the sole purpose of raising a revenue and that the enforcement provisions endangered American liberties.[3]

Despite the well-reasoned pleas of Dickinson and the other Presbyterian propagandists, the Pennsylvanians were slow to act against the Townshend Duties. Thomson's old opponent from Stamp Act days, Joseph Galloway, was speaker of the Assembly and a sworn opponent of Dickinson.[4] In February,

Thomson, who doubtless had a role as editor-critic of the "Farmers Letters," along with letter number twelve published his own letter signed "A Freeborn American."

The letter begins: "At a time when the judicious *Farmer* opens to view the terrible effects of a late act of parliament in all their native horrors, *do* I, my countrymen! *can* I still behold you *assenting* to the force of his arguments without *rousing* from your lethargy? Will not the chains of *slavery*, rattling in your ears, excite your attention?" He continued: "Shall the *freeborn* sons of BRITAIN become *slaves*?... Where are those *heroic resolves*, that zeal for the preservation of government and liberty, that shone so brightly in the time of the detestable *Stamp Act*?" After urgent exhortations to Americans to rouse themselves to oppose the acts, Thomson concluded:

> Revere the mother-country; but never, never let that veneration degenerate into a weak, pitiful submission to tyrannical measures. Encourage your own manufactories, expunge the superfluities of luxury, and let each one set an example of frugality. Consider, the prosperity of thousands yet unborn, depends in some degree on the conduct of each individual.
>
> Whenever it is possible, let the *representatives* be instructed by their *constituents*, to *such measures* as appear most advisable. Let the spirit of *liberty* and loyalty invigorate every breast, and, in the use of proper means, with the blessing of heaven, we may justly hope for success.[5]

Those who opposed the Townshend Duties realized that unless the colonies could be united their protests would achieve nothing. To unite those interested in their cause they formed committees designed to inform and influence the people of all the colonies. Charles Thomson, some twenty years later, wrote about these efforts to Dr. David Ramsay of South Carolina, who in 1786 was preparing his projected *History of the American Revolution*. Thomson told how the opposition leaders in Pennsylvania and the other colonies realized that the New England colonies possessed an invaluable asset in their regularly held town meetings.

The advantages derived from these meetings by uniting the whole body of the people in the measures taken to oppose the Stamp Act induced other provinces to imitate the example. Accordingly under the Association which was formed in opposition to the revenue laws of 1767 and which lasted for upwards of two years, Committees were established not only in the Capitals of every Province, but also in most of the county towns and subordinate districts.[6]

By these means any new information or defense of the colonial position was quickly spread from Boston, New York, or Philadelphia, where the opposition was centered, to the committees scattered over the colonies. The committees would then call public meetings to inform the people of the information received from the trading centers of the colonies.

A small committee, such as Thomson spoke of, arranged for the meeting of a large number of Philadelphia merchants at the London Coffee House in March 1768. A gathering of Boston merchants had recently signed a nonimportation agreement with the condition that it would go into effect when New York and Philadlephia joined. The radical core of Philadelphia merchants called the general meeting to try to secure Philadelphia's adherence to the pact. The merchants, however, fearing the heavy losses that would result from a cessation of trade with England opposed the proposal of nonimportation. The meeting limited its action to a resolution that the taxes were violations of American rights, and showed no intention of joining with Boston in their nonimportation plans. Thomson chafed at the delay and continued to apply pressure to the reluctant merchants.[7]

The radical group knew that if popular opinion was united firmly behind a boycott of British goods the merchants would be forced to accept nonimportation. To persuade the public the radical leaders utilized the same propaganda methods they had employed in their attacks on the Stamp Act. They distributed pamphlets, broadsides, and newspaper articles throughout the colonies in an effort to advance their cause. Frequently they used letters to the newspapers to present their case. Using several pseudonyms, a prolific writer could give the impression that a mass of public opinion favored nonimportation.[8]

Foremost among the propagandists in Philadelphia were Charles Thomson and John Dickinson. Thomson, who was more radical than Dickinson, worked avidly to enlist the other merchants in the cause of nonimportation. On May 12, 1768, an especially brusque letter by Thomson appeared in the *Pennsylvania Gazette*. Again using the signature "A Freeborn American," and this time addressing himself directly to the merchants of Philadelphia, Thomson appealed to the reluctant businessmen:

> we most ardently beseech you, join with New York and Boston. Shame us not, we intreat you. Let it not be a scandal to be a Philadelphian...a Pennsylvanian. Scorn all thought of delay. A few years more, and we shall not be able to buy, nor you to import...the people of England will throw upon you as much of their burden as they can. Union makes the weak strong and strength makes them safe. To be firm and true to the righteous cause of one's country can never be rebellion; it is a patriot virtue![9]

Thomson extended his propaganda efforts beyond the merchant classes of Philadelphia. Active himself in this year of 1768 in the American Society, Thomson realized that the many clubs and groups of Philadelphia could exert great influence in the struggle to unite the colonists. At the same time that he was involved in this struggle to preserve his country's liberties, Thomson was striving to advance its cause by promoting useful knowledge in America. Throughout the spring of 1768 Thomson's pen was busy pouring out letters in support of the American Society as well as the cause of American liberties. Typical was a June 2 letter in the *Pennsylvania Gazette* proposing that the various societies and clubs in the colonies write in defense of their invaded rights and liberties. He proposed that the clubs "establish the glorious fashion of wearing none but American manufactures." And he suggested that each society "resolve for a limited time to eat no lamb [to increase the native wool supply], ... encourage our own manufactories as much as possible, ... wear none but home-made clothes." All this was to be done "in the cause of liberty and their country."[10]

In May, the Massachusetts legislature, grown tired of waiting for the other colonies to join in a nonimportation agreement, sent a circular letter to the legislatures of all the colonies. The letter concisely set forth the case against the mother country and claimed that Parliament was violating the British constitution by depriving the Americans of their property through taxes levied without their consent. When the news of the letter arrived in England, it aroused charges of sedition and treason. Lord Hillsborough, secretary of state for the colonies, dispatched a letter to twelve colonies charging Massachusetts with proposing treasonable combinations to destroy the true British constitution.[11]

Lord Hillsborough's reply to the circular aroused a general cry of protest from the colonies. In Pennsylvania the Assembly received the circular letter from Massachusetts and adjourned without taking any action. In late July, after the receipt of Hillsborough's reply, a great mass meeting of Philadelphians was arranged. Thomson and John Dickinson addressed the crowd that had gathered before the State House and vividly denounced the usurpations of the British government. They implored the Philadelphians to support the radical movement opposing further importation of British goods. The meeting closed with the adoption of a resolution to the Assembly that the king, lords, and commons be petitioned immediately to end their unjust mistreatment of the colonies.[12]

When the Assembly met in September, the members showed a strong inclination to submit to the resolution signed by the citizens at the State House mass meeting. The speaker, Joseph Galloway, supported the authority of Parliament and the king and opposed any move to yield to the radicals. But the assemblymen had drawn away from his influence and adopted petitions as Thomson and Dickinson had demanded at the State House meeting.[13]

The merchants still refused to join the boycott against English goods so Thomson and the other radicals continued their propaganda activities. Thomson brought an additional element into the propaganda campaign by utilizing the contacts he had made while expanding the American Society. By November 1768 Thomson had corresponded with men of importance in all the American colonies as a part of the contest for members between the American Society and the Philosophical Society. The unification of the two societies into the American Philosophical Society in December-January 1768-69 signified a growing unity among the conflicting parties in Philadelphia. The Philosophical Society represented the conservative, more prosperous party, and its members, in general, opposed renewal of the nonimportation tactics. As other efforts to secure the repeal of the Townshend Duties failed, many of the wealthier merchants drew nearer to the position of Thomson and the American Society. Some even joined the "mechanics and tradesmen" to become supporters of the movement to accompany Boston and New York in refusing to import British goods.

On January 1, 1769, New York and Massachusetts began the enforcement of nonimportation. Still the Philadelphia merchants refused to yield to the demands of the radicals. Even those who agreed that some action was necessary debated as to whether the embargo should be on all British goods or only on those articles that were taxed. Thomson, with his fellow merchants, Thomas Mifflin, Thomas Clifford, and John Reynell, insisted that the embargo should be as complete as the one adopted by New York and Massachusetts. In February, Thomson proposed a drastic step. Those Philadelphia merchants who favored a complete embago were persuaded to sign an agreement to cut off all British goods until all of the Townshend Duties were repealed. About sixty of the more radical merchants signed the nonimportation agreement thus expressing faith in Thomson's assurances that public opinion would force the remainder of the merchants to join. A few weeks later, as Thomson had predicted, the merchants of the entire city joined the nonimportation association.[14]

The Philadelphia merchants subscribing to the nonimportation association appointed a Merchants Committee to enforce the agreement. The committee consisted of many patriots who were to become more important to the American cause as the movement toward a revolution continued. In addition to Thomson, who became secretary to the First Continental Congress in 1774, the committee included Thomas Mifflin, later a general in the Continental army; Robert Morris, the revolutionary superintendent of finance; and Tench Francis and John M. Nesbit, both associated with Morris and Thomson in the Bank of North America, which financed the government in the early days of its existence. The committee faced the problem of detecting violators of the embargo on British imports. As prices rose in the city and province, profiteers and merchants loyal to the crown attempted to smuggle shipments into Philadelphia or into hidden coves along the Delaware River. Those violators who were apprehended were brought before the committee, and the Philadelphia newspapers carried reports of the action taken against them. The merchants forced guilty individuals to return the goods and admit their "crimes" publicly.[15]

Soon after the boycott on British goods went into effect, the Philadelphia Committee of Merchants began to secure English allies working for the repeal of the Townshend Duties. Following the methods they had successfully initiated during the Stamp Act controversy, they gained the support of the merchant classes in London, Bristol, and other important British cities. In April 1769, Thomson wrote a letter signed by the entire committee that explained their position. The letter stated that the residents of the colonies had no choice in the election of members of Parliament, and because of their geographic and economic situation could never have representatives in London. Therefore, every act of Parliament made for raising a revenue in America deprived the colonists of property without their consent and consequently invaded their liberties.[16]

In November Thomson wrote to Franklin and discussed the matter in almost identical language:

> The colonies see plainly that the Ministry have adopted a settled plan to subjugate America to arbitrary power and that all the late acts respecting them lend to this purpose. ...It is true the impositions already laid are not very greivous; but if the principle is established, there is no

security for what remains. The very nature of freedom supposes that no tax can be levied on a people without their consent given personally or by their representatives. It was not on account of the largeness of the sum demanded by Charles Ist that ship money was so odious to the commons of England. But because the principle upon which it was demanded left nothing they could call their own. The continuation of this claim of the parliament will certainly be productive of ill consequences as it will tend to alienate the affections of the colonies from the mother country.[17]

During the month in which he wrote Franklin, Thomson left the dry goods business and became a manufacturer and distributor of rum. The prolonged period of difficulties with England had left its mark on the business of the colonies. Trade had declined considerably and the boycott on British goods created a situation in which it was almost impossible to prosper as a dry goods merchant. Thomson's father-in-law, John Mather of Chester, Pennsylvania, had died almost a year earlier leaving Thomson's wife with property that gave the Thomsons a moderate income.[18] Thomson sought to improve his own position and the condition of manufacturing in the colonies by establishing his rum distillery just outside Philadelphia near Kensington. He advertised his "Philadelphia Rum, of excellent Quality, and Cordials of all Kinds" for sale either at the distillery or at his house on Second Street a few doors above Race Street.[19]

Thomson had prospered as a merchant, but his strong adherence to the boycott of British goods had destroyed his greatest source of income. He now turned to the production of rum. He had long urged that Americans concentrate their efforts on locally producing goods that otherwise would have to be imported. Such activities are but another illustration of the application of "useful knowledge" in America. Thomson's motives were a convenient blend of self-aggrandizement and love of country. The manufacture and sale of rum seemed an excellent way to invest his funds.

Although Thomson left the mercantile business and was not directly affected by the Townshend Duties, he continued to work toward their repeal. In his November 26 letter to

Franklin he emphasized that the duties levied by Parliament were not the only grievances the colonies had with England. The arbitrary manner in which the taxes were to be enforced added to the opposition from the colonists. The extended jurisdiction of Admiralty Courts where no juries were permitted, the continued practice of stationing regular British troops in the colonies during peacetime, and the refusal of Parliament to consider the petitions from Americans seeking redress all increased discontent in the colonies. Franklin thought Thomson's letter "very judicious" and he showed it to several members of Parliament before having it printed in the *London Chronicle*, March 3, 1770.[20]

Despite continued discontent among the colonists, leading Philadelphia merchants still worked for an end to nonimportation. In Jaunary 1770 rumors spread that unless the embargo brought a quick response from Parliament, the merchants would seek to reopen trade with England. Leading dry goods importers who had been coerced into membership on the Merchants Committee now felt bold enough to resign and a collapse of nonimportation was threatened. Thomson responded with the publication of a letter that he received from Franklin, in which Franklin told how Thomson's arguments "had due weight" with members of Parliament and urged that nonimportation be continued until all external duties were removed. Franklin's letter was especially useful in keeping the allegiance of the mechanics and artisans. The workers of Philadelphia considered Franklin one of their own and respected his opinions. Franklin's letters seem to have had more effect than the reports of the Boston "Massacre," which aroused little interest in Philadelphia. Sentiment for resuming importation grew as summer neared, and Thomson, Mifflin, Morris, and the other radicals on the Merchants Committee faced difficulties as they stood firm against any talk of modifying the agreement.[21]

In June a meeting of the Merchants Association was called to consider possible changes in the agreement. Newspapers, largely supporting the radicals, reported that the meeting agreed "almost unanimously" to continue the embargo. But one critic reported that continuation of nonimportation was possible only because Charles Thomson, "the Leader, all along for the opposition. . . . Introduc'd tis suposed the body of disaffected Mechanics among the Subscribers, who were only appointed to meet & by this Artifice Carry'd his point."[22]

There is no evidence that the "mechanics" Thomson introduced into the meeting included the White Oaks (that group of ship carpenters who had hissed down Thomson's efforts to force John Hughes to renounce his stamp distributorship in 1765), but it is logical to assume that they were there. Less than a month later, they and the other mechanics would support Thomson and his Presbyterian party in the provincial elections. Thomson, who in 1765 "was one of the Son's of Liberty's generals without an army," by the fall of 1770 had acquired for his revolutionary movement "the troops which they needed to accomplish their aims in Pennsylvania."[23]

After the enemies of nonimportation were defeated in June, the Thomson elements thought that the embargo would stand until all the duties were repealed by Parliament. In this way the will of the colonies would be imposed on England, and the principle of no taxation without representation would be secured. But within a few days news reached Philadelphia that Parliament had repealed all of the Townshend Duties except that on tea. The pressure for resuming trade with England grew stronger as rumors reached the city that the merchants of the other colonies were making similar demands.

The radical leaders, backed by a united public opinion of their own creation, prevented any action modifying the nonimportation agreement until mid-July. Then news reached Philadelphia that the merchants of New York had dropped their boycott of all British goods except those that were still taxed. Thomson and the others realized that unless some sort of pressure was placed on the merchants an immediate end of the embargo was inevitable. To prevent a meeting of the merchants in which they feared they would be outnumbered, they hurriedly called the inhabitants of the city to meet at the State House on July 14. The principal speaker at the meeting was Charles Thomson. After condemning the New Yorkers, he introduced a resolution declaring that Philadelphia would continue its embargo and would also boycott New York until the merchants of that city reversed their decision. The merchants in the crowd protested against this method of imposing a further restriction on their trade, but Thomson through masterful oratory and an appeal to the patriotic "lower elements" of the city, carried the day.[24]

Events in the other colonies led to new attempts to break the association. The merchants of the colonies flanking Pennsylvania were taking advantage of Philadelphia's insistence on continuing nonimportation, and were supplying Pennsylvanians with goods that were not available in the Quaker city. In September matters came to a crisis. Although Thomson and the radicals were still in control of the Merchants Committee, the opposing group forced a call for a meeting on September 20. There a motion was presented to end the embargo on all goods except tea and other dutied items. When the motion passed, Thomson rose in protest for the radical members of the committee and declared that the agreement had been broken. He announced that he and the other members of the committee who shared his views were resigning as an indication of their dissatisfaction.[25]

A few days later Thomson, Mifflin, and the other radical committee members called a mass protest meeting at the State House. The action of the merchants' meeting was condemned and resolutions were adopted praising the action of those committee members who had resigned.[26] Although these resolutions had little effect, they indicated the popularity that Thomson and the others enjoyed with the inhabitants of the city. They could not completely control the actions of the large and prosperous merchant class but the mechanics, tradesmen, and small businessmen welcomed their leadership. This influential group had begun to realize their own strong position in the economy and politics of the province. It was only with their help that Thomson had maintained the nonimportation agreement in the face of growing protests from the conservative merchants. During the fight for repeal of the Townshend Acts, Thomson had become a leader of the radical elements of Philadelphia. The events of the next five years, which brought the Revolution to Pennsylvania and the other colonies, required the guiding hands of men in a position to back their demands with a strong voice of public opinion. Thomson was in a position to provide such guidance.

NOTES

1. For a detailed analysis of the many factions of Pennsylvania politics, see James H. Hutson, *Pennsylvania Politics, 1746-1770; The Movement for Royal Government and Its Consequences* (Princeton, 1972), pp. 202-4, and Benjamin H. Newcomb, "Effects of the Stamp Act on Colonial Pennsylvania Politics," *William and Mary Quarterly*, 3d ser. 23 (1966): 257-72. See also Hutson's "The Campaign to Make Pennsylvania a Royal Province, 1764-1770," *PMHB* 94 (1970): 427-63; 95 (1971): 28-49.

2. Robert J. Chaffin, "The Townshend Acts of 1767," *William and Mary Quarterly*, 3d ser. 27 (1970): 90-121.

3. David L. Jacobson, *John Dickinson and the Revolution in Pennsylvania, 1764-1776* (Berkeley and Los Angeles, 1965), p. 57.

4. Benjamin H. Newcomb, *Franklin and Galloway: A Political Partnership* (New Haven, 1972), pp. 180-207.

5. *Pennsylvania Gazette*, February 18, 1768. P. L. Ford, ed., *Writings of John Dickinson, 1764-1774* (Philadelphia, 1891), 1: 435, identifies "A Freeborn American" in the May 12, 1768, *Pennsylvania Gazette* as Thomson. A comparison of these two letters with others known to be Thomson's verifies the identification.

6. Thomson to Dr. David Ramsay, November 6, 1786. Paul H. Smith, "Charles Thomson on Unity in the American Revolution," *The Quarterly Journal of the Library of Congress* 28 (1971): 165.

7. *Pennsylvania Gazette*, March 31, 1768.

8. Arthur L. Jensen, *The Maritime Commerce of Colonial Philadelphia* (Madison, 1963), pp. 174-77 is an excellent discussion of the propaganda of the spring and summer of 1768. The traditional, more general accounts do not discuss Thomson's role at this point. cf. Philip Davidson, *Propaganda and the American Revolution, 1763-1783* (Chapel Hill, 1941) and Arthur M. Schlesinger, Sr., *Prelude to Independence: The Newspaper War on Britain, 1764-1776* (New York, 1957).

9. *Pennsylvania Gazette*, May 12, 1768. See note no. 5.

10. Ibid., June 2, 1768. Similar in language to much of Thomson's writing in support of the American Society, this letter, like both those from "A Freeborn American," is headed "Lancaster County."

11. The Massachusetts Circular received in Philadelphia is in *Pennsylvania Archives*, 8th ser., 7: 6181-84; Lord Hillsborough's letter is in ibid., Colonial Records, 9: 546.

12. *Pennsylvania Gazette*, August 4, 1768.

13. Theodore George Thayer, *Pennsylvania Politics and the Growth of Democracy, 1740-1776* (Harrisburg, 1953), p. 144.

14. The original articles of agreement, dated February 6, 1769, and signed by Thomson and about sixty other merchants, is in the Thomson Papers, Library of Congress.

15. *Pennsylvania Journal,* July 20, 1769; July 5, 1770; also, *Pennsylvania Gazette,* August 31, 1769, for a list of the eighteen members of the Merchants Committee.

16. "From the London Chronicle, June 10, 1769," *Pennsylvania Gazette,* August 31, 1769.

17. Thomson to Franklin, November 26, 1769, "Thomson Papers," N.Y.H.S. *Collections,* 11: 21. For the strength of the shift of opinion against the ministry and Parliament see Pauline Maier, *From Resistance to Revolution* (New York, 1972), pp. 172 ff.

18. Thomson served as his father-in-law's executor. *Pennsylvania Gazette,* January 12, 1769. John Mather's estate reverted to the Mather family following the death of Ruth Thomson, c. 1770. Lewis R. Harley, *Life of Charles Thomson* (Philadelphia, 1900), pp. 187-88.

19. *Pennsylvania Gazette,* November 2, 1769.

20. Thomson to Franklin, November 26, 1769, "Thomson Papers," N.Y.H.S. *Collections,* 11: 21.

21. Merrill Jensen, *The Founding of a Nation* (New York, 1968), pp. 357-58; Zimmerman, "Charles Thomson, 'The Sam Adams of Philadelphia,' " *The Mississippi Valley Historical Review* 45 (1958): 475-79.

22. *Pennsylvania Journal,* and *Pennsylvania Gazette,* June 7, 1770. Jensen, *Maritime Commerce of Colonial Philadelphia,* p. 189.

23. Hutson, "Philadelphia's White Oaks," p. 23. Hutson credits Franklin's great popularity among the White Oaks and other mechanics with assisting Thomson in achieving the shift in White Oak alliances. *Pennsylvania Politics,* pp. 233-37. R. A. Ryerson, "Political Mobilization and the American Revolution," *William and Mary Quarterly* 3d ser. 31 (1974): 566-77.

24. *Pennsylvania Journal* and *Pennsylvania Gazette,* July 19, 1770.

25. *Pennsylvania Gazette,* September 20, 1770; *Pennsylvania Journal,* September 27, 1770. Jacob Hiltzheimer, *Extracts from the Diary of Jacob Hiltzheimer of Philadelphia* (Philadelphia, 1893), September 20, 1770.

26. *Pennsylvania Gazette,* October 4, 1770.

5

"The Life of the Cause of Liberty"

Revolutions do not "just happen." However inexorable the movements of forces and events may be, in order for revolutionary change to occur an individual or a group of individuals must first decide that some goal is worth a struggle. The result may not be identifiable as the goal toward which the revolutionaries were working, but they are the men who set the revolution in motion and shape it to some degree.

In the American Revolution, Sam Adams is frequently cited as exemplifying the maker of a revolution. Adams' revolutionary activities in Boston are well known. His relationship to succeeding generations of Adams who were active in politics has assured him a continuing and well-earned place in our history. But it is rarely claimed that Sam Adams alone brought on the American Revolution. Instead hosts of men throughout the colonies pushed, led, cajoled, and sometimes shamed the Americans into a revolutionary stance from which there was no retreat. The remarkable thing about the American Revolution was that these men appeared in almost all the colonies at about the same time. Just as Massachusetts had Sam Adams, South Carolina had Christopher Gadsden, North Carolina had Cornelius Harnett, Virginia had Patrick Henry and Thomas Jefferson, and Pennsylvania had Charles Thomson, "the Sam Adams of Philadelphia, the life of the cause of liberty."[1]

Thomson guided the progress of revolutionary affairs in Philadelphia from a very advantageous position. His work with the Friendly Association and the American Philosophical Society kept him in a position of easy communication with the leading figures of the province, and also allowed him to continue his association with the artisans and workers of Philadelphia. From his position as a merchant and rum distiller Thomson led his townsmen's opposition to the Stamp Act and Townshend Duties. He worked with other Philadelphians to plan measures to be approved by gatherings at the Pennsylvania State House in much the same manner as Sam Adams controlled the town meetings of Boston.[2]

Thomson's radicalism and fervor prior to the Revolution are difficult to reconcile with his station in life and his later moderate republicanism. A prosperous businessman in his midforties, Thomson made an unlikely radical; but he used his tongue, his pen, and his organizational abilities effectively in the cause of colonial liberties. His letters to the press and to individuals show his great ardor for the American position. His public speeches and his behind-the-scenes organizational work show remarkable effectiveness as Thomson rallied the mass of public opinion behind movements to secure the repeal of oppressive British legislation. He was effective in shaping a movement that coerced unsympathetic merchants to join the boycotts of British goods that subsequently led to the repeal of the Stamp Act and all of the Townshend Duties except the tea tax.

With the repeal of the Townshend Duties and the end of the embargo on British goods in the colonies with the exception of the embargo still on the taxed tea, Thomson and the other patriots faced a new problem. Certain that the rights of the colonists would never be secure as long as Parliament claimed the powers to tax and to legislate in all matters, they saw a growing complacency at home and a willingness by the colonists to submit to the tea tax and other regulations in hopes that Parliament would not continue to exercise the arbitrary power that it claimed to possess. Thomson and the radical patriots across the colonies were determined to keep the issues before the people in order that the rights and liberties of Americans might be preserved.

After the merchants of Philadelphia refused to continue their boycott of British goods until the tea tax was repealed, Thomson realized that he must turn to other methods to assure the continued interest of the mechanics and artisans in their political rights. In the Assembly election of 1770, he worked to lead the artisan class against the conservative Quaker party. Headed by Joseph Galloway, the Quaker faction refused to support nonimportation and successfully prevented the Assembly from backing Thomson's radical program. This gave strength to the rising Presbyterian faction of which Thomson was the recognized leader. The Proprietary party and the Quaker party were faced with a union between the artisan groups of Philadelphia and Thomson's already established political following. In the Assembly election that was held in October 1770, Thomson's newly formed party began to make its political weight felt. With support from the White Oaks and other mechanics and artisans, John Dickinson defeated Joseph Galloway for a seat to represent the city of Philadelphia and forced Galloway to seek a seat in Bucks County.[3] Galloway, in the midst of the election, wrote Franklin "We are all in Confusion, the White Oaks and Mechanicks or many of them have left the old Ticket and 'tis feared will go over to the Presbyterians." In the same letter he warned Franklin against Thomson, "Be cautious what you write to that Man, who is void of Principle or Virtue. I have found him so on more Occasion than one, and I am confident you will also shd you continue your free Correspondence."[4]

By the activities that Galloway so condemned, Thomson was advancing one of the basic aspects of the coming revolution—the spread of political activity and power to classes that had previously submitted to rule by the upper levels of society. Though Thomson sought political power for the workers, primarily for the support that they could lend in the struggle for control of the Assembly, he realized that these groups were capable of participating and were entitled to participate in government. After the workers gained power they would move to positions far more radical than Thomson was willing to support, but for the moment he was the leader in their rise to political importance.

During most of 1771 and 1772 the political strife between Britain and her American colonies almost disappeared. Thomson, Sam Adams, and other Whig leaders attempted to keep the issues alive by reminding the people of the unrelenting claims of Parliament and the evils that would result from yielding colonial rights and privileges. They kept alive the memory of the Boston 'massacre' of March 5, 1770, for propaganda purposes and directed annual observances of a day of mourning on its anniversary. They continued to make exhortations against drinking taxed tea, which, combined with the low price of smuggled tea, helped reduce the importation of tea from England.[5]

In August 1772 the tradesmen, mechanics, and small shopkeepers of Philadelphia organized a "Patriotic Society." Disclaiming any intent of subverting "the happiness of our present constitution and liberties," they desired to unify their actions in Pennsylvania politics. After promising to "endeavor to promote the good and welfare" of King George III, they stated that they would strive to "Preserve, inviolate, our rights and privileges . . . against every attempt to violate or infringe the same, either here, or on the other side of the Atlantic."[6] By such devices Thomson and the other patriot agitators kept the subject of colonial rights and privileges fresh in the minds of the citizens of Pennsylvania and the other colonies. They frequently reminded the colonists of the infringements of Parliament during the preceding years and kept alive the question of the supremacy of Parliament.

During the fights against the Townshend Duties, Thomson had written to Franklin concerning the effect the acts were having on Americans. After speaking of the resentment aroused by the acts, Thomson spoke of the future of the American colonies:

> from the genius of the [American] people and the fertility of the soil, it is easy to foresee that in the course of a few years they will find at home an ample supply of all their wants. In the meanwhile their strength, power and numbers are daily increasing, and as the property of land is parcelled out among the inhabitants and almost every farmer is a freeholder, the spirit of Liberty will be kept awake and the love of freedom deeply rooted; and when strength and liberty combine it is easy to foresee that a people will not long submit to arbitrary sway.[7]

Thomson's forecast was accurate. The colonies grew rapidly and, as a result of movements begun during the nonimportation periods, their industries expanded and produced more of what was needed for life without the purchase of British-made goods. The spirit of liberty and the love of freedom matured quickly during a period of relative noninterference from England. Had Parliament been content to let matters remain in this state of comparative equilibrium, it is likely that the colonies would have remained restlessly but firmly under British control. In May 1773, however, Parliament passed a law that greatly intensified the anti-British movement and was to lead, step by step, to the calling of the Continental Congress and to the Declaration of Independence.

This act, known in the colonies as the tea act, tried to relieve the critical financial condition of the East India Company by giving it a preferred rate on the shipping of tea into the American colonies. Under the act the company sent tea to the colonies without paying the duties collectable in England. Although the tax levied at the American ports remained, the exemption enabled the East India Company to undersell the colonists engaged in smuggling tea from Holland. In addition to the duty exemptions granted to the company, warehouse outlets were established for their tea in the principal cities of the colonies. In this way, Parliament granted the East India Company an effective monopoly on the importation and distribution of tea in the colonies.[8]

It was not until late in 1773 that the colonial importers realized the extent of the monopoly that had been granted to the East Indian Company. The merchants of Boston enjoyed a profitable business importing both duties tea from England and smuggled tea from Holland. New York and Philadelphia continued an effective boycott of the duties tea but the merchants of both cities participated in widespread smuggling activities. When the tea importers realized that they were being deprived of one of the more profitable brances of their businesses, they immediately reunited with the patriotic groups who had continued to work against the payment of the tea duties. Parliament, in its attempts to aid the East India Company, thus alienated a group of substantial and respected merchants who were previously among the staunchest supports of Royal and Parliamentary power.[9]

The merchants and patriots of Philadelphia lost no time in organizing a demonstration against the new measures. On October 18, 1773, William Bradford, Thomson, and the other leaders who had opposed the Stamp Act and the Townshend Acts assembled the inhabitants of the city at the State House. The gathering adopted a series of resolutions declaring that any person who aided the East India Company in its attempt to sell tea while it was still subject to the payment of a duty upon importation into America was an enemy of his country. They named a committee to wait on the gentlemen appointed by the company to receive the tea and request their immediate resignations.[10]

Early in December 1773 the committee elected at the protest meeting in October assumed additional authority when it inventoried the tea stock in the city and set a maximum price for the remaining supplies of the beverage. Thomson and the other colonial patriots worked to prevent the merchants with large stocks of tea from raising the price of that tea as a result of the renewed controversy over its importation. The tea committee continued its work and laid plans for the action to be taken when the first shipload of tea arrived in the city. Although sentiment was united in opposing the tea act, some of the members feared that harsh measures would be needed to prevent the landing of the tea. Thomson urged that any action necessary should be employed and took an active part in the planning, which resulted in the return of the tea to England.[11]

In a frenzy of radicalism over the tea issue, Thomson chose to initiate a correspondence with Sam Adams in Boston. The two had not previously corresponded; but his contacts in Boston apparently informed Thomson that Adams and John Hancock would like to hear from him. In his letter Thomson spoke of the need for a union between the colonies and Great Britain—but a union with the relationship spelled out in a constitutional fashion. Assuming that this end was desirable but unlikely, Thomson proposed that preparations be made for a break with the mother country. The leadership of the colonies should correspond with each other in order to more thoroughly link the colonies together; the people should be given arms to keep up their military spirit; and young men should establish friendships and connections in foreign courts, by visits if possible. Unless these things were done, Thomson inferred, to attempt a break with England would invite disaster.[12]

The tone of Thomson's letter to Adams reflects the nature of the Philadelphian's revolutionary activities. Thomson was a radical but a cautious one. He was willing to risk all in the cause of colonial rights but he worked meticulously to assure success. In his correspondence, in his organizing efforts among various groups, and in his public image Thomson called for immediate action. Between friends and fellow revolutionaries he urged caution and careful preparation lest the revolt fail. Thomson concluded his letter to Sam Adams with a report of how he was presently pushing Philadelphians toward a determined resistance to the landing of tea. He had distributed handbills showing the East India Company to be "the ravagers of Asia, the corrupters of their country, the supporters of arbitrary power, and the patrons of monopoly." He concluded "I do not think it unworthy the cause sometimes to borrow aid from the passions."[13]

And passions were at work in Philadelphia because of Thomson's activities. The committee to oppose the landing of the tea, with Thomson its most adamant member, laid plans to prevent the landing and sale of the taxed tea. Shortly after Thomson sent his letter to Boston, word came that the *Polly* had entered the river and was on its way up to Philadelphia. The tea committee located Abel James and Henry Drinker, tea agents, and demanded that they resign as Thomas Wharton had already done. When James hesitated, a crowd gathered before his home and shouted threats until he complied. Thomson and another member of the committee went down river to meet Captain Ayres of the *Polly* and suggest that he not bring his ship all the way into the city, where a crowd was demanding that the tea be dumped into the harbor as had been done in Boston a week earlier. Captain Ayres agreed and accompanied the committee members back to the State House. Thomson and Bradford had circulated handbills giving directions as to what should be done if attempts were made to land the cargo. When Ayres saw the temper of the crowd of about eight thousand, he agreed to return to England with his entire cargo. The citizens of

Philadelphia, with Thomson in the lead, had shown effectively that they were determined to resist this new attempt to collect the tea duty.[14]

The tea embargo continued in effect during the spring of 1774. Believing that Lord North's ministry had introduced the tea act as a maneuver to revive the dispute over American rights, the revolutionaries worked to unite the colony in opposition. Thomson, Mifflin, and others who had fought the earlier British acts grew convinced that the question of Parliamentary supremacy would not be settled peacefully. In order to unite the colony they worked to establish committees in every county of Pennsylvania to lead the resistance. These committees, similar to those organized during the Stamp Act and Townshend Act debates, kept in constant touch with the Philadelphia Committee, and in this manner could keep the citizens of the outlying counties informed as to the events that were taking place across the colonies.[15]

While the Pennsylvanians were establishing correspondence committees in every county, the British government considered actions that, when accomplished, would drive the colonies another step down the road to rebellion. The ministry of Lord North, when faced by the destruction of the tea in the port of Boston, resolved that the colonies must accept the authority of Parliament. As the first of a series of "Intolerable Acts" designed to coerce Massachusetts into obeying Royal regulations, Parliament passed the Boston Port Bill in March 1774. The bill closed the port of Boston to commerce until the inhabitants of the town compensated the East India Company for the loss of its tea. Almost everyone in Philadelphia joined in condemning the bill when the news of its passage reached the city. Many who had disapproved of the action of the Bostonians proclaimed that the use of force by Parliament would only lead to more active resistance in all the colonies. Expressions of sympathy with the people of the city of Boston came from all who opposed the unlimited claims of Parliament, and the partisan leaders of Philadelphia inaugurated plans to organize a mass expression of support to the Massachusetts city.[16]

On May 19, Paul Revere arrived in Philadelphia bearing letters from the Boston Committee of Correspondence. The letters requested the aid of the Philadelphians in opposing the closure of their port. Until the colonies could assemble in a congress to take united action against the measures, they proposed that New York and Philadelphia join Boston in a pledge of nonimportation of British goods. When the letters arrived in Philadelphia, Charles Thomson, Thomas Mifflin, and Joseph Reed, a young lawyer who had recently moved to Philadelphia and joined Thomson in his fight for colonial rights,[17] quickly gathered at the London Coffee House to discuss what action should be taken.[18]

Thomson, Mifflin, and Reed recognized that the dispute with Great Britain had reached a crisis and that stronger action would thereafter be necessary. It was of the utmost importance that the entire population of the colonies unite in the cause of overcoming the authority claimed by Parliament. Thomson and his two friends realized that unless they planned carefully and wisely, the many political factions of their own colony of Pennsylvania would never be united in support of the closed port of Boston and the threatened rights of all Americans.

After discussing the need for careful handling of the various political factions, Thomson and his two friends agreed that a public meeting, well planned in advance, would secure the adherence of the majority of the people to resolutions supporting Boston. They then read the Boston letters to all those who were present at the Coffee House and announced that a meeting would be held the next evening at the City Tavern to decide what measures should be taken. The three plotters knew that in a public meeting, the Quakers, who saw the threatening dangers but opposed involving Pennsylvania further in the dispute, would be well represented. Unless they were carefully controlled they could easily defeat any measures of which they did not approve. In Thomson's words, "...it was necessary to devise means so to counteract their designs as to carry the measures proposed and yet prevent a disunion, and thus, if possible, bring Pennsylvania's whole force undivided to make common cause with Boston."[19]

In order to accomplish this goal the three men decided to enlist the aid of John Dickinson. Dickinson, long a political associate and Thomson's friend (Thomson, a widower since about 1770, would marry Dickinson's niece before the end of

1774), was known and respected among all groups in Pennsylvania. He had opposed the Stamp Act, his "Farmer's Letters" had made his name widely celebrated in all the colonies, and as a leader in the Assembly he would add a note of authority to the gathering. Dickinson had taken no part in the agitation that resulted in the return of the taxed tea to England. Consquently, the Quakers and moderates felt him to be less radical than Thomson and his known associates. With Dickinson's support, Thomson had little doubt that the measures would be accepted by all those present at the meeting.

In the afternoon prior to the meeting at the City Tavern on March 20, 1774, Thomson, Dickinson, Mifflin, and Reed gathered at Dickinson's home to decide what action should be taken and what means would be necessary to assure the adoption of their program. Since there was little point in Pennsylvania's and Massachusetts' attempting to challenge the authority of Great Britain without the aid of the other colonies, they decided that the meeting should only send a friendly answer to Boston pledging Philadelphia's support and calling for the convening of a congress to consider what action should be taken. To accomplish this, in the face of the expected opposition, Thomson, known as a rash man for his actions in the earlier disputes, proposed that he press for an immediate declaration in favor of Boston. Some of the other radicals would support Thomson and Dickinson would then "oppose and press for moderate measures; thus by an apparent dispute prevent a farther [sic] opposition and carry the point agreed on."[20]

That night a large crowd met in the City Tavern. The group heard the letters from Boston and the text of the Boston Port Bill; Thomson's plan of action then went into effect. Reed and Mifflin spoke condemning the English injustices. Thomson rose and began to urge an immediate declaration in favor of Boston. During the violent opposition and arguments that resulted from these proposals, Thomson fainted from the heat and fatigue and friends carried him from the room. Dickinson then put his more moderate proposals before the group. Thomson conveniently recovered and returned to the disorderly meeting and moved that a committee be appointed to write an answer to the Boston letters. When his proposal passed Thomson discovered that two lists, one moderate and one radical, had been submitted for appointment to the committee. To keep the meeting unified they combined the two lists and appointed a committee of twenty men. By preconcerted action Thomson and his friends had led the Philadelphians into support of Boston. They brought into a somewhat official existence a corresponding committee that was to be of invaluable aid in the growing struggle to unite Pennsylvania and the other colonies in opposition to England.[21]

The committee met the next day to frame a reply to the Boston letter. Among its members were Reed, Mifflin, Dickinson, and Thomson, who guided the contents of the reply along the lines already agreed upon. The letter began by expressing hopes that, if the dispute could be settled by paying for the destroyed tea, Boston should agree to such a settlement; but, if the British authorities continued to threaten to use force to extract payment for the tea, then Boston was assured that the Philadelphians would regard this as a violation of the common rights of the American colonies to agree to their own taxation and would stand firmly behind Boston's support of American liberties. The letter then proposed a congress of deputies from the colonies to consider measures to restore harmony with Great Britain and prevent the dispute from advancing to an undesirable end.[22]

When Paul Revere left Philadelphia carrying this declaration of the Philadelphia committee, he also had with him a letter from Thomson to Sam Adams. In his letter to Adams, Thomson expressed his concern for the cause of Boston and the colonies. He sought to strengthen the determination of Adams and the other Bostonians by assuring them that the people of the rest of the colonies were supporting Massachusetts in her time of trouble. However, he urged Adams to restrain the violent elements of Boston following so that no irreparable split might be formed with the mother country. Thomson indicated that if Adams' mob took any more violent action such as the Boston Tea Party, the British troops stationed in the city would be engaged and an armed conflict would begin.[23] In addition to the letter to Boston, the Philadelphia committee sent news of its action to all of the colonies south of Pennsylvania. With this notice went a letter to each colony suggesting the necessity of calling a general congress from all colonies to consider the problem. This suggestion, combined with a similar call from the Virginia House of Burgesses, met with approval all through the colonies; planning began for the First Continental Congress to meet at Philadelphia in September 1774.

Meanwhile Thomson, Dickinson, and other members of the committee published a series of letters designed to make the people aware of the effects of the acts that Parliament had passed to punish Boston and Massachusetts. The Philadelphia revolutionaries denounced Britain's plans to subjugate her colonies and directed numerous blasts in newspaper propaganda articles against the Boston Port Bill, the Massachusetts Government Act, which destroyed the old provincial charter and restricted local government in Massachusetts, the re-enacted Quartering Act, and the Administration of Justice Act. On June 1, when the bill closing the Boston port went into effect, Thomson and other patriots urged the citizens of Philadelphia to observe a day of mourning. Shops closed, churches held services, and thereafter the people remained quietly in their homes. The patriots were conditioning the minds of the people of Philadelphia and Pennsylvania for the active opposition to English acts, which they feared must come.[24]

The committee requested that the governor convene the Pennsylvania Assembly. More than nine hundred freeholders signed a petition requesting that the Assembly be convened to consider sending delegates to an all-colony congress that would work to restore harmony and peace to the Empire. When the petition was presented to Governor Penn on June 8, 1774, he refused to call the Assembly saying that he could see no need for a special session at that time. This, according to Thomson, was what he and the other members of the committee had expected. The committee had proposed that the Assembly be called only to demonstrate their desire that the elected representatives be allowed to act.

Thomson had taken another step toward overthrowing established authority in America. By showing the people that the established government was not willing or able to act, the revolutionaries justified action outside the established order. By acting in the name of the will of the people the revolutionaries could be assured of popular support. Thomson, wanting to take action opposed by the leaders of the Assembly, first made the government's position clear to the people. When the governor refused to accept Thomson's demand to call the Assembly into session, he played even further into the hands of Thomson and the radical committeemen who wanted to name the delegates to the Continental Congress.

Thomson recorded the revolutionary process. "On Friday, June 10th, 1774 a number of Gentlemen of different classes, societies & parties met to prepare questions for a general meeting of the Inhabitants." Agreeing upon "certain resolutions" they decided on ways of manipulating the various groups in order to insure their support.[25] A call was issued for a town meeting to be held on June 18. The original committee of twenty was too conservative, and the radical leaders wanted a new group that would be more representative of the popular interest. Thomson, Reed, and Dr. William Smith, a conservative, addressed the almost eight thousand Philadelphians. When the speakers finished, the assembled citizens loudly resolved that the closing of the port of Boston was unconstitutional and called for a Continental Congress to meet to secure the rights and liberties of the colonies. They added twenty-three men of liberal views to the old committee to form a Committee of Forty-Three to "Determine what is the proper mode of collecting the sense of the Province, and appointing Deputies for the same to attend a general Congress. ..."[26] The meeting adjourned having accomplished exactly what Thomson desired.

Thomson saw that it was going to be difficult to assure that Pennsylvania was represented in a colonial congress. Joseph Galloway, speaker of the Pennsylvania Assembly, opposed all of the measures that had been taken in support of the people of Boston. He and the Quaker and proprietary factions believed that the use of popular mass meetings and irregularly elected committees was nothing less than rebellion against the established government and would undoubtedly result in anarchy. Yet, when the members of the committee approached him, Thomson agreed to call an unofficial meeting of the Assembly to appoint delegates to the congress. He realized that he could exercise a control over the choices of the Assembly that were not possible by any other method. The committee recognized this potential and sent out letters to the corresponding committees in all the counties, requesting that they send delegates to a provincial convention to meet at the same time as the Assembly and make certain that the wishes of the populace were regarded.

Governor Penn, realizing that Thomson and his associates were determined to elect delegates to the Continental Congress in some manner, decided to call the Assembly in official session in which he believed the members would be subject to less pressure from the people. On the pretext of considering some reported Indian hostilities in the Ohio region, Governor Penn sent out a call for the Assembly to meet in July. Thomson and his friends on the committee decided that it would be unwise to allow the Assembly complete freedom in the choice of delegates to the Continental Congress. Accordingly, they followed their earlier plan and called a convention of delegates from the county committees to meet in Philadelphia on July 15, two days prior to the Assembly meeting. They intended that the members of this convention advise and assist the Assembly in the preservation of the liberties of the colony.[27]

Dickinson, Mifflin, and Thomson began preparations for the Provincial Convention. To guarantee that men of the proper political views would be nominated as delegates, the three made a tour of two or three of the frontier counties visiting the county committees as they went. They traveled under the pretense of an excursion of pleasure and attempted to enlist support for their cause at the same time. They worked particularly among the Germans, who had traditionally supported the more conservative Quakers but were becoming interested in exercising their political power. On the basis of their tour they, not surprisingly, concluded that the majority of the people of the province supported their actions even though they were in opposition to the elected Assembly.[28]

The Provincial Convention met on July 15. The delegates elected Thomas Willing, a radical Philadelphia merchant, chairman of the convention and made Charles Thomson their clerk. The convention adopted a series of resolutions proclaiming that it was necessary for the colony to send delegates to the Continental Congress and instructed the Assembly to appoint such delegates. At the same time, according to Thomson, the convention resolved that, if the Assembly refused to name delegates, the convention itself would assume the authority to appoint the deputies.[29]

When the Assembly opened, the delegates to the convention swarmed into the State House to see their resolutions presented to the members. Faced with the resolutions and obvious eagerness of Thomson and some of the other more active liberals to appoint their own deputies, the Assembly yielded and agreed to name a delegation to the Congress. But they chose neither Thomson, Dickinson, or Reed as a deputy. Joseph Galloway, still a power in the Assembly, succeeded in limiting the deputies to members of the House and in this way was able to prevent the election of the more radical leaders. Galloway, Samuel Rhodes, Thomas Mifflin, Charles Humphreys, John Morton, George Ross, and Edward Biddle were elected.[30] Thomson, Dickinson, and the other agitators on the Philadelphia committee of correspondence had hoped that in some manner they would be sent as delegates to the Congress. Still they realized that their revolutionary activities in the province had been extremely successful. As evidence of their success they only had to look at the deputies who had been named to represent Pennsylvania in the first political meeting of the colonies. Led by Thomas Mifflin, a wealthy merchant who had joined Thomson in opposing the Stamp Act, the liberals of the group would be able to control its conduct in all matters; Thomson and Dickinson, though not representatives, could easily make their influence felt through their confederates.

Thomson had succeeded in organizing Philadelphia and Pennsylvania. By various methods of propaganda he and others kept the protest movement alive among the Pennsylvanians during the period from the repeal of the Townshend Acts until the passage of the Tea Act. Much as Sam Adams was doing in Boston and other parts of Massachusetts, Thomson worked to prevent the enforcement of the tea duty which threatened to destroy the tea merchants of the colonies. In an effort to unite the colony of Pennsylvania in action against the Tea Act and the Boston Port Bill, Thomson and his confederates worked avidly to form committees of correspondence in all the counties. Their earlier work among the artisans and mechanics of Philadelphia had brought them into full participation in the decision-making process in Pennsylvania. A revolution was already at work. A new group of citizens were forcing their way into the governmental process of Pennsylvania and the other colonies. A more formal recognition of that shift of power would not come until later and would be accompanied by a complete break with England. Such action was as yet unanticipated by most of Thomson's followers, but Thomson, in his letter to Sam Adams and John Hancock on December 19, 1773, showed that he was already considering the possibility of separation from England. So, by working to accomplish a shift in political power, and by working to prepare Pennsylvanians for a break with England, Charles Thomson was well advanced along the path to Revolution. The plotting that preceded Philadelphia's response to the Boston Port Bill illustrated the careful planning and intrigue necessary to lead the people of Pennsylvania successfully into measures of resistance. Thomson utilized the reputation for rash actions that he had gained from his work in forcing the return of the tea to England. By introducing resolutions of more force than those really desired, the revolutionists gained approval of the more moderate measures they actually favored. Thomson used these and many similar devices to secure people of Philadelphia and Pennsylvania as adherents to the colonial cause.

Thomson's organizing labors with the corresponding committees and the tour of the frontier that he and his friends made contributed to the patriotism and loyalty of the members of the Provincial Convention. With the support of the Provincial Convention behind him, Thomson convinced the Assembly that it would be wise to send delegates to the Continental Congress. Accordingly, the Congress met without the handicap of the absence of one of the older and larger colonies.

In the months prior to the convening of the First Continental Congress, Thomson was one of the most active revolutionaries in Pennsylvania. John Adams would shortly refer to Thomson as the "Sam Adams of Philadelphia," and certainly Thomson deserved this praise. Like Adams, Thomson was an organizer of his province, a propagandist, a correspondent with radical leaders both within his province and in other colonies, a developer of middle-class patriotism and a leader and manipulator of mobs and assemblies. But Thomson not only worked to destroy the authority claimed by Parliament, he worked also to further the development of America in many other ways. His activities with the American Philosophical Society included working to improve agriculture and manufacturing and encouraging cultural union and advancement. His own investments and business activities advanced American manufacturing, economy, and trade. Along with these additional interests and activities, Thomson occupied himself principally in the months before the meeting of the Continental Congress with efforts to organize the fight for the rights of the people of British America. John Adams' other phrase in his description of Thomson showed the regard in which he was held by fellow Pennsylvanians— "This Charles Thomson is . . . the life of the cause of liberty, they say."

And it was for the cause of liberty that Thomson labored. Convinced that the British Empire as it was established did not advance freedom, Thomson urged that the Empire be modified. Seeing no modification, and instead seeing further measures of oppression coming from Britain, Thomson slowly developed the determination that American freedom and liberty be established whatever the cost. The American Revolution came from the kind of leadership and conviction that Thomson manifested.

NOTES

1. John Adams, *The Adams Papers: Diary and Autobiography of John Adams*, ed. L. H. Butterfield (Cambridge, Massachusetts, 1961), 2: 115.

2. *cf.* John C. Miller, *Sam Adams: Pioneer In Propaganda* (Stanford, 1936), p. 48-53.

3. *Pennsylvania Gazette*, September 27, 1770; *Pennsylvania Chronicle*, September 24, October 1, 1770; Theodore George Thayer, *Pennsylvania Politics and the Growth of Democracy, 1740-1776* (Harrisburg, 1953) pp. 149-50; James H. Hutson,

Pennsylvania Politics 1746-1770; The Movement for Royal Government and Its Consequences (Princeton, 1972), pp. 235-36.

4. Galloway to Franklin, September 27, 1770, American Philosophical Society.

5. Hiller B. Zobel, *The Boston Massacre* (New York, 1970), p. 214.

6. *Pennsylvania Journal,* August 26, 1772.

7. Thomson to Franklin, November 26, 1769, "Thomson Papers," N.Y.H.S. *Collections,* 11: 24.

8. Benjamin Woods Labaree, *The Boston Tea Party* (London, 1964), pp. 58-73.

9. L. H. Gipson, *The Coming of the Revolution 1763-1775* (New York, 1954), pp. 217-18.

10. Thomson's leadership in the earlier movements assured him a place on the committee, but he seems to have become even more radical at this point. Perhaps this explains Dickinson's withdrawal from the movement. *Pennsylvania Gazette,* October 20, 1773.

11. *Pennsylvania Gazette,* December 8, 1773.

12. Thomson to Sam Adams and John Hancock, December 19, 1773, Sam Adams Papers, New York Public Library; Merrill Jensen, *The Founding of a Nation* (New York, 1968), p. 443.

13. Thomson to Adams and Hancock, December 19, 1773; Labaree, *Boston Tea Party,* pp. 157-58.

14. Thayer, *Pennsylvania Politics,* pp. 153-54; Labaree, *Boston Tea Party,* pp. 158-59; *Pennsylvania Gazette,* December 29, 1773.

15. Thomson to William Henry Drayton, n. d., "Thomson Papers," N.Y.H.S. *Collections,* 2: 279; also *PMHB* 2 (1878): 411-23.

16. The text of the act that closed the Boston port was printed in the *Pennsylvania Gazette,* May 18, 1773.

17. John F. Roche, *Joseph Reed* (New York, 1957), p. 41.

18. The following description of the action taken by the Philadelphians is taken from Thomson's reports to Dr. David Ramsay and to William Henry Drayton, both of South Carolina, as information for each gentleman's projected history of the Revolution. "Thomson Papers," N.Y.H.S. *Collections,* 11: 215-29, 274-86; Smith, "Charles Thomson on Unity in the American Revolution," 163-71.

19. Thomson to Drayton, "Thomson Papers," N.Y.H.S. *Collections,* 11: 275.

20. Ibid., p. 276.

21. Ibid., p. 277.

22. Thomson to Ramsay, Smith, "Charles Thomson on Unity in the American Revolution," p. 166.

23. Adams to Thomson, May 30, 1774, *The Writings of Samuel Adams,* ed. H. A. Cushing (New York, 1904-1908), 3: 122-23.

24. Thomson to Sam Adams, June 3, 1774, Sam Adams Papers, New York Public Library.

25. Thomson Notebook, Historical Society of Pennsylvania.

26. *American Archives,* 4th ser. (Washington, 1837-1846), 1: 426.

27. Thomson to Ramsay, Smith, "Charles Thomson on Unity in the American Revolution," pp. 167-68.

28. Thomson to Drayton, n.d., N.Y.H.S. *Collections,* 11: 279.

29. Ibid., 11: 260; *Pennsylvania Archives,* 8th ser., 8, p. 67098.

30. "Votes," July 22, 1774, *Pennsylvania Archives,* 8th ser., 8: 7098.

6

Provincial Politician and Congressional Secretary, 1774-1776

The development of a revolution is a complex process that needs careful leadership. The direction of the energies of a restless body politic into controlled channels requires extraordinary devotion and effort or the revolt will never progress beyond the formless early stages. Once begun, a revolution must be carefully managed or the passions engendered will sweep control from the instigators into even more radical hands. The American rebellion is an excellent example of one which went beyond the intent of its perpetrators yet its excesses were mild when compared with revolutions before and after. Perhaps the American rebels were of a more careful breed and possessed greater talents of political management than did those of other rebellions.

The development of a revolutionary is even more complex than the process of the revolution itself. Charles Thomson entered the Revolution as a radical—careful but nonetheless radical. He led Philadelphia's protest against the Stamp Act, the Townshend Duties, and the tea act. He brought the city's mechanics and artisans into the revolutionary cause and served as their leader. He aroused the political awareness of the western Pennsylvania Scotch-Irish and Germanic elements and contributed to their entrance into politics. But as the Revolution progressed, Thomson himself seemed to lag behind the onrushing political tide. The man who had been "the life of the cause of liberty" and who had urged appeals to passion in the revolutionary cause opposed the radical Pennsylvania Constitution of 1776.

In one sense Thomson had moved from the local to the national scene and in the process he had lost some of his radicalism. In another sense the Revolution had simply progressed too far for Thomson to follow. The situation in Pennsylvania between the opening of the First Continental Congress on September 5, 1774, and the adoption of the Declaration of Independence on July 4, 1776, illustrates the course of the American Revolution on a local level. Revolutionaries such as Charles Thomson worked ardently to bring the province to the point of supporting independence only to find that the radicals they had brought into the colony's political life were demanding a voice of their own. From this demand came the Pennsylvania Constitution of 1776, promulgated in the same summer that the Declaration of Independence was adopted. Thomson, by now a moderate Whig, opposed this most radical of the new state constitutions but was not successful in defeating it.

The situation began with Thomson and the Whigs as the radical element in Pennsylvania politics. When the First Continental Congress met, sentiment in the Quaker province opposed any talk of independence and the official instructions to its delegates in Congress reflected this sentiment until mid-1776. Opposition to independence changed only because of the work of Thomson and others like him. Thomson and those other Pennsylvania patriots who sometime during this period decided that independence from the mother country was necessary walked carefully along the path toward revolution. Only prudent management prevented several of the competing factions from unifying in opposition to independence. Had they done so they would have blocked the movement toward separation from England.

The two most powerful groups with which Thomson, Mifflin, Dickinson, and the other Whig leaders constantly dealt were the proprietary and the Quaker parties. The proprietary party had long headed the most conservative faction of Pennsylvania politics. The large landowners and prosperous merchants and traders who composed the party could lose much and gain little from a conflict with England. When independence did come, many of these Pennsylvanians became active Tories and supported Great Britain.

The other major group, Thomson's old associates the Quakers, had long before condemned the radical principles and violent actions of their former schoolmaster and his friends. Opposed to force of any fashion and believing that peaceful petitions would achieve the restoration of colonial rights, the Quakers protested against the turbulent methods that were used to secure the repeal of the Stamp and Townshend Duties and that had been recently employed to enforce the boycott of taxed tea. As the conflict with England progressed and more pressure was applied in the Assembly for organizing and equipping militia units and for other such warlike measures, the pacifist Quakers joined with their old enemies, the proprietary party, in opposition to Thomson and his Whig confederates.

Thomson and his fellows in 1774 controlled another important faction in the politics of the province—the corresponding committees representing the western counties and the mechanics and artisans of Philadelphia. These rural and urban citizens, many of them excluded from active participation in the Assembly by a fifty-pound property requirement for voting, had for the first time moved into an important position in the political life of the colony. Prior to 1774 they had confined their actions to the endorsement of preconcerted resolutions at mass meetings called by Thomson, William Bradford, and others. With the meeting of the Provincial Convention in July 1774, however, they entered into a new phase of politics.[1]

At their first gathering in 1774 Thomson, Mifflin, and the other radicals on the Philadelphia Committee of Correspondence secured the adherence of the representatives of the western counties to a program aimed at putting pressure on the Pennsylvania Assembly to support the Continental Congress. But with this exercise of power many of the convention members realized the strong position they could occupy in directing the actions of the province. As a result, leaders developed among the westerners and at the same time the Philadelphia artisans demanded that they and their compatriots be allowed equal opportunities for participation in the Pennsylvania government.

Thomson and his friends recognized that this demand would never gain the approval of many of the more prosperous and well-to-do elements of the Whig party. Although such Whigs were vitally interested in preventing the execution of the English "Intolerable Acts" (the Boston Port Act, the act for quartering soldiers in all the colonies, and other oppressive measures), they would never consent to the participation of the lower classes of Philadelphia and the Pennsylvania frontiersmen in the political life of the province. Thomson wanted to secure the adherence of as many groups as possible in support of the Continental Congress and worked with all factions, hoping that by preventing a serious break in the ranks of the radicals he could assure that Pennsylvania would present a united defense of the rights of Americans.

While seeking to compromise the democratic demands and conservative position of the two wings of the Whig party, Thomson also faced the problems of gaining as much support as possible from the Quaker pacifists who dominated the Assembly. He, as well as others, thought it of supreme importance that the people of the colonies should unite to defend their rights against British usurpations. Although he opposed the popular democracy that resulted in the extremely liberal Pennsylvania Constitution of 1776, his interests lay primarily in securing the backing of its proponents and its detractors and all Pennsylvanians in the movement toward separation from England which bore fruit in the Declaration of Independence in July 1776.

Still there were few hints in September 1774 that in less than two years independence would be declared, though some viewed the meeting of the First Continental Congress as an opening move in that direction. For the first time all of the colonies (except Georgia) gathered to consider means to prevent the enforcement of British acts that the colonists held as a violation of the rights of all British-Americans. The Boston Port Bill, the destruction of the Massachusetts charter by the Massachusetts Government Act, and opposition raised by the Quebec Act aroused all of the colonies and had at last brought about a unification of their efforts to secure recognition of their rights.

The delegates to the Congress began gathering in Philadelphia around the first of September and Philadelphians of all ranks and opinions welcomed them. Both the conservative and radical elements exerted themselves mightily to greet the colonial leaders as they arrived in hopes of influencing them to their respective views. Though the foremost Philadelphia patriots, Thomson and Dickinson, were not delegates to the Congress, they met and conversed with the representatives as they came into town.

Thomas Mifflin, Thomson's associate who had succeeded in being elected a delegate to the Congress, had a spacious and elegant home within the city, and the Philadelphia Whigs used this as a meetingplace. With Thomson and Dickinson as his guests, Mifflin practically help open house for the visitors. In this way Thomson and Dickinson, excluded from the Pennsylvania delegation by Joseph Galloway's astute maneuvering, became acquainted with many members of the body that was to convene on September 5, 1774. As Thomson met with these colonial leaders it was evident that he was anxious to have a part in the Congress. He knew that if he could maintain direct contact with the proceedings he could help advance the radical cause.

Prominent among the more radical representatives who visited Mifflin's home and conversed with Thomson concerning the organization and activity of the coming convention of the colonies were John Adams and the rest of the Massachusetts delegation. On August 30, Adams recorded in his diary that he and his fellow delegates had "had much conversation" with this "life of the cause of liberty" of Pennsylvania.[2]

The delegates to the Congress were divided almost equally between radical and conservative viewpoints. The conservative faction, led by Thomson's bitter opponent Joseph Galloloway, eagerly sought to take any measures possible to repair the break with Great Britain and restore friendly relations with the Empire. The radicals, who had led the protests that brought about the break, worked zealously for a determined resistance against the British usurpations.

Tests of the strength of the two groups came on the first day of the meeting. Galloway, hoping to fortify his position in the Pennsylvania Assembly by establishing himself in a strong place of leadership in the Congress, offered the Pennsylvania State House as a place where Congress could hold its sessions. The radicals immediately proposed Carpenters'

Hall as being more suitable, knowing that this would please the mechanics and carpenters of the city. After inspecting the Carpenters' Hall, the more radical delegates defeated the Galloway faction's proposal and voted to stay. This point settled, the election of chairman proceeded without dispute as Peyton Randolph of Virginia was elected unanimously. When the question of the election of a secretary was raised the two parties again divided. The Galloway faction wished to choose a member of the Congress and apparently favored Silas Deane of Connecticut. Then, to Galloway's surprise and disappointment, the radical group proposed that Charles Thomson be elected secretary. Galloway believed that he had ruined Thomson's chances of having any part in the Congress by preventing his election as a delegate, but Thomson's reputation and the contacts he had made with the delegates as they arrived in Philadelphia assured his election. Galloway reported to his fellow Tory, Governor William Franklin of New Jersey, that Thomson "(one of the most violent sons of Liberty, so called, in America) was unanimously elected. The New Yorkers [John Jay and James Duane] and myself and a few others, finding a great majority, did not think it prudent to oppose it. Both of the Measures, it seems, were privately settled by an Interest made out of Doors."[3]

Thomson may not have had prior knowledge of the actions of the Congress and did not join the curious spectators who that day accompanied the delegates to Carpenters' Hall. He did conveniently arrange to arrive in Philadelphia, accompanied by his bride, just about the time the matter was settled. He and his second wife, Hannah Harrison, the niece of Mrs. John Dickinson, journeyed into Philadelphia to visit with Mrs. Dickinson on the day that the Congress assembled. The newlywed's carriage was stopped in the street by a messenger from Congress who informed Thomson that the Congress desired his presence. Thomson immediately accompanied the messenger, and President Randolph told him of his election. He accepted the position and promised to begin his duties as soon as possible. He little realized that he would serve as secretary of this body until it relinquished its governmental powers in 1789, when the federal Constitution went into effect.[4]

Thomson assumed his position as secretary to the Continental Congress on September 10, five days after his election. By this time the delegates were organized, had established rules of procedure, and were ready to settle down to the business at hand. Thomson's duties as secretary included recording business transacted by the Congress and later preparing this record for publication as the official journal. In keeping the congressional minutes Thomson partially adopted a method proposed by Patrick Henry, a delegate from Virginia. Henry suggested that since many differing proposals would be made before a final suggestion was adopted, the secretary should only record the measures that finally were approved by Congress. Thomson recorded all the measures voted on by the Congress, whether they were approved or not, and even included many roll-call votes, but did not record the discussion of the issues. This method unfortunately left no official record of the debates of the delegates but enabled Thomson to verify the minutes with much less difficulty than any other plan would have allowed. As secretary, Thomson also attended to all correspondence the Congress found necessary, and served as custodian for all letters and documents received and copies of all official documents issued.[5]

The duty that brought Thomson most before the public eye was that of publishing all orders, resolutions, and declarations approved by the Congress. Congress made public reports of military and naval engagements and of foreign negotiations and treaties, all of which bore the signature of Secretary Charles Thomson. Thomson's meticulous care assured that no incorrect information was issued and added a great deal to the popular prestige of the Continental Congress. The people, accustomed to relying on rumors both true and false about actions of the British government taken months before, respected a governing body which published the truth whether it concerned defeat or victory, gains or losses. Thomson's endorsement of an official announcement became so well known that a common method of asserting the truth of a particular fact was to state that "It's as true as if Charles Thomson's name was to it."[6] In this way, Thomson aided Congress by establishing a reputation for himself and that body for integrity and truthfulness. Perhaps the Delaware Indians possessed some rare foresight in 1756, when they named Thomson "the man who talks the truth."

As secretary to the Congress, Thomson informally exercised strong influence on the measures that body considered. Since he was known to all of the members as the leader of the radical party in Pennsylvania, Thomson's opinions carried much weight in the after-hours councils where proposals were discussed and agreed upon for presentation. As time passed and the more radical delegates discovered that they could control the actions taken if they could agree among themselves, Thomson's experience at organization proved invaluable. He and men of his kind from the other colonies realized that the conservative group could be controlled and led into supporting measures showing the people of England that the colonies were determined to secure their rights from any attempt at their destruction.

In this manner, the "violent element" of Congress defeated a plan of union proposed by Thomson's foe Joseph Galloway. This plan would have given the colonies a position in the empire with a colonial legislature but still subordinate to Parliament. The radicals, sure that Parliament would not agree to such a plan and that their rights would not be secure if the plan were put into effect, defeated this proposal and began work on plans to unite the colonial resistance to the "Intolerable Acts."

Before the Congress adjourned on October 26, the radicals adopted a policy of nonimportation of British goods to begin December 1, 1774, and a nonexportation resolution to go into effect September 1, 1775, unless grievances of the colonies were redressed by that time. Then, to satisfy the moderate elements throughout the colonies that the delegates were indeed trying to reconcile the colonies and England, they had two petitions prepared, one to the king and the other to the people of England, requesting the recognition of colonial rights. To complete their presentation of the American position, the delegates adopted a Declaration of Rights and Grievances stating the political theory on which they based their stand against English authority. Further, the radicals planned an "Association" to enforce the nonimportation resolutions throughout the colonies. This measure built a system of committees in all the colonies, similar to that which Thomson had developed in Pennsylvania, by which each community would enforce its own embargo on British goods. The lessons learned in Massachusetts, New York, and Pennsylvania were applied in all the colonies in hopes that by united efforts the British trade might be completely stopped until the mother country granted the demands of the colonies.[7]

Meanwhile Thomson engaged in more than just his work as secretary of the Continental Congress. During the years 1774-1776 he remained active in the politics of the province he had helped bring into the quarrel with Britain. The various factions in Pennsylvania were persuaded to back the convening of the First Continental Congress; now they must be led to support the resolutions that it adopted.

Thomson and his fellow Pennsylvania patriots first exerted themselves toward gaining control of the Assembly. They carried out a concerted campaign among all elements of the city and province, urging the election of representatives who supported the Continental Congress and who would work diligently to enforce its proposals. The patriots succeeded, particularly in the Philadelphia city and county elections. Thomson joined Thomas Mifflin as a representative from the city, and the county elected John Dickinson. The newly elected Assembly added Dickinson to the list of delegates to the Second Continental Congress. The three leading agitators of Pennsylvania were now in Congress—Mifflin and Dickinson as delegates and Thomson as secretary. Galloway and the conservatives had fought to prevent their participation, but by careful planning Thomson had obtained a place for himself and Dickinson in the Congress.[8]

In addition to his work in the Assembly, Thomson continued to guide the activities of the Committee of Forty-three, which had assumed control of the Philadelphia nonimportation resolutions. As soon as the Continental Congress adopted its recommendations for a union of all colonies in enforcing the embargo on British goods, the Philadelphia committee maneuvered to join the Association. On November 2, the Forty-three issued a call for a mass meeting on

November 12 to elect a new committee pledged to carry out the recommendations of the resolves of the Continental Congress.

When the citizens gathered in front of the State House, they received a plan to expand the city's committee and to instruct the new committee to obey the rules of the Continental Association. Thomson and his friends sought to gain the adherence of Philadelphia to the Association while not alienating any of the more moderate elements who had thus far cooperated. They realized that the old Committee of Forty-three was too conservative to agree to the violent methods that might be necessary to enforce the association. They realized also that any attempt to weed out conservative committeemen would create ill feeling and division. Therefore, the proposal suggested that the meeting expand the committee membership from forty-three to sixty and appoint enough men of more liberal views to give Thomson and his fellows a majority of the membership. The meeting approved this suggestion and set up a new Committee of Sixty that Thomson, Mifflin, Dickinson, and William Bradford easily dominated. [9]

All the counties of the province also formed new committees early in November, and by the end of the month they began functioning throughout Pennsylvania. As Congress had directed, the committees regulated the use of scarce articles such as wool and controlled the prices of goods likely to become scarce under the embargo. At a December 5 meeting the Philadelphia Committee of Sixty created six subcommittees of Inspection and Observance to carry out more effectively the resolutions of Congress. Thomson and Dickinson headed the Inspection and Observation group in the Northern Liberties section of the city. They busied themselves checking the utilization of the scarce embargo goods and dealing with the infractions of the Association that occurred in their area. [10]

In January 1775, the Philadelphia Committee of Sixty issued a call for a second Provincial Convention. In the meeting, Thomson, along with other leaders of the Association, attempted to unify the work of the county committees and make them more effective. They also discussed plans for further development of the manufacture of gunpowder, iron, nails, and other articles that would be needed in the absence of British imports. The committee urged all of the people of the province to use American-made goods and requested them to report violations of the Association to their local committees. By such public suggestions and resolutions, Thomson and Dickinson again sought to gain the backing of the people of the province for the various objectives of the nonimportation Association.[11]

In February and March 1775, the quarrel between Joseph Galloway and Thomson and Dickinson broke into the open again. Galloway had James Rivington, a New York Tory printer and editor, publish a pamphlet called *A Candid Examination of the Mutual Claims of Great Britain and the Colonies*. In this pamphlet Galloway attacked the Whig claims to inherent rights and said that Parliament controlled all the empire. Thomson and Dickinson published a carefully reasoned answer in March, declaring to Galloway that "you have laboured to shew, that America has no rights at all; and that we are the most abject slaves on earth."[12] This attack by Thomson and Dickinson completely discredited Galloway in Pennsylvania politics. Before the meetings of the Second Continental Congress in May of that year, Galloway resigned from the Pennsylvania delegation and entered even more determinedly into Tory opposition.

In April the news of the battles at Lexington and Concord aroused the fears of the people of the colonies. This open British attack upon Americans, although forced on General Gage by the accumulation of patriot arms, brought home to the American people the fact that Parliament was determined to use violence to subdue the colonies.

In early May, the Philadelphia Committee of Sixty called a public meeting to petition the Assembly to prepare for the defense of Pennsylvania. The Assembly received the petition and after much debate named Thomson, Mifflin, Dickinson, and ten others as a committee to provide stores for the use of the colony in the event that the war between Britain and her colonies already begun in Massachusetts should come to the Quaker province.

While the Assembly took these steps, Governor Penn showed how little he recognized the temper of the province by recommending that the Assembly approve a plan of colonial self-taxation proposed by the British House of Commons. The Assembly named Dickinson and Thomson to direct the committee preparing an answer to his message. The answer adopted on May 4 evidenced the success of Thomson's work toward creating a firm colonial union. "We should esteem it a dishonourable Desertion of Sister Colonies, connected by an Union," the Assembly declared, "to adopt a measure, so extensive in Consequence, without the Advice and Consent of those Colonies engaged with us by solemn Ties in the same common Cause."[13] Thomson, Dickinson, and the other radicals had joined Pennsylvania firmly to the newly formed colonial union and had adopted measures for an active defense against Britain. They had forced the province into a position from which there was little, if any, chance of retreat.

The Second Continental Congress met in Philadelphia on May 10, 1775, and again chose Thomson as secretary. The members realized that they faced a crisis in the relations of the colonies with the mother country. The conflicts at Lexington and Concord had revealed Britain's determination to enforce her policies and the king's refusal to answer their petitions for redress of grievances showed that the American "Union" was not recognized by the British government. At home even the patriots were divided between advocating the adoption of forcible measures of defense and proposing new petitions to the king in a more submissive tone in hopes that he would yield to this show of loyalty. As the summer progressed the Congress wavered between these two methods of approach. While they talked of peaceful petitions they made George Washington commander-in-chief of the newly created Continental army. The Battle of Bunker Hill, which occurred immediately after this action, renewed the feeling of the radical element of the Congress that no peaceful solution was possible. In Thomson's words "much blood was now shed, and it was evident that the sword must decide the contest."[14]

These words, it would seem, indicate that Thomson had become an advocate of complete independence from Britain by the time of the Battle of Bunker Hill in June 1775.

Although *Common Sense*, Tom Paine's pamphlet that reflected the shift of public opinion toward the independence movement, was not published until January 1776, many of the more radical Whigs already believed that the colonies should declare their independence. No contemporary statement by Thomson remains to show that he was irrevocably on the side of independence at this time. But his active support of the military preparations undertaken by the Continental Congress and by the Pennsylvania Assembly, and his maneuverings to convince his fellow Pennsylvanians that a peaceful settlement was impossible, show clearly Thomson's conviction that the colonies should no longer remain subject to Britain and King George III.

Thomson and Dickinson, who was still a deputy to the Congress, both realized that the people of Pennsylvania were not yet convinced of the impossibility of reconciliation with Britain. If the people were to be united in support of the actions of the Continental Congress, the Congress must make some further effort to obtain a peaceful settlement. To accomplish this, Thomson worked to gain the backing of some of the delegates for a new petition to the king. The petition, framed in humble terms, was adopted, and Richard Penn was sent to London to present it to George III. But when Penn, grandson of William Penn and a powerful Pennsylvania conservative, arrived in England in August 1775, the king refused to see him or to receive the petition. Thomson and other Philadelphians portrayed the king's rejection of this second, or "olive-branch," petition as proof of Great Britain's determination to subdue the colonies completely. Thomson recorded later that the rejection "had a powerful effect in ... bringing the Province in a united body into the contest."[15]

But Thomson and his friends Dickinson and Mifflin faced a new and difficult situation within the ranks of the Whigs. By artful management they had directed the province of Pennsylvania into support of the nonimportation Association and the militant measures taken by the Continental Congress. They had been elected to the provincial Assembly and led that body as it took action, without the consent of the governor, to arm the colony. However, in organizing Philadelphia's Committee of Sixty to enforce the Association, they had included as members a large number of mechanics and artisans. The Philadelphians who had never before taken part in the proceedings of government became impatient with the apparent hesitancy of the Assembly in supporting measures leading to independence. These rabid revolutionists particularly disapproved of the Assembly's instructions to the Pennsylvania deputies in the Continental Congress. These instructions directed the delegates to continue seeking means of reconciliation with Britain and prevented them from voting for any measure that would lead to official separation from the mother country.

Thomson and his two fellow Assembly members believed that the Assembly could be controlled and as matters progressed could be led into unified adherence to the cause of independence. But Benjamin Franklin, George Clymer, James Cannon, and Benjamin Rush, leaders of the impatient mechanics, began a movement to wrest the government of the province from the Assembly and give the power to a provincial convention controlled by the more radically democratic elements of Pennsylvania. This movement threatened the colonial unity for which Thomson and many others like him had so strenuously worked.

In the spring of 1775, Thomson learned of plans to organize a special committee to rally support for the dissolution of the Assembly. He, Dickinson, and Mifflin began to work to prevent any action from being taken. The three, all members of the Assembly and also of the Philadelphia committee, attended a meeting of the special committee to urge them not to continue their ruinous program. Thomson and his associates pointed out that if such measures were pushed at this time much damage would be done to the cause of American rights in Pennsylvania. They reminded the committee that the united support of the entire province was needed to prevent the triumph of British pretensions to supremacy. Any attempt to unseat the Assembly, they declared, would create divisions and factions in Pennsylvania that could not easily be repaired.

At this point Thomson appears to have moved away from the radicalism that had thrust him to leadership in Pennsylvania. His apparent shift is even more remarkable since Benjamin Franklin, who had lagged behind Thomson's radical position in the days of the Stamp Act, now supported the movement for the dissolution of the Assembly and so surpassed Thomson's radicalism. Such was indeed the case. Thomson, a part of the Continental government, had moved from a radical Whig to a moderate Whig and would soon be classed as a moderate Republican. He saw the need for democratic reform in Pennsylvania but felt it was overshadowed by the need to unite the colonies behind the independence movement.

Fortunately for the success of the program of the Continental Congress, the advice of Thomson, Mifflin, and Dickinson was heeded. The plans to replace the Assembly with a provincial convention were dropped for a time and the established government, with all the respect and authority inherent in an already functioning ruling body, was preserved.[16]

Thomson and his two compatriots had won only a temporary solution to a problem that occurs in almost all revolutions. As in Pennsylvania, those who organize and begin a revolt against the constituted authority by hard work and organizing effort can secure control of the political powers. They are then content to utilize this control in a manner that is not very different from the old authority in an effort to accomplish the ends for which they began the revolt. At this point they discover that they have aroused desires and ambitions that are even more radical than their own. A new group works to replace the original revolutionary leaders.

This happened in Pennsylvania. Thomson and the early revolutionaries, by organizing the mass of the people in support of their program, had aroused the political ambitions of the lower classes. The mechanics, artisans, and frontier farmers had united under the leadership of Franklin, Clymer, Rush, and others, and were demanding equal representation and participation in the provincial government as well as stronger support for the independence movement in the Continental Congress. Thomson opposed their movement not because he opposed their desire for participation in government but because he feared that the destruction of the established government in Pennsylvania would hinder the movement toward independence for all the colonies.

The reluctant manner in which the Assembly supported the Continental Congress gave Franklin and the more democratic elements of Pennsylvania a ready excuse to push their demands for a provincial convention and for a new type of government. Thomson and the Whig Assembly leaders then faced a group which demanded either immediate action favoring independence or the dissolution of the Assembly. Unless Thomson and his moderate-liberal associates could bring the Assembly into a firm support of the Continental Congress, the end of the established government in Pennsylvania would soon come.[17]

In the October 1775 elections to the Pennsylvania Assembly Thomson did not run for re-election. Devoting more and more time to his duties with the Continental Congress, Thomson yielded his seat in the Assembly to Benjamin Franklin, who had recently returned from his long stay in England as the colony's agent. Thomson soon realized that Franklin favored a new, more democratic form of government for Pennsylvania, and his election even further weakened the hope that the Assembly as it was established under Penn's charter might survive.

Thomson's hopes were dampened to a large degree by the elections but rose when the new Assembly, although the Quakers and conservatives still possessed a majority, proved itself more willing than its predecessor to cooperate with the Continental Congress. The Assembly passed a militia law and strengthened the Pennsylvania Association, and Thomson began to think that Franklin, Clymer, Rush, and their followers would accept this new trend and allow the Assembly to continue as the government of Pennsylvania. His hopes grew as the Assembly authorized bills of credit amounting to 80,000 pounds and appointed a committee of safety to assume the executive powers of the government of the province. The governor was practically ignored in all governmental matters as the Assembly took unto itself the transaction of almost all business by legislative resolutions.

Before the end of November 1775, Thomson saw the Assembly fail in its attempt to lead the movement toward independence. On November 9 the Assembly refused to instruct the Pennsylvania delegates to Congress to work for independence. Franklin and the mechanics and artisans expressed much displeasure when they learned that the instructions still directed the delegates to work for reconciliation with Britain. The Assembly's refusal to go along with the tide of sentiment in the province marked its downfall, and Franklin began anew to plan for its destruction and the establishment of a new government of Pennsylvania. Thomson responded by shifting his attention to the situation in Congress and leaving Pennsylvania affairs to others.[18]

As the winter passed the question of the provincial government became more embroiled with the growing sentiment for independence. Tom Paine published his pamphlet *Common Sense* in January 1776 and spread powerful arguments for independence through all of the colonies. Some of the most ardent Pennsylvania advocates of independence, such as Franklin, also wanted to replace the charter government with one possessing a more democratically elected assembly. Others who were more moderate in their position as to the type of provincial government followed the lead of their associate Charles Thomson and desired independence, but proposed to achieve it through the already existing Assembly. Still others among the moderates, who had until now supported the radical movements, stood with John Dickinson who favored at least one more attempt to reconcile Britain and the colonies.

In Febraury 1776, the Assembly continued its contradictory policy of providing large sums for the defense of the province while at the same time refusing to alter its instructions to the delegates to Congress opposing independence. The Assembly did yield to the democratic westerners when it voted on March 8, 1776, to admit seventeen more members from the underrepresented western counties. This partly met the demands for a more proportionate system of representation but did not entirely satisfy Franklin and the western leaders. Unless the independence-minded mechanics and artisans gained control of the Assembly in the election for new members to be held on May 1, the Assembly had little chance of continuing. Revolutionary committees already had assumed much of the Assembly's authority in the outlying counties.[19]

When the election for the additional assemblymen was held on May 1, the Quaker and Conservative factions retained a small majority. The Assembly had carefully apportioned the new seats to areas in which they could control the elections and be assured that they would maintain control of the government of the colony. They had succeeded, but in so doing they dealt a death blow to the Pennsylvania government as established under William Penn's charter. The mechanics, artisans, and farmers saw their defeat in the election as an indication that they would never wrest control of the province from the Assembly by legal means. The years before, Benjamin Rush, George Clymer, James Cannon, and others had listened to Thomson's assurances that the Assembly could be brought to favor independence. A year had passed and this change in the Assembly's attitude had not taken place, so the radical leaders decided that the time had come to establish a new government in the province.

On May 20, 1776, Franklin, Rush, and Clymer called a meeting of the inhabitants that was attended by almost seven thousand people. The large attendance proved conclusively that the control of provincial politics had passed into more radical hands than those of Thomson. The "Sam Adams of Philadelphia" was conspicuous by his absence among those guiding the crowd into making demands for a new constitution with no property requirements for voting and with equal representation for all of the counties. The final resolutions called for a Provincial Convention to establish a new government and directly conflicted with Thomson's firm belief that the government under the charter could better lead Pennsylvania in the war with England than could any newly founded, radically inspired, convention government.[20]

While plans were being made for the Provincial Convention, which was to meet on July 15, Thomson continued his duties as secretary of the Continental Congress. Much to his disgust, Congress became involved in the question of a suitable government for Pennsylvania and for some of the other colonies who were proving reluctant to back a movement for independence. On May 15, five days before the State House meeting, John Adams led in the adoption of a resolution urging the people to suppress all governments established under the crown. The crowd before the Pennsylvania State House cheered the reading of this resolution and based their actions on its request. Thomson, working earnestly and long to bring Pennsylvania into complete union with Congress, saw the two objects of his allegiance join together in defeating the charter government that he believed best for his home province.[21]

While Congress debated the proper form of government for Pennsylvania and the other colonies, the surge toward independence increased daily.

On June 7, Richard Henry Lee introduced resolutions declaring the thirteen colonies independent of all ties with England. From that day until the adoption of the Declaration of Independence most of the time spent by Congress in debate concerned this question. On June 8 the Pennsylvania Assembly made one last effort to redeem itself and allowed the Pennsylvania delegates to vote for independence. The action came too late to save the Assembly; it was replaced by the ultrademocratic Pennsylvania Constitution of 1776. But the delegates could now follow their desires without violating their instructions. After the introduction of the resolution for independence, Congress spent almost an entire month debating the advisability of the measure. On July 2, 1776, Congress finally gave approval to Richard Henry Lee's resolution declaring the colonies independent, and on July 4 Jefferson's Declaration of Independence, with minor alterations, was approved.[22]

Thomson may have played a significant role in the writing of the Declaration of Independence. As secretary to the Congress he knew its thinking better than anyone, so what better source could Jefferson have consulted? There is, however, no evidence that this is what happened and certainly the circumstances surrounding the writing of the Declaration of Independence have been thoroughly explored.[23] It is certain that Thomson's role in the events involving the adoption of the Declaration has been both exaggerated and minimized. The Northern Ireland Tourist Board proclaims in a blurb accompanying a photograph of Thomson's birthplace "It was he who penned the American Declaration of Independence." This is accurate—it was Thomson who wrote the draft from which the printer made the copy that is wafered into the *Journals* of the Congress—but it is misleading. Deborah Logan's belief that it was Thomson who first read the Declaration to the assembled Philadelphians a few days after it was adopted is completely erroneous. It was, in fact, a fellow Philadelphia radical, John Nixon, who first publicly read the document on July 8, 1776.[24]

On the other hand, Thomson is rarely mentioned in accounts of the "Signers" of the Declaration of Independence. Yet his printed signature and that of the president of Congress, John Hancock, were the only two names officially linked with the Declaration for months after its adoption. The familiar "engrossed" copy of the Declaration was not signed until August 1776, and the names of the "signers" were not recorded in the *Journals* even then. No public announcement of those who signed was made until January 1777, more than six months after Thomson and Hancock's names were publicly and officially linked with the treasonable document.[25] The recent payment of more than four hundred thousand dollars for one of the few remaining copies of that first printing with Thomson's and Hancock's names boldly affixed may be an indication that Thomson's association with the Declaration is about to receive belated but well-earned recognition.[26]

Thomson had another, more personal problem with the adoption of the Declaration of Independence. His good friend, fellow radical, and a relative by marriage, John Dickinson, had refused to vote for the Declaration and was being politically exiled for his actions. Dickinson, who believed that one last try for reconciliation should have been attempted before independence was adopted, had petulantly retired to private life and his "books and fields." In August, as the members of Congress were gathering to sign the Declaration that Dickinson had refused to support, Thomson wrote to his friend: "You and I have differed in sentiment with regard to propriety of certain public measures—not so much the measures themselves, as the time, which you thought was not yet come." In urging Dickinson not to be too peeved with his countrymen's reaction to his refusal to support the Declaration, Thomson commented with an Americanized version of a familiar Shakespearean maxim. Where Shakespeare had Brutus say "There is a tide in the affairs of men, Which taken at the flood, leads on to fortune," Thomson, apostle of progress and the American fetish of seizing control and shaping the future, commented to his friend, "There is a tide in human affairs, which if improved, things go on smoothly but if neglected, tis in vain to loose from the wharf." The tide of revolution was at its flood, and for the next several years Thomson would be involved in attempts to "improve" it.[27]

Congress declared independence. The United States was loosed from the wharf. The efforts of patriot revolutionaries had succeeded in wearing down the opposition and had paved the way for the creation of an independent nation. Thomson saw this as the greater victory, but it grieved him that, in obtaining his province's support for independence, the provincial leaders had sacrificed the charter government. It would have saddened him if he had realized that it was he who had stimulated the desire for governmental participation in the masses who supported the Pennsylvania Constitution of 1776. Thomson's utilization of the mobs of Philadelphians to protest against British oppression had been these citizens' first taste of government.

Thomson had devoted his time and energy to the cause of American independence. Prior to the meeting of the First Continental Congress, Thomson concentrated his efforts in Pennsylvania but with increasing regular contacts with the other colonies. This was his radical Whig period. From September 1774, when the Congress first met, until July 1776, when independence was declared, Thomson divided his time between the colony and the new nation. During this time Thomson appeared to waver between a radical and a moderate Whig position. By July 4, 1776, he had become a part of the revolutionary establishment as a moderate Whig. From this point it was an easy step to moderate republicanism. He never entered the radical republican phase that many revolutionaries were to experience and that is frequently a part of the world's revolutions. He turned his attention to his job as secretary to the Continental Congress—the body whose task it was to make the independence of the United States a certainty.

NOTES

1. The most incisive study of Pennsylvania and the adoption of the Constitution of 1776 is David Hawke, *In the Midst of a Revolution* (Philadelphia, 1961). The relationship between Philadelphia and the backcountry is discussed, pp. 59-86.

2. John Adams, *The Adams Papers: Diary and Autobiography of John Adams,* ed. L. M. Butterfield (Cambridge, Massachusetts, 1961), 2: 115.

3. Galloway to William Franklin, September 5, 1774, *New Jersey Archives*, 1st ser. (Newark, 1880-1886), 10: 477. A good account of the opening of the First Continental Congress is Lynn Montross, *The Reluctant Rebels: The Story of the Continental Congress* (1950; reprinted, New York, 1970), pp. 33-38.

4. Thomson's account of his election and notification is found in "American Biography," *American Quarterly Review* 1 (1827): 30.

Hannah Harrison, Thomson's second wife, was the daughter of Richard Harrison, a wealthy Quaker farmer. Since Thomson was not a Quaker, her marriage to him in 1774 caused her to be dismissed from the Friends Meeting to which she belonged. The Quakers felt little kindness for their former schoolmaster who was now one of the more rabid revolutionaries in the province.

The marriage brought Thomson a considerable amount of property in addition to that he already owned. Most valuable was the 700-acre "Harriton" estate a few miles from Philadelphia near present-day Bryn Mawr. Thomson and his wife resided in Philadelphia during the revolutionary years, but after the Continental Congress was dissolved in 1789, Thomson left the service of the federal government and retired to the "Harriton" estate. Lewis R. Harley, *Life of Charles Thomson* (Philadelphia, 1900), pp. 187-95.

5. "American Biography," pp. 30-31. See also Frederick S. Rolater, "The Continental Congress: A Study in the Origin of American Public Administration, 1774-1781" (Ph.D. diss., University of Southern California, 1970), pp. 57-61.

6. So reported a contemporary, Ashbell Green, a Philadelphia minister as recorded in Joseph H. Jones, *The Life of Ashbell Green* (New York, 1849), p. 48; see also, Watson, *Annals of Philadelphia and Pennsylvania in the Olden Time* (Philadelphia, 1850), 1: 568.

7. For a full discussion of the actions of the First Continental Congress, see E. C. Burnett, *The Constitutional Congress* (New York, 1941), pp. 35-59.

8. "Votes," *Pennsylvania Archives*, 8th ser., 8: 7148, 7152.

9. *Pennsylvania Journal*, November 16, 1774.

10. Ibid., December 7, 1774.

11. Ibid., January 26, 1775.

12. Ibid., March 8, 1775; that Thomson and Dickinson were the authors of the "Answer" is attested by Galloway himself in a letter to Samuel Verplank, April 1, 1775, *PMHB* 21 (1897): 481. Julian P. Boyd, *Anglo-American Union* (Philadelphia, 1941), pp. 45-50.

13. "Votes," *Pennsylvania Archives*, 8th ser., 8: 7224-34.

14. Thomson to Drayton, n.d., N.Y.H.S. *Collections*, 11: 284.

15. Ibid., p. 285.

16. Ibid., p. 284.

17. Theodor George Thayer, *Pennsylvania Politics and the Growth of Democracy, 1740-1776* (Harrisburg, 1953) pp. 173-75.

18. Thomson to Drayton, n.d., N.Y.H.S. *Collections*, 11: 284; for the record of the Assembly's actions, see "Votes," *Pennsylvania Archives*, 8th ser., 8: 735 ff.; Thayer, *Pennsylvania Politics*, pp. 172-75. Though inaccurate in putting Thomson as Franklin's associate in the autumn of 1775, this is a good account of the period.

19. "*Votes*," *Pennsylvania Archives*, 8th ser., 7: 7428, 7436; Thayer, *Pennsylvania Politics*, pp. 176-77. John Adams indicates that Thomson was among those working in Congress for independence in February 1776. Adams, *Adams Papers*: *Autobiography*, 3: 362-63. Shortly thereafter, however, Adams condemned Thomson's method of recording the minutes as favoring the "opposition." Ibid., p. 365.

20. *Pennsylvania Gazette*, May 22, 1776. Thomson's opinions as to the desirability of retaining the Assembly as the government of the province were expressed later to William Drayton, n.d., N.Y.H.S. *Collections*, 11: 282.

21. Burnett, *Continental Congress*, pp. 158-59; Hawke, *In the Midst of a Revolution* is by far the best account of the events of 1776 in Pennsylvania. Charles H. Lincoln, *The Revolutionary Movement in Pennsylvania 1760-1776* (Philadelphia, 1901) and J. Paul Selsam, *The Pennsylvania Constitution of 1776* (Philadelphia, 1936) add full coverage to this complex period. Charles J. Stille, *Life and Times of John Dickinson* (Philadelphia, 1891) discusses Dickinson's role.

22. John H. Hazelton, *The Declaration of Independence, Its History* (New York, 1906), pp. 156-80; David Hawke, *A Transaction of Free Men* (New York, 1964), pp. 140-206.

23. A thorough account of Jefferson's construction of the Declaration is in Julian P. Boyd, et al, eds., *The Papers of Thomas Jefferson* (Princeton, 1950-   ), vol. 1; see also Hawke, *A Transaction of Free Men*, pp. 140-75.

24. Information accompanying photographs of "Gorteade Cottage," Thomson's birthplace near Londonderry, Northern Ireland. Northern Ireland Tourist Board, Belfast. Deborah Logan, "Diary," Historical Society of Pennsylvania. Hawke, *A Transaction of Free Men*, p. 208.

25. T. R. Fehrenbach, *Greatness to Spare: The Heroic Sacrifices of the Men Who Signed the Declaration of Independence* (Princeton, 1968), is an exception in that he mentions, albeit briefly, Thomson's role. pp. 5, 7-8. Worthington C. Ford, ed. *Journals of the Continental Congress* (Washington, 1904-1937), 5: 507, 590-91, 626.

26. For an account of the discovery and sale of the sixteenth known copy of the first printing of the Declaration see the *New York Times*, January 4, 1969; May 8, 1969. F. R. Goff, *The John Dunlap Broadside: The First Printing of the Declaration of Independence* (Washington, D. C., 1977) is an account of all known extant copies of the Dunlap printing. See also J. Edwin Hendricks, "The 'Signer' Who Didn't Get to Sign," *Furman Studies*, June 1978, 3-9.

27. Thomson to Dickinson, August 16, 1776, Logan Papers, Historical Society of Pennsylvania. Printed in PMHB 35 (1911): 499-502; *Julius Caesar*, act 4, scene 3, line 218.

7

Secretary to a Nation

*F*or *fifteen* years Charles Thomson was secretary to the government that joined the thirteen former British colonies together into the United States. He was the only person associated with the First Continental Congress that convened in 1774, the Confederation Congress that gave way to the government under President George Washington in 1789, and all the Congresses in between.[1] Thomson's services bridged the period that included the Declaration of Independence, the successful war with Great Britain, the depression and economic doldrums of the 1780s, and the framing of the federal Constitution. As secretary to the United States in Congress Assembled from 1774 until 1789, Charles Thomson was indeed secretary to a nation in the making.

As secretary to Congress, Thomson recorded its minutes and edited its journals; he handled much of its correspondence and kept his office as a repository of records, books, laws of the various states, newspapers, paper, ink, quills, and all the other materials necessary for the conduct of a legislative body. As the most effective executive officer the Congress possessed, Thomson corresponded with the states to urge their compliance with the laws and requisitions from Congress. He even at times had to plead for the states to send representatives to Congress in order that a quorum might be present to transact business. He issued passports, letters of marque and reprisal, news releases, and public proclamations. He presided over Congress for brief periods, served as secretary of foreign affairs in addition to performing the duties of his own office, and maintained an extensive correspondence with Washington, Jefferson, Franklin, Jay, and

John Adams. He served the Revolution from its inception to its conclusion.[2]

During his entire career Thomson's primary duty was to keep a record of the actions of Congress. Even though the secretary did not record the discussion of issues by the Congress, keeping their records was a heavy task. Congress convened at nine in the morning and worked until midafternoon. Night sessions were not unknown and, whatever the adjournment hour, Congress expected its minutes ready for reading upon convening the next morning. Thomson took rough notes while Congress was in session and transcribed them into a journal for presentation the next day. Most of the journals are in Thomson's handwriting and, even when a clerk was given the task of transcription, Thomson supervised the activity and lined out and inserted sections where he deemed it advisable or where Congress directed. At one time nine different journals were being kept on the same proceedings. This included a Secret Domestic Journal; an "Imperfect" Secret Journal; a "Secret Journal A;" a volume of "letters of instruction, commissions, letters of credance, plans of treaties, ratification of contracts and the like;" and a Journal of Foreign Affairs. There was also a "More Secret Journal" that contained material not found elsewhere, related exclusively to peace efforts.[3]

Thomson's previous duties as secretary to Teedyuscung, as secretary to the Philadelphia committee of correspondence, and to the Pennsylvania provincial assembly had prepared him somewhat for his job as secretary to Congress. His experience, the fact that he was a resident of Philadelphia, his known radicalism, and his excellent penmanship were factors that probably led to his appointment. None of his experience prepared him for the intrigue and secrecy that accompanied his new job. Even the proceedings of Congress were secret. High-level correspondence between Thomson's office and officials abroad, and even with other departments within the government, sometimes was conducted in code. The British made at least two attempts to infiltrate Thomson's office with spies, and Thomson himself had an "understanding" with a double agent, *New York Gazette* editor, James Rivington. No wonder earlier historians repeated the

claim that Thomson was in charge of the secret service during
the Revolution![4]

Thomson and two members of Congress directed the publication of the first printed *Journal* of Congress. Thomson
prepared the rough copy of the records for publication by
extracting the Articles of Association, and the Bill of Rights,
along with occasional resolutions, memorials, and measures
passed by the Congress. The Bradfords in Philadelphia published the *Journal*, which circulated widely enough to go
through several printings in a few months. Thus, Thomson
continued his work of making the proceedings for liberty
known to the people of America.[5]

Additional duties imposed by Congress upon their secretary were many and varied. In January 1776, Congress asked
Thomson to present to the Congress an account of the unsuc-
cessful Quebec campaign. After the resignation of the president of Congress, John Hancock, Thomson officiated over
Congress until a new president took office. For a time in 1778
Thomson had the duty of attesting all military commissions
in addition to issuing commissions for privately armed vessels. As the *Journals* of Congress were printed, Thomson
assumed the task of sending copies to the several states. He
accomplished these tasks while attending the usual debates
and proceedings of Congress. Congress moved frequently,
and Thomson transported the papers and records safely and
with dispatch. Thomson's functions and his influence em-
braced many of the actions of Congress and placed his im-
print on much that emerged from that body.[6]

With each succeeding Congress, Thomson's office increasingly came to be a place of reference for the members. New
members found that the secretary could best inform them of
the manner in which Congress accomplished its business. In
his office was a complete set of the *Journals*, both the printed
and the more complete manuscript versions. Thomson subscribed to at least one paper from all the states and most of
the New York and Philadelphia papers. He sought to have
"as compleat a collection of the public papers of every State
as I can deposited here, where the delegates from the several
states may have access to them." He collected census returns
from those states that had recorded them. It was natural then

that with the coming of peace an attempt would be made to authorize him to establish a library for Congress. In 1782 and 1783, a committee investigated the matter and made such a proposal, but the measure never passed. Thomson, nonetheless, continued to keep what amounted to a library of Congress attached to his office for as long as he served.[7]

Congress depended greatly upon the work of its secretary, and individual members frequently commented on the amount and quality of work that proceeded from that office. Jefferson wrote to Thomson in 1781 of "the load of business under which you labor."[8] That same year Franklin sought to aid Thomson in his work by sending him a copying device from France.[9] John Adams illustrated the trust placed in news received from the secretary's office by referring to the "sacred" nature of Thomson's signature.[10] John Jay, on a peace commission in France in 1781, wrote to Thomson inferring that his was the only office that kept the foreign representatives in touch with events at home.[11] Deborah Logan, observer and historian of revolutionary Philadelphia, recorded:

> The value of his great integrity was felt in the implicit credit with which the public received whatever was published with the sanction of his name; his services were also very great in the House, in a variety of ways, such as reconciling the members, repressing extravagancies, & detecting errors, in whatever came within the sphere of his business.[12]

Thomson's integrity and his conduct of his office did not always meet with complete acceptance from the members of Congress. John Adams once accused him of favoring the "opposition," and Tom Paine felt that Thomson did not treat him fairly. Jonathan Trumbull sought president Henry Laurens' assistance in compelling Thomson to address him as "paymaster general." Thomson's continued refusal carried over into a later dispute with Laurens, which resulted in a confrontation on the floor of Congress, a struggle between the president and the secretary over copies of the *Journals*, and a consequent congressional investigation. The quarrel is thoroughly covered by accounts from both participants in the *Journals of the Continental Congress*. The intensity of the

battle between two otherwise reputable gentlemen is an indication of the height of tension in Congress as the war with
Britain wore on into its fifth year in 1779. And both men had
recently returned from visits to their dying colleague William
Henry Drayton of South Carolina. Less is known of a later
incident in which Pennsylvania delegate James Searle
"cained the Secretary of Congress and the Secretary returned
the salute." It is reported that both Searle and Thomson
returned to Congress on the next day, apparently no worse
for the incident. Perhaps this too was a result of the tensions
of the day, but it is an indication that Thomson had lost none
of his youthful fire and vigor in his service to his country.[13]

The war was going tragically for the Americans. Congress
had spent almost a year in exile from Philadelphia in 1777-
1778; when they returned, Thomson and other Philadelphia
patriots found that their homes had been destroyed. Steady
inflation of the Continental currency resulted in the near
bankruptcy of the government and probably contributed to
Benedict Arnold's decision to side with the British. Arnold's
treason came to light in the fall of 1780 immediately following General Horatio Gates' disastrous defeat at Camden,
South Carolina. While much of the nation was blaming
Gates for his defeat, Thomson wrote to John Jay, "to our
want of money may be ascribed the Enemy's success in
Carolina."[14]   That November the patriot ladies of Philadelphia went from door to door, canvasing for funds for the
struggling government "H[annah] Thompson [sic], Mrs.
[Robert] Morris, Mrs. [James] Wilson, and a number of very
genteel women, paraded about streets in this manner, some
carrying ink stands, nor did they let the meanest ale house
escape."[15] A considerable amount of gold and silver money
was collected in this manner along with two hundred thousand dollars of Continental currency (still not completely
depreciated). Hannah Thomson and three other ladies collected eleven guineas, thirty-four silver dollars, seven half-
joes along with 19,959 continental dollars in the Arch to
Market Street district.[16]

But better financial days were coming. On June 24, 1781,
Secretary Thomson prepared a nine-page report on the income of Congress for the previous year for the new secretary
of finance, Robert Morris. It presented a bleak picture, and

Morris was forced to resort to chartering the Bank of Pennsylvania in an attempt to provide supplies for the army for an additional two months. Several congressional leaders subscribed pledges to be paid out of their own funds in case Congress could not repay the bank. Thomson subscribed for four thousand dollars, but fortunately Morris' financial genius was such that the subscribers did not have to pay. Thomson, Morris, Benjamin Lincoln, Robert R. Livingston, and George Washington, when he was in town, met daily at Morris' office before the convening of Congress in what came to be a sort of semiofficial cabinet meeting to consider the conduct of the war and other pressing matters of business.[17]

One pressing matter that was constantly before Congress was the precise nature of the government that was directing the fortunes of the nation. Although the Articles of Confederation had been proposed in 1777, they had not yet been ratified by all of the states, and therefore had not gone into effect. The Congress and the various departments of the government were operating in much the manner that they proposed, however, and it was with great relief that they saw the Articles ratified in 1781. The secretary had been operating his office under a resolution of Congress of March 22, 1777. With the formal adoption of the Articles of Confederation there was an attempt to tighten the administrative practices of the government. Additional duties were assigned to the secretary by Congress in January 1782. "In order that the President may be relieved from the business with which he is unnecessarily incumbered . . . and that business may be conducted with regularity and dispatch," the new act instructed the secretary to record, authenticate, and make available the proceedings, reports, acts, and ordinances of Congress. Under these instructions Thomson furnished the heads of all departments of government with copies of each act, order, or resolution that concerned their department. He recorded all communications received by Congress in a register and made notes of action taken respecting them. The secretary replied to all communications except those directed to the attention of the president or some particular department. He kept a register of all treaties, conventions, and ordinances and made a copy of each ordinance or report that was not of secret nature for each state. The secretary was to safeguard the Great Seal of the United States and affix it to documents as directed by Congress. He maintained records of the members' attendance and directed publication of the *Journals of Congress* and other documents. In return for these and many other services not fully detailed, Thomson's salary was raised to three thousand dollars a year.[18]

During the whole of Thomson's service as "Secretary of the United States in Congress Assembled" he received his salary irregularly. He was given no pay at all for his services to the First Continental Congress except for a silver bowl that Congress presented to his wife. The bowl occupied a place of honor in the Thomson home. Congress made no arrangements for other compensation until June 1776—almost two years after he began his task. At that time he was given twelve hundred dollars for the year just past. In 1778, Thomson received two thousand dollars and he was paid three thousand dollars for 1783. These figures were apparently based on specie dollars, whereas the fourteen thousand he received in 1780 was doubtlessly paid in inflated Continental currency. Throughout the period Thomson was among the highest paid officials of the new government though he never received the highest salary (that honor usually went to the secretary of foreign affairs). When Thomson left the government in 1789, he had Joseph Nourse, register of the treasury, prepare a statement that showed that Thomson received approximately thirty-two thousand dollars in specie or equivalent value for his services from 1774 to 1789.[19]

Even this would have been a handsome salary for the period, but Thomson frequently had to pay his office expenses from his own pocket and hope that Congress would reimburse him later. The frequent moves of Congress made further inroads on Thomson's wealth as he moved his residence from city to city and met the expenses of moving himself and his household. Early in the war his home had been destroyed. Although the house he was occupying at Summerville belonged to John Dickinson, Thomson's loss was great as books, clothing, and other personal effects were destroyed, presumably by orders of Sir William Howe, in

November 1777. The next month two regiments of Pennsylvania militia encamped on Thomson's fields at "Harriton" and attacked the enemy from that position. When Congress returned to Philadelphia after the British had evacuated, Thomson was forced to turn to the wife of his old enemy Joseph Galloway for a house to rent (Galloway had fled with the British and was to end his life in exile in Great Britain). The damage done to Thomson's estates, combined with the expenses of maintaining his office and his residence as he followed Congress, meant that Thomson emerged from the revolution financially poorer than he had entered it. Fortunately his own wealth and that of his wife permitted him to make such a sacrifice without a serious blow to his comfort and fortune.[20]

The 1782 resolution on the operation of the secretary's office had included the duty of safeguarding the Great Seal of the United States and of affixing it to such documents as Congress should direct. No such seal was then in existence but Congress had been debating the precise form of this seal since July 4, 1776. After six years and a profusion of ideas from Franklin, Jefferson, Adams, and others, Congress agreed that it could not accept the recommendation of the third committee it had appointed to resolve the issue. On June 13, 1782, Congress turned the entire matter over to Thomson, directing him to prepare a suitable seal. The secretary to Congress chose some features from the designs submitted by all three committees and arranged them in a simple, definite scheme. In his rough drawing and written description, Thomson designed a seal that was quite similar to the one finally adopted and in use today. His seal presented the American bald eagle in a glowering and menacing position and included all the attributes of the present seal. An olive branch in the eagle's right talon, a bundle of arrows in the left (though not the thirteen arrows of the final design), the motto *E Pluribus Unum* held in the beak, and a summit of thirteen stars completed the device. For the reverse of the seal, Thomson combined several suggestions and included some new parts that were his own. The most prominent feature was William Barton's unfinished pyramid topped with an all-seeing eye. Thomson contributed from his own extensive knowledge of the Latin classics by changing two lines from Virgil to produce the inscriptions *ANNUIT COEPTIS* (He has favored our cause) and *NOVUS ORDO SECLORUM* (A new order of the ages). These two phrases certainly encapsulate Thomson's religious and political attitudes and indicate a full understanding of the significance of the work in which he and the Congress were involved.[21]

Thomson's varied duties included more than those listed in the outline of his work made in 1782. When Congress received the French minister to hear the announcement of the birth of the dauphin, Thomson planned the ceremony, issued tickets to members and officials, and stood on the platform at the right of the president. When Congress declared peace in 1783, it was Thomson who drew up the declaration. In 1783 members of Congress suggested that questions of voting procedure be left to the secretary for settlement. Several members successfully objected because they believed that this would make the secretary more powerful than Congress.[22]

In June 1783, when Robert Livingston resigned as secretary for foreign affairs, he suggested an even more potentially powerful secretariat. Congress resolved that Thomson be directed to receive all papers until a successor was appointed. Livingston and others urged Thomson to assume the duties of that office in addition to his own, but Thomson "determined to have nothing to do with the business of the office."[23] Livingston believed that Congress had Thomson in mind for the position and hoped that "They may & will, I hope, prevail upon you to change your determination with respect to the business of the office."[24] Thomson conducted the business of foreign affairs officially only until 1784 when John Jay took office as the new secretary for foreign affairs. But throughout his tenure as secretary to Congress, Thomson had frequently served as an unofficial foreign affairs officer. His correspondence with Franklin, Jefferson, Jay, and others is filled with information concerning the attitudes of Congress, the progress of the war, the state of the economy, and other such matters as were pertinent to the actions of our representatives abroad.

Congress meanwhile continued its travels from city to city in search of a suitable home. Located at first in Philadelphia, the seat of government had at different times settled in Baltimore, Lancaster, York, and Princeton. It then moved to Annapolis, to Trenton, and finally in January 1785, Congress convened in New York where it met until it was replaced by the government established under the Constitution. Thomson generally attended wherever the Congress met—at times moving his entire household as Congress moved, and at other times leaving Mrs. Thomson at their home in Philadelphia. In the summer of 1784, Congress was in recess and the Committee of the States, a sort of interim executive committee, conducted the business of the nation in Annapolis. Thomson obtained leave to return to Philadelphia on condition that one of the deputy clerks maintain the secretary's office. Thomson remained in touch with the government by corresponding with the two clerks, Bankson and Remsen, while he was in Philadelphia. It was with no small difficulty that the committee kept enough members in attendance to continue conducting business, especially since the Congress next convened in Trenton rather than Annapolis.

Thomson hoped that the capital eventually would return to Philadelphia, but he wished even more that a permanent seat would be chosen. He commented on the matter to Jefferson: "I wish Congress were settled. This mode of rambling is neither consistent with dignity nor convenience."[25] His wish was eventually fulfilled at the end of 1784, when after a long debate Congress adjourned its session in Trenton to meet again after the first of the year in New York. Though Thomson believed that Philadelphia was a more suitable choice than New York, and it certainly was more to his convenience, Congress and the Confederation Government had a permanent seat.

As 1785 approached, Charles and Hannah Thomson prepared to move to New York. "Harriton," their estate just north of Philadelphia, was still suffering from the ravages of war but was in the hands of tenants. The Thomsons closed their house in Philadelphia, and Hannah arranged for the transportation of their household goods and Thomson prepared the records of Congress for relocation in their new home in New York.

The Thomsons enjoyed a prominent role in the social life of the nation's new capital. Hannah doubtlessly missed her relatives and friends of a lifetime but she seemed to make the most of her situation. In a series of letters written during her stay in New York she leaves a vivid picture of the difficulties and joys that the Thomsons experienced. Writing to John Mifflin, a young cousin living in Philadelphia, Hannah Thomson spoke of the difficulty of writing while the carpenters were working on the house in which they were living. After stepping "into Mr. Thomson's parlor (where Penn, Ink & paper stand always ready)" she recorded that "I find N. York more agreeable than I expected. The Ladies are gay & agreeable [and] there are a number of belles here."[26] In May, she reported that they were not yet settled and unpacked, for their landlord was still preparing the house in which they were to live (probably a different one than that mentioned in her previous letter). In describing the city, Hannah Thomson reported that she had "met with several frights at the ferries. They are dangerous and disagreeable in blustering weather."[27]

Though Mrs. Thomson apparently enjoyed her life in New York and wrote often of the parties, weddings, and romantic alliances in progress, she did wish that she and her husband were permanently settled. Once after seeing a "beautiful seat on the East river" she remarked that:

Were we permanently fixed here I would wish Mr. T. to possess it as the present owners are going to the West Indies this fall. But instead of fixing anywhere, I consider myself a Sojourner or a traveller that holds himself ready to start when the Stageman calls.[28]

Despite the bad New York winters during which she was often confined to the house by the snow, and the ill health that confined both Thomsons for a time in the winter of 1788, Mrs. Thomson continued to relate with apparent enjoyment the lively social life of the city. Winter outings, plays, teas, and other social events helped make life more bearable for this lady who aided her husband throughout his career, even to the extent of helping him make copies of the *Journals* of Congress in the early years of the Revolution. A lively sense of humor is indicated in a letter written in 1788 in which she speaks of two recent Philadelphia weddings. Commenting that one of the matches brought to mind a poem relating two minds made in the same mold, she said of the other alliance:

How can the soft enchantment hold
Two jarring Souls of angry Mold
The rugged and the keen.
Sampson's young foxes might as well
In bonds of chearful wedlock dwell
With firebrands tied between.[29]

The life of the Thomson family in New York was a full one for the age in which they lived and, with the aid of his wife, Charles Thomson enjoyed his time as secretary of the Congress.

At the time of the move of Congress to New York, some members attempted to remove Thomson's influence from the government. Thomson confided to his wife on April 3, 1785, that his enemies in Congress sought to establish a new secretariat and require a new election or, failing that, to require an annual election of the secretary.[30] The attempt produced only a new ordinance regulating the office in a manner similar to the ordinance that had been passed in 1782. Congress directed their secretary to keep his office in or near the building where the Congress was meeting and, as before, to preserve the *Journals* and other papers. Either Thomson or his deputy must attend Congress or the Committee of States at all times and notify all states of the acts and regulations of the national government. The secretary corresponded with the states concerning the execution of the measures of Congress and reported the results of this correspondence to Congress. It was a weak government in which only the secretary to Congress dealt with the execution of the laws, but with the cooperation of the states and the industriousness of the secretary he accomplished much.[31]

The attempt to remove Thomson as secretary or lessen his influence apparently passed with little effect. Thomson continued to perform his usual duties and to aid in the conduct of affairs in other ways. He served as master of ceremonies for the July 4 dinner, a few months after the move to New York in 1785, and sent invitations to the members of Congress and fifty other guests. He composed a list of thirteen toasts while the secretary of war arranged for a band and for a cannon to fire salutes at appropriate times. In a more executive capacity, Thomson advised Congress on several matters, including such questions as whether or not Congress should give an interpretation of a treaty with France, what action Congress should take on the petition from four Indian chiefs, and what should be done with respect to Canadian refugees.[32]

The fact that Thomson had the responsibility for getting the states to abide by the laws and treaties of the new government, and yet had no authority to force the states to comply, is a good indication of the things that were wrong with the government under the Articles of Confederation. Congress had little faculty other than to make recommendations to the states and had no means to coerce reluctant states into acting. With no power to levy taxes or tariff duties it found it difficult to arrange payment of debts incurred during the Revolution and this led to a decline in prestige abroad. With no authority to enforce its acts within the states, the confederation government could expect little respect at home. Some men, Thomson among them, had feared this from the beginning of the Revolution.[33] Thomson expressed similar feelings to Jefferson.

> Unless a different spirit prevail from what has of late appeared there is reason to apprehend a dissolution of the Confederacy ... I wish the states would send forward men of enlarged Minds and conciliating tempers ... that time might be given for consolidating and strengthening the Confederacy.[34]

In October 1784, he wrote to Jefferson again concerning the inaction of Congress and the need for an executive organ of government. "Though this invisibility of a federal head will have little effect on our affairs here ... I am apprehensive it will have an ill aspect in the eyes of European Nations."[35] There was much that was wrong with the Confederation, and many desired to improve it in order to provide the nation with a government that could command respect at home and abroad. But as long as the various states insisted on preserving their individual rights and powers, little could be accomplished toward a strong national government.[36]

From time to time, Congress recognized the failings of the Confederation and attempted to strengthen the government in various ways. Attempts were made to give the Congress the power to tax and to give Congress the power to levy a duty on goods coming into the country. These were attempts to provide the government with a source of revenue that in turn would have given it new stature and authority at home and abroad. Thomson, in his correspondence with state officials concerning their obligations to Congress, urged them to adopt those measures that would have made the government feasible by strengthening it. He prepared reports for Congress on the futile attempts to amend the Articles of Confederation, and he fretted at the weakness of the government that he served.[37]

Thomson's view of the United States under the Articles of Confederation was not wholly dark, and as time passed it became more favorable. In 1786, he wrote to Jefferson:

> I will venture to assert, that there is not upon the face of the earth a body of people more happy or rising into consequence with more rapid stride, than the Inhabitants of the United States of America. Population in encreasing, new houses building, new lands clearing, new settlements forming and new manufactures establishing with a rapidity beyond conception. And what is more, the people are well fed, well clad and well housed.[38]

Yet within a few months the crisis posed by Shays's Rebellion in Massachusetts caused Thomson to send out urgent pleas to the states to send representatives to Congress so that it might, at least, attempt to deal with the matter. Congress assembled and increased the size of the army, but found it impossible to deal with the issues of state sovereignty that were involved and so took no action.[39]

At the same time events were under way for the production of a new type of government that would be vested with the powers necessary to govern. The Mount Vernon meeting in 1785 had led to the Annapolis Convention in 1786, and from there a call had gone out for a meeting to revise the Articles of Confederation. It seems doubtful that Thomson had a role in these conferences but he was in Congress when that body, faced with the fact that Virginia had already chosen its delegates to the convention, approved a call for the convention to meet in Philadelphia. What met in Philadelphia in May 1787 was, of course, not a body to amend the Articles, but a group of delegates who quickly decided that the only hope was to form a completely new government. This decision was made in secret, the meetings that followed were held in secret, and much that happened there is shrouded in secrecy.[40]

It is known that somewhere between May 2 and May 5 Thomson, secretary to the Congress then supposedly in session in New York, quietly left for Philadelphia on "private business." No record exists to show that he ever appeared at the meetings of the Constitutional Convention. But, by the time Thomson left Philadelphia to return to New York, the convention had decided on a new form of government and was well about its work. It is logical to assume that Thomson spoke to some of his old friends and associates in the convention—ranging from presiding officer Washington to the fourteen convention members who were also delegates to the Congress striving to keep a quorum in New York—and certainly his thoughts on government would have been most valuable.[41]

More interesting yet is the role that Thomson assumed upon his return to Congress. He may have been back in New York as early as June 21, but he was certainly back at his old post as secretary on July 2. He almost immediately began to assemble Congress "for the great purposes of the Union." He managed a quorum by enticing enough delegates away from the constitutional convention to obtain representation from eight states, and on Friday, July 13, 1787, the Northwest Ordinance was passed. During this period, the president of Congress, Arthur St. Clair, was on a trip to western Pennsylvania and Thomson was the only executive in Congress. So, with the government in shambles, a convention meeting to devise a replacement government, and the presiding officer gone, Secretary Thomson virtually forced Congress into session and held the delegates there long enough to pass one of the most far-reaching pieces of legislation to come out of any Congress, and certainly one of the most significant laws passed under the Confederation.[42]

The Northwest Ordinance (Ordinance of 1787) provided for a staged, democratic process by which territories could become states on an equal basis with those already within the union. It made provision for the regular support of public education, guaranteed civil rights and freedom of religion, and, perhaps more significantly, prohibited slavery within the Northwest Territory. The political and moral implications of slavery had long plagued Thomson, and he greatly favored the inclusion of the prohibition against slavery in the Northwest Ordinance. Shortly after the measure passed he wrote, "I shall be sorry if any of the worthy French inhabitants suffer by the article against slavery in the western Country, but I am so much a friend to that article that let the consequences be what they may I would not wish it altered."[43] Thomson seemed to have had an important part in giving the ordinance its final form. So, far from being merely a good secretary, Thomson, even in the last days of his service to Congress, gave shape to the future in securing the passage of the ordinance that was predecessor to many of the parts of the Bill of Rights and the freedom amendments to the constitution.

The Northwest Ordinance prohibited slavery in the territory, and Thomson had a long involvement with the slavery issue. His papers include notes taken from several state enactments dealing with the problem.[44] Although Thomson, at times owned slaves; in 1785, he actively urged Congress to abolish slavery in the territories that were under its control:

If it is or ought to be the object of government not merely to provide for the necessities of the people, but to promote and secure their happiness, and if the felicity of happiness of a people can only be promoted and secured by the exercise of humanity, virtue, justice and piety, it would be unpardonable in Congress in creating new States, not to guard against the introduction of slavery, which has a direct tendency to the corruption of manners, and every principle of morality or piety.[45]

A further statement by Thomson on the slavery question indicates that he knew well the problems that the national government was to face both in the immediate and distant future. Thomas Jefferson had been critical of slavery in his *Notes on the State of Virginia* and feared that the Southern states might be irritated by his comments. On learning of these fears Thomson replied:

> It grieves me to the soul that there should be such just grounds for your apprehensions respecting the irritation that will be produced in the southern states by what you have said of slavery. However I would not have you discouraged. This is a cancer that we must get rid of. If it cannot be done by religion, reason and philosophy, confident I am that it will one day be by blood. I confess I am more afraid of this than of the Algerine piracies or the jealousy entertained of us by European powers of which we hear so much of late. However I have the satisfaction to find that Philosophy is gaining ground on selfishness in this respect. If this can be rooted out, and our land filled with freedom, union preserved and the spirit of liberty maintained and cherished I think in 25 or 30 years we shall have nothing to fear from the rest of the world.[46]

Thomson misplaced his faith in the advance of "philosophy," and he unfortunately proved correct in his prediction that if slavery were not wiped out by "religion, reason and philosophy" it would be done by blood. Thomson's ideas were advanced for his day and illustrate a movement in the minds of man that failed to gain ascendancy in America although upheld by men such as Thomson and Jefferson.

The Ordinance of 1787 became one of the most successful actions of the Confederation government. Its passage provided for the future growth of the nation and, as its provisions were re-enacted by the new federal Congress in 1789, it provided for the growth and expansion of the country by furnishing a method for the admission of new states. Unfortunately the proslavery elements in the country were strong enough to prevent an antislavery section in the new Constitution.

September 1787 was a busy month for Thomson. The new Constitution was published by the convention and submitted to Congress for action. First it was necessary to obtain a quorum, and again Thomson's talents at persuasion and coercion were put to work. A quorum assembled and the delegates could not agree on the proper manner to treat the document, which would in essence bring an end to the government under which the United States had existed for so long. Finally, the Congress determined merely to submit the new constitution to the state legislatures in order that it could then be submitted to conventions of delegates. Thomson drew up a resolution to that effect, issued it under the name of "the United States in Congress Assembled," signed it as he had signed so many other resolutions, "Charles Thomson, Secretary," and ordered it published. His work as secretary was nearing an end.[47]

Despite a reluctance to see old and familiar things pass away, and despite a foreboding that the new government might not have a place of service for him, Thomson supported the new constitution. He wrote to James McHenry in Maryland on April 19, 1788, expressing his hope that the constitution would be adopted.

> For unless that take place, I confess to you my fears for the safety, tranquility and happiness of my country are greater than at any period of the late war. The present federal government is at the point of expiring. It cannot I think survive the present year and if it could, experience must have convinced every man of reflection that it is altogether inadequate to the end desired. What remedy then have we prepared for the train of disastrous events which must necessarily ensue from a dissolution of the union, what security for our independence, peace and happiness as a nation?

Along with his letter Thomson sent the first volume of the *Federalist Papers* and said that he would send the second volume as soon as it was published.[48]

As state after state ratified the new Constitution, it proved more and more difficult to get members of the Confederation Congress to attend its sessions. It was nearly impossible to obtain a quorum, and at times days passed with no Congress assembled. October 10, 1788, was the last day of any official business of the Congress. The last Congress never adjourned, and the secretary kept his office open until the new government took the reins of the country in hand. From time to time various members of the Confederation Congress dropped into the office and Thomson duly recorded these members as having attended Congress. This continued until March 2, 1789, only two days before the new Congress was to assemble. On that day, Secretary Thomson dutifully recorded that Mr. Philip Pell, member from New York, "attended" the Confederation Congress. He was the last member to do so.[49]

While waiting for the new Congress to assemble, Thomson, as the only semblance of government that the country possessed at the time, received the electoral votes that the various states cast for president and vice-president. On April 6, 1789, he delivered these votes to the Congress and they were opened and counted before a joint session of the House of Representatives and the Senate. George Washington was unanimously elected president and John Adams was elected vice-president. Thomson was chosen "with the concurrence of both houses of this present Congress ... to wait on his Exy gen Washington with the information of his being elected to the office of President of the United States of America."[50] Thomson traveled to Mt. Vernon, informed Washington of his election, and escorted him to New York in the midst of triumphant rejoicing. The task was a fitting honor for one who had served his nation long and well.

At this time Thomson was negotiating with several members of the new Senate concerning his relationship with the government. After fifteen years as secretary to the Congress Thomson had mixed emotions about his future. He spoke on the one hand of "the determination I had taken to retire to private life,"[51] and yet in the same letter proposed that he be continued in office at the same salary and with the title

"Secretary of the Senate and the United States or Congress." He would be custodian of the seal, acts, and archives of Congress but would not "be under the necessity of attending except on special Occassions and when the great business of the Nation is under deliberation."

> If this proposition be approved by the Senate and acceptible I am ready to serve them to the utmost of my power, at least till the present government be organized and begin to take its due tone. If other wise I must pursue my first determination and retire to the private walk but with an anxious wish and most earnest prayer that the measures of the present government may prove effectual to secure the tranquility and promote the happiness and glory of the United States.

Thomson's sincerity concerning this desire to retire to private life is brought in question by his vociferous comments a few weeks later, when he was not included in the ceremonies accompanying Washington's inauguration. "I cannot conceal that I was struck with surprise at being passed by unnoticed in the arrangement ..." he stated and expressed again his desire to be released from his old duties as keeper of the seal and the records of Congress.[52]

However, the super-secretaryship that Thomson proposed to occupy was rejected by the Senate. Thomson refused the position of clerk to the Senate, and Samuel Otis was elected its secretary. Thomson continued his duties of winding up the business of his office. He advised several officers in the new government concerning such matters as the laws relating to piracies and felonies. He mailed the final volumes of the *Journal* of the Continental Congress to the various states, and on Washington's inquiry, he advised the president that the constitutional authorization for the appointment of ambassadors and other officials was adequate basis for such appointments, and that no enabling act from Congress was needed.[53] But Thomson encountered further difficulties. Although many of his friends protested his not being included in the new government, others were delighted by his exclusion, and he began to run into problems.[54] One of the greatest of these was that the board of the Treasury refused to continue his salary without authorization from the Senate. Thomson protested, settled his accounts with the Treasury, and, on July 23, 1789, submitted a letter of resignation to President Washington.

Washington was an old and respected friend and it was with great pleasure that Thomson received a testimonial letter from him. Washington spoke of the "unsullied reputation" with which Thomson had always conducted himself in the execution of the duties of his office and commented that "Posterity will find your Name so honourably connected with the verification of such a multitude of astonishing facts." Washington concluded, "your services have been as important as your patriotism was distinguished."[55] On June 25, Thomson turned over the records of his office to a deputy clerk, and the duties of the "perpetual secretary" to the Continental Congress came to an end.

With the end of his official association with the government Thomson left New York and returned to "Harriton." The estate was in poor repair, and all of Thomson's old interests in science and agriculture were revived in an attempt to care for it. Timothy Pickering, who visited Thomson in December after he returned to "Harriton," reported:

> He has fitted up a small stone house very neatly, and has a fine farm of six hundred acres, on which he intends to live the residue of his days. It is in bad order, owing to its having been many years in the hands of tenants. It will take him the rest of his life to bring into complete order. . . . He retired from Congress about August last, I think somewhat chagrined. But this will wear off; and as he and his wife have a competent fortune, they will live more happily than ever in their present retirement.[56]

Thomson had contributed more than his share to the Continental Congress and to the Confederation. He served faithfully and worked to keep Congress active and productive until it passed from the national scene. His talents had been invaluable to the new government in its time of need, and by continuing in office as the membership of Congress changed from year to year, Thomson tended to give to the government an air of permanence and stability that it otherwise might not have possessed. He had devoted his energy and wealth in war and in peace to the establishment of a great nation that would be worthy of respect both at home and abroad. He was to go into a somewhat reluctant retirement and devote himself to improving "Harriton" and to translating the Old and New Testaments from the Greek. But the greatest service he rendered to the new nation was his work as "perpetual secretary" to the Continental Congress.

NOTES

1. Thomson served as secretary to many congresses: The First Continental Congress, the Second Continental Congress, and the congresses that followed the Declaration of Independence until the Confederation Congress was formed after the adoption of the Articles of Confederation were ratified March 1, 1781. The practice of referring to all of these congresses as the Continental Congress is used by such historians of the period as E. C. Burnett, *The Continental Congress*; Jennings B. Sanders, *Evolution of the Executive Departments of the Continental Congress, 1774-1789* (Chapel Hill, 1935); and Lynn Montross, *The Reluctant Rebels; the Story of the Continental Congress, 1774-1789* (1950; reprint, ed., New York, 1970).

2. A full account of Thomson's work as secretary will probably never be known. Much of his work was personal—a word here, a suggestion there, an omission here, an insertion there—and by its nature left no record. When the indexing of the Papers of the Continental Congress is completed by the National Archives, these indexes, combined with the papers either in Washington or in their microfilm edition (Microcopy No. 247, Papers of the Continental Congress), will give a more complete view of Thomson's importance. In addition to the volumes listed in note 1, Thomson's duties are most thoroughly discussed in Frederick S. Rolater, "Charles Thomson, Secretary of the Continental Congress, 1774-1789" (M.A. thesis, University of Southern California, 1965) and in shorter form in his chapter "The Secretary of Congress," in "The Continental Congress: A Study in the origin of American Public Administration, 1774-1781" (Ph.D. diss., University of Southern California, 1970), pp. 57-103. Rolater's excellent "Charles Thomson, 'Prime Minister' of the United State," *PMHB* 101 (1977): 322-48 was not available when this work was completed. A good summary of Thomson's role as secretary is Kenneth R. Bowling, "Good-by 'Charlie': The Lee-Adams Interest and the Political Demise of Charles Thomson, Secretary of Congress, 1774-1789," *PMHB* 100 (1976): 316-17.

3. Herbert Friedenwald, "The Journals and Papers of the Continental Congress," American Historical Association *Annual Report* 1 (1896): 89-93; Rolater, "Charles Thomson, Secretary," 36-37.

4. Thomas Scharf and Thomson Wescott, *History of Philadelphia; 1689-1884* (Philadelphia, 1884), 1:275. The John Jay Papers, Columbia University, contain ciphers and codes used by the secretary of Congress. Catherine Snell Cary, "The Double Life of the Tory and the Spy; James Rivington," *William and Mary*

Quarterly, 3d ser. 16 (1959): 65. Rolater, "The Continental Congress," pp. 83-93. Rivington, as part of his role as a Tory editor, frequently downgraded the Congress and its secretary. On December 21, 1777, Rivington commented in the *New York Gazette* about the work of "old Nosey Thomson"—a most unkind reference to Thomson's penchant for keeping abreast of all that was going on, as well as a jibe at his most prominent physical feature.

5. Friedenwald, "Journals of the Continental Congress," p. 93.

6. Worthington C. Ford et al., eds., *Journals of the Continental Congress* (Washington, D.C., 1904-1937), 1: 102; 4: 79; 11: 547; and Sanders, *Executive Departments*, pp. 174-75.

7. Rolater, "Charles Thomson, Secretary," p. 171; Thomson to Jonathan Trumbull, March 23, 1780, Edmund C. Burnett, ed., *Letters of the Members of the Continental Congress* (Washington, D. C., 1921-1936), 5: 94; Papers of the Continental Congress, Item 70, Roll 84, folio 539. *JCC* 24: 83-92; Fulmer Mood, "The Continental Congress and the Plan for a Library of Congress in 1782-1783," *PMHB* 72 (1948): 12-14.

8. Jefferson to Thomson, December 20, 1781, The *Papers of Thomas Jefferson* ed. Julia P. Boyd et al (Princeton, 1ᶜᶜ0-   ), 6: 142.

9. Franklin to Samuel Huntington, September 13, 1781. *Writings of Benjamin Franklin*, ed. A. H. Smyth (Princeton, 1905) 8, 303.

10. John Adams to William Lee, July 20, 1780, *Works of John Adams*, ed. Charles Francis Adams, (Boston, 1850-1856), 7: 231.

11. Jay to Thomson, April 23, 1781, Thomson Papers, Library of Congress.

12. Deborah Logan Diary, Historical Society of Pennsylvania.

13. Rolater, "Continental Congress", 84-89; Montross, *Reluctant Rebels*, pp. 275, 315; *JCC*, 14: 1008; Burnett, *Letters*, 5: 392-408; Thomson Papers, Library of Congress. The Thomson Papers contain materials not printed in Burnett's *Letters*, 5: 392-408; Thomson Papers, Library of Congress. The Thomson Papers contain materials not printed in Burnett's *Letters*. The Library of Congress' Bicentennial staff has begun publication of a more comprehensive edition of the *Letters* that should throw light on this and other matters relating to the actions that took place in Congress, 1774-1789. Paul H. Smith et al. eds., *Letters of Delegates to Congress, 1774-1789* (Washington, D.C., 1976-   ).

14. Thomson to Jay, October 12, 1780, Burnett, *Letters*, 5: 420; Montross, *Reluctant Rebels*, 302-5.

15. Anna Rawle as quoted in William B. Rawle, "Laurel Hill, and some Colonial Dames who once lived there," *PMHB*, 35 (1911): 398.

16. William B. Reed, *Life of Joseph Reed* (Philadelphia, 1847), 2: 260, 429.

17. Papers of the Continental Congress, roll 68, folio 229-37; Scharf and Wescott, *History of Philadelphia*, 1: 409; Max M. Mintx, *Gouverneur Morris and the American Revolution* (Norman, 1970), p. 148; E. James Ferguson, *The Power of the Purse* (Chapel Hill, 1961), pp. 119-21.

18. *JCC*, 22: 55-57; and Sanders *Executive Departments*, p. 179.

19. Elizabeth Commetti, "The Civil Servants of the Revolutionary Period," *PMHB* 75 (1951): 159-69; Sanders, *Executive Departments*, p. 180; extracted from the *JCC* pertinent information regarding Thomson's salary. The Nourse statement (June 2, 1789) is in the Thomson Papers, Library of Congress.

20. "Extracts from the Journal of Mrs. Henry Drinker," *PMHB* 13 (1889): 301-2; *PMHB* 5 (1881): 15-16, 134; *PMHB* 17 (1893): 423; "Diary of Grace G. Galloway," *PMHB* 55 (1931): 37.

21. Department of State, *The Seal of the United States* (Washington, D. C., 1957), pp. 7-10; The committee reports and Thomson's original sketch on which the two inscriptions first appear are in the Papers of the Continental Congress, Item 23, Roll 31; and are published in part in the Jefferson *Papers*, 1: 494-97. Cf. Vergil, *Georgics*, 1: 40, and *Eclogues* 4: 5.

22. *PMHB* 29 (1905): 497-99; Burnett, *Letters*, 6: 348-50; A Proclamation declaring the Cessation of Arms, April 11, 1783, Thomson Papers, Library of Congress; Sanders, *Executive Departments*, pp. 180-81.

23. Thomson to Robert Livingston, June 4, 1783, N.Y.H.S. *Collections* 11 (1878): 170.

24. Livingston to Thomson, June 5, 1783, ibid. 11 (1878): 170-71.

25. Thomson to Jefferson, June 18, 1784, Jefferson *Papers*, 7: 307.

26. Hannah Thomson to John Mifflin, January 15, 1785, "Letters of Hannah Thomson," *PMHB* 14 (1890): 28-29.

27. Hannah Thomson to John Mifflin, May 12, 1785, ibid., 14 (1890): 29.

28. Hannah Thomson to John Mifflin, August 28, 1786, ibid. 14 (1890): 34.

29. Hannah Thomson to John Mifflin, August 17, 1788, ibid. 14 (1890): 40.

30. Thomson to Hannah Thomson, April 3, 1785, Thomson Papers, Library of Congress.

31. Sanders, *Executive Departments*, p. 183.

32. Ibid., p. 184; *JCC* 28: 238, 485-586; 29: 688-89.

33. Thomson to Benjamin Franklin, August 13, 1784, Historical Society of Pennsylvania; and printed in Lewis R. Harley, *Life of Charles Thomson* (Philadelphia, 1900), pp. 106-13.

34. Thomson to Jefferson, May 19, 1784, Jefferson *Papers*, 7: 272-73.

35. Thomson to Jefferson, October 1, 1784, Jefferson *Papers*, 7: 431.

36. Although the Confederation government was weak, there is much dispute among historians concerning the extent of its weakness. John Fiske, *The Critical Period of American History* (New York, 1888), presents the view that the era was one of near chaos from which the country was only rescued by the Constitution. Merrill Jensen, *The New Nation: A History of the United States During the Confederation, 1781-1789* (New York, 1950), stresses the more positive aspects of the Confederation period and believes that with a few major changes the Confederation could have been made into a workable system of government.

37. Rolater, "Charles Thomson, Secretary," pp. 162-64, 208. Papers of the Continental Congress, Charles Thomson Letter Book A, Item 18, Roll 25, folios 128-32; Charles Thomson Letter Book B, Item 18, Roll 25, folios 104-5; Reports of the Secretary, Item 196, Roll 180, folios 16-21. See also Thomson's History of the Confederation, Item 9, Roll 22.

38. Thomson to Jefferson, April 6, 1786, Jefferson *Papers*, 9: 380.

39. Burnett, *The Continental Congress*, pp. 671-73; Thomson Letter Book A, Papers of the Continental Congress, Item 18, Roll 25, folios 107-8.

40. Montross, *Reluctant Rebels*, pp. 393-99.

41. Rolater, "Charles Thomson, Secretary," pp. 200-2; *JCC*, 32: 244-97; Burnett, *Letters*, 8: 595-99; Papers of the Continental Congress, Charles Thomson Letter Book B, Item 18, Roll 25, folio 120.

42. *Letters*, 7: 602, 614, 618; *JCC* 32: 334-43.

43. Thomson to George Morgan, July 28, 1787, George Morgan Papers, Library of Congress.

44. "Act, March 1, 1780," "Act, 29 March 1788," Thomson Papers, Library of Congress.

45. Statement by Thomson quoted in Frederick D. Stone, "The Ordinance of 1787," *PMHB* 13 (1889): 335.

46. Thomson to Jefferson, November 2, 1785, Jefferson *Papers*, 9: 9.

47. Broadside, Evans no. 20790, September 28, 1787.

48. Rolater, "Charles Thomson, Secretary," p. 207; Thomson to James McHenry, Bernard C. Steiner, *The Life and Correspondence of James McHenry* (Cleveland, 1907), pp. 108-10.

49. Burnett, *The Continental Congress*, p. 726.

50. Thomson Statement, Burnett, *Letters*, 8: 833.

51. Thomson to Robert Morris, April 7, 1789, Burnett, *Letters*, 8: 829.

52. Burnett, *Letters*, VIII, 833-34.

53. Burnett, *Letters*, VIII, 827-38. Thomson to George Washington, May 19, 1789, Papers of the Continental Congress, Item 49, Roll 63, folios 191-207.

54. Bowling, "Good-by 'Charlie'," presents evidence that a coalition of Thomson's old political enemies consisting of Arthur Lee, John Adams, Samuel Otis, and others prevented Thomson from continuing in the service of the new government. Bowling concludes: "As the living symbol of the old government which the Federalists disdained and wished forgotten, Thomson was too indelibly marked by its internal politics. Too much so for the politically conscious Washington to take a risk" (p. 334). Similar conclusions, although not so sharply detailing the strength of Thomson's enemies, are in Bill B. Lightfoot's paper "A Time to Cast Away: The End of the Public Career of Charles Thomson" Missouri State Conference on History (1968). See also William Maclay, *The Journal of William Maclay* (New York, 1927), pp. 6-8.

55. George Washington to Thomson, July 24, 1789, *The Writings of George Washington*, ed. John C. Fitzpatrick (Washington, D. C., 1931-1944), 30: 359.

56. O. Pickering and C. Upham, *Life of Timothy Pickering* (Boston, 1873), 2: 436-37. "Harriton" is discussed more fully in chapter nine.

8

Contributions to a National Culture

The American Revolution was a multifaceted movement including the War for Independence, the political revolution within the colonies becoming states, the social changes occurring in many areas of national life, and the beginning of a national culture for the United States. Developments in the national culture included advances in science, agriculture, and many other practical fields. Advances were also made in historical, linguistic, literary, and other of the more intellectually oriented areas. Such men as Noah Webster, the Hartford Wits, Royal Tyler, and others are well known for their cultural contributions but many of the revolutionary leaders contributed to the new nation in fields other than the political and military. Charles Thomson's work also extended beyond his activities as a Philadelphia revolutionary and Congressional secretary.

His contributions to the cultural development of the nation began in the 1760s when he directed the formation of the American Philosophical Society and proposed such suggestions as his "Plan for an American University." During the next two decades Thomson's primary contributions were in the economic and political areas as he became a colonial revolutionary leader and then a figure of significance in the Confederation government. As the political and military revolution progressed Thomson also made contributions to the developing American culture. Much of his work took the form of suggestions about projects that his associates were considering. He encouraged Thomas Jefferson to publish his *Notes on the State of Virginia* and contributed lengthy "commentaries" that Jefferson had printed as an appendix to his book. Two South Carolina delegates to the Continental Congress, David Ramsay and William Henry Drayton, requested Thomson's assistance on their projected histories of the American Revolution, and Thomson wrote lengthy accounts of various aspects of the struggle. His work for Congress included many reports such as his brief "History of the Confederation," a short account of the origin and legislative history of the nation's government. And in 1787, Thomson published *Notes on Farming*, a book encouraging experimentation as a means of improving American agriculture. Through his work in many fields, Thomson made considerable contributions to the emerging American culture.

Significantly, the American Philosophical Society provided the stimulus for Thomson's collaboration with Thomas Jefferson on the *Notes on the State of Virginia*. The Society, which Thomson had helped establish, went through a period of doldrums during the early years of the Revolution, but reorganized in 1780 in an effort at revitalization. Early in 1781, several prominent American leaders were notified that they had been elected "councellors" to the Society. Thomson and Jefferson, among others, were elected in an effort to "shew to posterity that in the midst of a bloody and unparalleled war, where every moment was indeed precious, men of the first imminence in America cherished the arts and sciences and dedicated a part of their time to Philosophy."[1]

In late 1781 and early 1782, Thomson and Jefferson exchanged letters indicating their mutual ignorance as to the specific duties of the "councellors" and lamenting the lack of time they had to spend pursuing activities that the American Philosophical Society encouraged. Jefferson also asked Thomson to examine a manuscript that Jefferson was sending to Francois Marbois, secretary to the French legation at Philadelphia, in answer to twenty queries concerning the state of Virginia. The queries, part of an information-gathering movement by the French government, encompassed the government, geography, religions, education, minerals, Indians, and several other aspects of the life and history of Virginia. Jefferson requested that Thomson, upon receiving the manuscript, go over the answers to the queries and determine if any of the subjects treated might be expanded upon and presented to the American Philosophical Society for publication.[2]

Thomson's reply indicated that the manuscript had not yet arrived, but that the American Philosophical Society included "the whole circle of arts, science and discoveries especially in the natural world . . . therefore I am persuaded your answers to Mr. Marbois queries will be an acceptable present." In late April 1782, Thomson received the manuscript from Marbois, and studied it with great care and made detailed notes on both its wording and content. Thomson then returned the manuscript to Jefferson along with lengthy notes and a suggestion that the work be published.[3]

Thomson's proposal led Jefferson to inquire into the possibility of getting the manuscript published. Finding printing costs and delays excessive in Philadelphia, Jefferson wrote to Thomson on the eve of his departure for France where he would replace Franklin as diplomatic representative for the United States. Jefferson stated, "My matter in the printing is dropped . . . Perhaps I may have a few copies struck off in Paris if there be an English printer there. If I do you shall assuredly have one. I shall take the liberty of adding some of your notes."[4] Some months after Jefferson's departure for France, Thomson commented further concerning the book. "I hope by this time you have found leisure to revise and compleat that work and have committed it to the press or at least struck off some copies for the satisfaction of your friends, among whom I hope to be ranked." Speaking of Jefferson's earlier intimation that he might publish the answers under the title "Notes on the State of Virginia in answers to queries . . .," Thomson suggested that "you . . . owe to your reputation to publish your work under a more dignified title." Thomson suggested that the book was indeed "a most excellent Natural History not merely of Virginia but of No[rth]. America and possibly equal if not superior to that of any Country yet published."[5]

Even before receiving Thomson's letter, Jefferson had made arrangements in Paris to have the book printed for private distribution under the title *Notes on the State of Virginia*. The favorable reception of the private printing led

Jefferson to have John Stockdale, an English publisher, issue the first public edition in 1787. In both the 1785 Paris and and 1787 London editions, Thomson's "commentaries" were included as an appendix.[6] The first commentary listed three trade routes to the West that Jefferson had not included in his list of such passages. In the second commentary, Thomson showed his acquaintance with the new convulsive theory of geology, and used his knowledge of the spot where the Potomac River passes through the Blue Ridge Mountains to illustrate the possibility of sudden convulsive changes being responsible for the present appearance of the surface of the earth. The third note had to do with the Jamestown or Jimson weed, which produced temporary mental derangement when eaten. To this note Jefferson added several comments to further identify the plant.[7]

Thomson's fourth and fifth "commentaries" were the longest and dealt with the American Indian. The fourth is a lengthy refutation of the widely held European belief that the American continents had a debilitating effect on plants, animals, and men. "Mons. Buffon had indeed given an afflicting picture of human nature in his description of the man of America," Thomson wrote, "but sure I am there never was a picture more unlike the original." He then proceeded to deny that Indian "organs of generation are smaller and weaker than those of Europeans;" to insist that they did indeed have beards, and to describe the painful and tedious process by which they divested themselves of whiskers; to deny the prevalence of "frigidity, or want of ardour for the female;" and to insist on the bravery of Indians. The fifth commentary begins with a discussion of several of the Indian tribes that Jefferson had failed to include in his discussion of the American aborigines. Thomson included a discussion of the tribal organization of the American Indians and their method of choosing a chief ("Sachem"), which corresponds with the current interpretations of Indian life. He also included an account of the formation of the Lenopi tribe (his old friends the Delawares).

The last two commentaries also deal with Indians. In the sixth commentary, Thomson adds to Jefferson's statement on the burial customs among the Indians a discussion of the "custom among the Indians to gather up to bones of the dead, and deposit them in a particular place." The seventh and final commentary provided information as to the parent tribe or nation of several subgroups of Indians that Jefferson had failed to identify. Jefferson introduced Appendix No. 1, which was composed of Thomson's seven commentaries, with the statement "The preceding sheets having been submitted to my friend Mr. Charles Thomson, Secretary of Congress, he has furnished me with the following observations, which have too much merit not to be communicated." Thomson certainly added much to the comprehensiveness of Jefferson's volume.[8]

Thomson and Jefferson corresponded regularly during the years 1781-1791. During much of this time Jefferson was in Europe, but the correspondence continued even after Jefferson returned home to take his place as secretary of state to the new government. These two "men of the first imminence in America," like the Society for which they were "councellors," were interested in all aspects of knowledge—especially anything that would serve to advance their native land. Their correspondence is filled with discussions of matters both practical and theoretical.

Thomson, for example, was most appreciative of a pamphlet that Jefferson sent from Paris that helped "allay the evil" of Franz Anton Mesmer's "animal magnetism," a theory that Lafayette had popularized in Philadelphia. Commenting later on the phenomenon of mesmerism and its popularity, Thomson concluded "that Mr. Mesmer and his disciples had discovered no new property in nature," and commented on the "degree the imagination can operate on the human frame."[9]

Thomson wrote to Jefferson of another European import—the practice of ballooning. In 1785, Jefferson wrote lamenting the death of de Rozier, one of the pioneer balloonists, in an attempt to cross from the coast of France to England.[10] Thomson related in the year following that several others had lost their lives in experiments.

[Ballooning, however,] has had a rapid rise and has been pursued with great spirit as a rare show. But unless some skill artist can find out some method of directing its course and preserving the gas, I fear the remembrance of it will only furnish a figure in poetry and Oratory, like Phaeton's attempt to guide the chariot of the Sun.

Thomson then turned to a general comparison of European and American developments.

The people of Europe and America seem to be pursuing different amusements. While the former are diverting themselves with bubbles of air and quarreling with one another for toys and rattles, the latter are employed in the encrease of their species and providing the means of subsistance.[11]

Thomson, like most Americans of his day, was concerned lest the United States be criticized for not making significant contributions in intellectual and scientific fields, and frequently hastened to point out that his countrymen were more concerned with building a stong, efficient nation than with theoretical experimentation.

The new nation was contributing to the expanding knowledge of mankind. During this period many new and unusual plants were discovered and transported from their native habitat in America to the botanical gardens of Europe. In May 1786, Jefferson requested that his friend in New York pay for and see to the successful shipping of some plants and seeds for one of the ladies of his acquaintance in Paris.[12] Thomson replied promptly that he would gladly perform this service, and in the same letter he informed Jefferson of "a circumstance I have heard touching the introducing the native plants of one country into another." The duke of Argyle had engaged the captain of a vessel sailing to America to go into the woods and scrape off about one quarter inch of the earth there and bring it in hogsheads to the duke's garden. There the soil was spread over a prepared bed in the original depth and from this grew a number of plants including some that had not before been described or classified by botanists.[13]

The correspondence between Thomson and Jefferson shows the interest that both men had in the application of steam as a motive power. Jefferson first encountered this means of power while visiting in London in 1786. He wrote to Thomson describing this advancement as "simple, great, and likely to have extensive consequences."[14] The application that Jefferson described ran a gristmill. The mill turned eight pairs of stones and burned one-hundred bushels of coal a day. Thomson questioned whether the mill in London used the steam as an immediate moving agent or raised water that would then become the moving power. Thomson also mentioned American proposals for building a steamboat, but stated that he had heard of none being built or in use.[15] Jefferson then informed Thomson that the steam was indeed the immediate mover of the machinery and worked with such efficiency that a peck and a half of coal would perform as much as a horse could do in one day.[16]

The correspondents discussed other matters of more personal interest and usefulness. One of these concerned advances made in the art of lighting—a serious problem at the time. Jefferson sent Thomson a description of a newly invented "Cylinder lamp," which was said to give light equal to that of six or eight candles. "The improvement is produced by forming the wick into a hollow cylinder so that there is a passage for the air through the hollow."[17] Franklin had tried the same idea a few years before, but he had attempted to use a rush instead of a large cylinder as a wick, and found this too small to allow the air to intensify the flame. The lamps burned olive oil or whale oil and produced excellent light.

At Thomson's request, Jefferson sent him such a lamp from Paris. When the lamp failed to arrive, Jefferson sent a similar one from London. Some two years after the first mention of the invention by Jefferson, one of these lamps finally reached Thomson in New York, and an industrious craftsman had already begun to produce the lamps in the United States.[18] This exchange demonstrates important points concerning life in this era. Communication was slow and uncertain, though inventions and ideas quickly traveled from the Old World to the new, and were as eagerly developed here as in Europe.

The phosphorus match, another development in lighting, also gained quick acceptance in America. Jefferson said of this invention:

They are a beautiful discovery and very useful, especially to heads which like yours and mine cannot at all times be got to sleep. The convenience of lighting a candle without getting out of bed, of sealing letters without calling a servant, or kindling a fire without flint, steel, punk &c. are of value.[19]

Thomson's reply of a few months later noted that these matches were, as Jefferson had heard, already being sold in America.

I think them a pretty invention, but am not much disposed to make use of them in the way you hint. . . if I chance to awake in the night which is but seldom, I find that solemn stillness a good opportunity to resolve some subject which I want to trace through its various relations and probable effects and consequences.[20]

Men of similar minds welcomed the additions to knowledge, though Thomson at this time had few spare moments to devote to science and "those philosophical researches I once was fond of."[20]

Yet in one of Thomson's letters he gave a detailed picture of an occurrence of Northern Lights (aurora borealis). His description of the event showed the care with which even common events in America were reported. The displays he wrote about occurred on several succeeding evenings in the summer of 1786. A short section from his account illustrates the matters with which Thomson was concerned, and the manner in which he recorded them.

As I viewed them on friday evening the 30 June there appeared just over the tops of the houses a white luminous cloud extending in a horizontal position from NE to NW. From this. . . streams of light tapering to points, some of them to the heighth of 50 degrees. The stars were bright and the north pole clearly discernable among the streamers, so that by it I could judge of their height.... The light was so great as to cast a shadow from my body and my hand against a wall.[21]

Thomson's records included accounts of the general state of the weather and atmosphere before and after the lights were seen. Thomson made no attempt to explain the phenomena but contented himself with having meticulously recorded the events as they happened. This was a normal procedure for men who were interested in American science and one for which they were often criticized. Jefferson, however, wished that Americans seeing new places and observing new things "would make very exact descriptions of what they see ... without forming any theories. The moment a person forms a theory, his imagination sees in every object only the tracts which favor that theory. But it is too early to form theories."[22]

Despite a pragmatic inclination Thomson, like most American investigators, could not avoid theorizing—especially when it pertained to religious matters. In a refreshing attempt to blend traditional religious theory with the facts of reason, Thomson wrote Jefferson:

I have sometimes had it in contemplation to hazard some thoughts on the general Deluge and endeavor by an hypothesis somewhat different from any I have seen to prove not only the possibility but the probability, I had almost said the certainty of the waters covering the whole Earth. ...I wish you to consider what would be the probable effects of a sudden change of the position of the earth, say for instance by an alteration of the poles, an inclination of the axis 23 degrees or a change in the Annual Orbit.[23]

Jefferson responded with the suggestion that the Creator had made the earth in a solid form as an "oblate spheroid" (the nearly spherical form with flattened poles that gives the earth stability), and that there could be no shifting of the axis.[24] Here are two of the more enlightened of American minds, one attempting to prove the truth of the Biblical story of a universal flood and the other holding to a single creative act in which the earth was made as a solid in its final form. The men of American science were not free from preconceptions that affected their thinking along many lines.

Thomson's association with Jefferson was but a small part of his activities as contributor to the nation's cultural heritage. A nation needs tales of heroism, identification of national goals, and national causes. Some of this is accomplished naturally but the haphazard creation of a national ethos can result in a misdirected emphasis on particular men and ideals. Thomson, who later in life would refuse to tamper with the mythology that had developed around the Revolution, made at least two efforts to direct the nation's mythmakers.

Sometime in 1778 or 1779, and again in 1786, Thomson wrote lengthy accounts of the Revolution in Pennsylvania. The first account was to William Henry Drayton of Charleston, South Carolina, who had shown Thomson a manuscript of his history of the Revolution. Thomson felt that Drayton's account did injustice to John Dickinson's role in the coming of the revolution in Pennsylvania. In his account of the events, Thomson not only sought to give credit to Dickinson but also revealed some of the careful, behind-the-scenes maneuvering in which he, Dickinson, and John Mifflin were involved. Although written long after the events of the opposition to the Stamp Act and the Townshend Duties, this account offers an inside view of the making of a revolution. Thomson showed how he and his associates carefully worked to "bring Pennsylvania with its whole force undivided" into the struggle against Great Britain. His account revealed that the rebel leaders recognized the dangers that disunion could bring to the revolution. The divisions that did arise over the adoption of the Declaration of Independence and the Pennsylvania Constitution of 1776 were proof that Thomson was accurate in his anlaysis. Thomson told of a public meeting where he urged radical actions, even to the degree of working himself into a faint, so that the moderate measures that they really wanted adopted would be approved. He told of a trip through the frontier counties, "under colour of an excursion of pleasure," to rally support for independence. And through the entire account Thomson spoke of the efforts at maintaining unity within the colony.[25]

The same stress on unity, and the efforts of the revolutionary leaders to maintain it, occurs in Thomson's other more lengthy account of the revolution. Writing to David Ramsay, another South Carolina delegate to the Continental Congress who was engaged in writing a history of the Revolution, Thomson emphasized the process by which a unified opposition to Great Britain was achieved. He showed great respect for history—insisting that Ramsay delete a story that was "too low for history" and change some phrases "which did not please" and "which seemed too common to comport with the dignity of history." He insisted that the success of the revolutionary activities "depended on the wisdom with which they were planned & the Union of the whole people in carrying them into execution." He spoke of "prudent management" in "tempering immoderate zeal, giving time to prepare the public mind and suffering matters to ripen gradually." And above all, he demonstrated the efforts made to preserve a united front among the revolutionaries.[26]

Like most historians, Thomson's emphasis and his interpretation of the events of the Revolution were shaped by the times in which he wrote. In 1778-1779 the Revolution was still in progress and unity and goodwill were necessary if the nation were to be successfully formed. In 1786, the war with Britain had been won, but the nation appeared foundering on disunity and lack of cooperation. In both instances Thomson's insistence on the unity of the revolutionaries and the methods by which this had been achieved was in part a reflection on a continued need that Thomson doubtlessly observed. Nonetheless Thomson's accounts add considerably to our understanding of the Revolution and the period immediately following.

A final example of Thomson's contribution to the culture of the new nation is his book on American Agriculture— *Notes on Farming*, published in New York in 1787.[27] Thomson had long been interested in agriculture. In the early days of the "Young Junto" and the American Society, many of his questions had to do with such matters as the best time to transplant strawberries or whether some new plant might not be suitable for growing in America. When he acquired the "Harriton" estate by his marriage to Hannah Harrison in

1774, he gained property with a rich agricultural heritage. "Harriton" had been the site of some of the most extensive and profitable production of tobacco in the northern latitudes. Although devoted to crops more common to the region, "Harriton", under Thomson's direction, continued to be a place for experimentation. In 1785, before the Confederation government had permanently located in New York, Thomson participated in the formation of the Philadelphia Society for Promoting Agriculture. At the first meeting Thomson presented an extended review of Arthur Young's *Farmer's Tour through the East of England* (4 vols., London, 1771).[28] After he moved to New York, Thomson apparently continued his interest in agriculture. He corresponded with his tenants at "Harriton," with young Jonathan Mifflin of Philadelphia, and with George Morgan of Princeton on agricultural topics. He also expanded his review of Young's volumes with several suggestions for improving American agriculture, and, in 1787, he published *Notes on Farming*.[29]

Shortly after the book was published, Thomson wrote George Morgan who had provided several pages for the book in the form of information contained in his letters. Thomson sent Morgan fourteen copies of *Notes on Farming* with the following comment:

> I wish they may do good; and would be much oblidged if some of those into whose hands you may put them would, after trying the experiments hinted at, favor me or the public with an account of the success. Farming is a branch of natural philosophy and it is only by experiments that we can hope for success in improving it. A few successful experiments clearly pointed out are better than a whole volume of theory.[30]

Thomson's book is only thirty-eight pages long and obviously was not a complete survey of agriculture in America. Despite the claim on page 1 that the notes "are chiefly collected from Mr. Young's Farmer's Tour through England; published in 1771," the book contained much that was not in Young's volumes and devoted much space to peculiarly American problems. After discussing the proper ways of collecting and applying manure to the soil, crop rotation, and the advantages of root crops, Thomson shifted to such topics as the use of Indian corn as a substitute for turnips and the use of pumpkins as food for cattle and hogs. *Notes on Farming* illustrates the transfer of eighteenth-century English enlightened agricultural practices to the United States and also demonstrates the development of an experimental American agriculture.

Like his *Notes on Farming*, Thomson's contributions to American culture are suggestive rather than comprehensive. Thomson experimented in many areas and contributed much in some and little in others. But he made significant contributions in science, anthropology, geography, history, politics, and experimental agriculture. And while much of this was in process, Thomson was also at work on his translation of the Bible from the Greek, which was to become his greatest cultural contribution of all.

NOTES

1. Timothy Metlack, Secretary APS, to Thomas Jefferson, February 7, 1781, Thomas Jefferson *The Papers of Thomas Jefferson*, ed. Julian P. Boyd et al. (Princeton, 1950-   ). 4: 544.

2. Jefferson to Thomson, December 20, 1781, Jefferson *Papers*; Thomson to Jefferson, March 9, 1782, Jefferson *Papers* 6, 163.

3. Thomas Jefferson, *Notes on the State of Virginia*, edited with notes by William Peden (Chapel Hill, 1955), p. 296.

4. Jefferson to Thomson, May 21, 1784, Jefferson *Papers*, 7: 282. Thomson's manuscript notes from which Jefferson prepared the Appendix are in the Coolidge Jefferson Collection in the Massachusetts Historical Society.

5. Thomson to Jefferson, March 6, 1785, Jefferson *Papers*, 8: 16.

6. Jefferson, *Notes on Virginia*, Peden ed., p. 296.

7. Appendix No. 1, Charles Thomson's Commentaries, Jefferson, *Notes on Virginia*, pp. 197-209. All seven "Commentaries" along with references to the appropriate pages in the text of the *Notes* are here.

8. Thomson also assisted Jefferson in the preliminary work that led to the adoption of a decimal system of coinage for the United States, Jefferson *Papers*, 7: 150-60, 175-88; Jefferson to Thomson, July 14, 1785, Jefferson *Papers*, 8: 295.

9. Thomson to Jefferson, March 6, 1785, Jefferson *Papers*, 8: 15-16.

10. Jefferson to Thomson, June 21, 1785, Jefferson *Papers*, 8: 245.

11. Thomson to Jefferson, April 6, 1786, Jefferson *Papers*, 9: 379-80.

12. Jefferson to Thomson, May 10, 1786, Jefferson *Papers*, 9: 505-6.

13. Thomson to Jefferson, July 30, 1786, Jefferson *Papers*, 10: 175-76.

14. Jefferson to Thomson, April 22, 1786, Jefferson *Papers*, 9: 400-401.

15. Thomson to Jefferson, July 8, 1786, Jefferson *Papers*, 10: 102.

16. Jefferson to Thomson, December 17, 1786, Jefferson *Papers*, 10: 608-10.

17. Jefferson to Thomson, November 11, 1784, Jefferson *Papers*, 7: 518-19.

18. Discussed in several letters that passed between Thomson and Jefferson, Jefferson *Papers*, 8: 599; 9: 379, 400-401; 10: 102.

19. Jefferson to Thomson, November 11, 1784, Jefferson *Papers*, 7: 518-19.

20. Thomson to Jefferson, March 6, 1785, Jefferson *Papers*, 8: 15-16.

21. Thomson to Jefferson, July 8, 1786, Jefferson *Papers*, 10: 103.

22. Jefferson to Thomson, September 20, 1787, Jefferson *Papers*, 12: 159.

23. Thomson to Jefferson, July 8, 1786, Jefferson *Papers*, 10: 104.

24. Jefferson to Thomson, December 17, 1786, Jefferson *Papers*, 10: 608-9.

25. Thomson Papers, Library of Congress. Printed with some errors in transcription in *PMHB* 2 (1878): 411-23, and in New York Historical Society *Collections* 11 (1878): 269-86. For a discussion of the issues involved see David L. Jacobson, *John Dickinson and the Revolution in Pennsylvania, 1764-1776* (Berkeley and Los Angeles, 1965), pp. 71-82.

26. Thomson Papers, Library of Congress. Like the Drayton letter printed with some errors in transcription in New York Historical Society *Collections* 11 (1878). For an accurate, annotated rendering see Paul H. Smith, "Charles Thomson on Unity in the American Revolution," *Quarterly Journal of the Library of Congress* 28 (1971): 158-72.

27. Evans No. 20599 indicates copies in the Boston Atheneum and the American Antiquarian Society. The American Philosophical Society copy has "said to be published by the order of Chs. Thomson Esq." inscribed on the title page. Manuscript pages in Thomson's handwriting in the Thomson Papers, Historical Society of Pennsylvania, and Thomson's letter to George Morgan, July 28, 1787, George Morgan Papers, Library of Congress, confirm Thomson's authorship.

28. Minutes of the Philadelphia Society for Promoting Agriculture, February 11, 1785, not paged, Veterinary School Library, University of Pennsylvania. Brooke Hindle, *The Pursuit of Science in Revolutionary America 1735-1789* (Chapel Hill, 1956), pp. 359-60. The work of the Philadelphia Agricultural Society is discussed at length by Olive Moore Ganbril, "John Beale Bordley and the Early Years of the Philadelphia Agricultural Society," *PMHB* 65 (1942): 410-39.

29. Hannah Thomson to John Mifflin, May 12, 1785, *PMHB* 14 (1890), Thomson to George Morgan, July 28, 1787, George Morgan Papers, Library of Congress.

30. Thomson to George Morgan, ibid.

9

Greek and Biblical Scholar

O *ne* of the most definite signs of the emerging nationalism of the United States was the development of a native literary tradition. From the beginning of settlement there were historians and chroniclers in each colony. Writers of fiction appeared in the eighteenth century but recognition beyond the United States would not come until later. Poets were not numerous and wrote in a European style and for a limited audience. Nonetheless literature was developing in the New World.

The Puritan background of many of the early settlements made it natural that some of the interest in literature would involve the sacred scriptures of Christianity. Bibles accompanied Sir Walter Raleigh's settlers on Roanoke island, and came to Jamestown in 1607 and, of course, to Plymouth in 1620. As the colonies matured and attempted to establish their freedom from the mother country, interest developed in producing an American printing of the Bible. As a result of this feeling, Robert Aitken, a Philadelphia publisher, printed an edition of the New Testament in 1777, and his "First complete English bible printed in America" was authorized by Congress and printed in 1782.

Not satisfied with imitative efforts or with publishing even so great a work as the Bible, many Americans consciously worked to produce cultural advancements that would give credit and respect to the new nation. Native artists, literary and otherwise, produced mediocre works and received acclaim far beyond their merits. Native historians turned out tedious accounts of the colonial and revolutionary period, and were regarded as advancing nationalistic sentiments even though they did not attempt to glorify the movement that had made the new nation. Many who were involved in the movement that was developing a native culture turned to an emphasis on the classics. Knowledge of the Greeks and Romans was after all the standard of an educated man, but for the citizens of the new nation, it was not enough. A classical education bespoke too much of the Old World and things European. Some way was needed to merge the cultural aspects of the classical world with the native aspects of New World culture.

Charles Thomson was a man well suited to do this. His interests in science, agriculture, manufacturing, politics, and other fields prove that he was a versatile as well as a learned man. His eagerness for knowledge is illustrated by his actions throughout his life from the time of his confession of a desire for an education to the unknown lady in New Castle, Delaware, until his death in 1824. For almost a century his inquiring mind grappled with problems that varied from the maintenance of the friendship of the Delaware Indians to the proper execution of his duties as the secretary of Congress. Thomson's early education established a good foundation of knowledge upon which he could draw as his attention shifted from one area of thought and action to another. Though his training at the Thunder Hill School of Dr. Alison emphasized the classics, it also extended into the realms of literature, mathematics, and science. This, combined with his continued self-education after he moved to Philadelphia, gave Thomson a more than adequate base upon which to build as his interests grew in new fields of thought.

After his retirement from public life in 1789, Thomson devoted himself almost exclusively to caring for his estate near Philadelphia, and to the translation of the Bible from the Greek. To obtain the most accurate available version of the Old Testament, Thomson made his translation from a copy of the Septuagint published at Cambridge, England, in 1665 by John Field. This publication was descended from the Sixtine edition based on Codex Vaticanus, the earliest known manuscript, which as the name implies, is in the Vatican Library in Rome.

"Septuagint" refers to "seventy" and the work is frequently listed as "LXX," alluding to the legend that the Septuagint was translated by approximately seventy Greek scholars in Alexandria in the third century B.C. The translation of the Old Testament from the Hebrew into the Greek was made for the Greek-speaking Jewish community in Alexandria. It is of great value to biblical scholars because it was the text in use at the time of Christ and, when the New Testament writers wished to quote from the Old Testament, they usually cited the Septuagint version.

Prior to discoveries in the twentieth century few manuscripts of the Hebrew Bible were known to have survived from a time earlier than the ninth century A.D. Fragments of the Septuagint dated from as early as the second century B.C., with most of the manuscripts being from the fourth century A.D. From these manuscripts scholars determined with considerable accuracy the Hebrew text from which the Septuagint came. In this manner the Septuagint served as a valuable tool for the recovery of the Hebrew Bible as it existed prior to the time of Christ.[1]

It was as a part of the search for the true texts of the scripture that Thomson provided the world with its first English translation of the Septuagint. He gave to the general reader, as well as to the biblical scholar, a version of the Bible that was older and more historically accurate than the sources then in use. English scholars had already translated parts of the Septuagint, and Thomson made use of these translations as he worked. Thomson also consulted leading Greek authorities such as Sebastianus Castellio as he rendered the Septuagint into English.

In addition to an authoritative text, biblical scholars constantly seek for translations that can be readily understood by those who read them. Even the King James version of the Bible, which was prepared from Hebrew as well as from Greek sources, used a language different from that used by most Americans. At times this led to difficulty in understanding some passages and it was a factor in Thomson's desire to publish a translation of the Bible. His translation of the New Testament was apparently made from one of the readily available Greek versions and was valuable, not only for its scholarly contribution but also for its clear, felicitous language.[2]

It seemed natural that after his resignation as secretary of Congress, Thomson should return to his studies in the classical languages. His early training was classically oriented, and his first teaching duties had been those of instructing Latin and Greek to the students at the Academy of Philadelphia and then at the Friends' Public School. Concern for matters of a biblical nature also seemed natural for a man who, even though a rationalist, was active in the Presbyterian Church for most of his life.

Though it is not surprising that Thomson was interested in the translation and eventual publication of the Septuagint, there is some question as to why he chose this particular fashion of utilizing his time for a period of almost two decades. Two Philadelphians, somewhat contemporary with Thomson and acquaintances of his in his latter years, indicated that his interest was first whetted by the purchase of a half of the Septuagint at an auction in 1760, and the discovery of the other half of the book for sale at the same spot some two years later.[3] Later research has attributed Thomson's work in this area to another motive. On a page preserved with some of the remaining manuscript copies of his translation, Thomson left an unfinished statement that, as he attempted to discover whether Jesus Christ truly fulfilled the predictions of the Old Testament prophets, his research led him into a study of the Septuagint as the source to which the New Testament writers most often referred.[4] It is likely that there is truth in both views—Thomson bought the two sections of the Septuagint at auction for mere trifles and then decided to translate his purchase because of his inquiries into the New Testament and his concern with religious matters.

Other factors also influenced him in this project. After a visit with Thomson in May 1810, Benjamin Rush recorded that "He was induced to translate the Septuagint in order to relieve his mind from the distress he felt after the war was over, from the feebleness of the old Confederation and its incompetency to preserve the Union or the states."[5] Though Rush erred regarding the period during which Thomson worked on the translation, it is likely that Thomson engaged in his work at least in part to "relieve his mind from ... distress." Thomson's resignation as secretary to Congress came only after it was evident that he was not to be appointed to a similar office in the government established under the Constitution in 1789. Friends who visited him soon after his return to "Harriton" found Thomson disturbed over his rejection by the new government and inclined to be rather bitter over his ouster from public affairs. In this state of mind, Thomson turned to his work of translation and, when the manuscript was about to be published in 1808, he confided to his friend Jefferson:

> I am thankful to that kind over-ruling Providence which directed my attention to this work. It had kept my mind employed so that I can say that I have not during the last 19 years found one hour hang heavy on me.[6]

Once the translation neared completion Thomson decided to have it printed. Publication was a natural goal as Americans took pride in their new nation and labored to advance its culture in any way possible. American scholars worked to provide books of all kinds that were written and printed in America. Before 1800, American printers issued some twenty different editions of the Bible. Efforts to popularize knowledge on all levels of society accompanied these attempts to develop a strictly American culture. The upper levels of society directed thought during this early national era, but the spirit of the times was such that the aristocrats worked to spread culture and knowledge among the masses. Thomson's translation and publication of the Bible may have been related to this movement.

Thomson's religious beliefs influenced his desire to study and translate the Bible. His inquiring mind made it necessary that he find the best sources available to provide the answers to his religious questions. He was not as radical in theology as he was in politics, though his close association with the Quakers led some to believe that he was one of that sect, and others associated him with the "Godless" Franklin and Jefferson. Thomson's late-nineteenth-century biographer merely states that Thomson "accepted the truths of Christianity in his early youth" and confines further comments to this statement: "Some have called him a Presbyterian; others insist that he inclined towards the Friends, while a few claim that in later years he worshipped with the Baptists."[7]

Thomson's position in education, politics, and other areas indicate that he was a rationalist and a Deist. A statement that he wrote to Reverend Samuel Miller in 1801 seems to support this idea. Thomson stated, "attached to no system nor peculiar tenets of any sect or party, I have sought for truth with the utmost ingenuity. . . ."[8] This is in the tradition of the Enlightenment. To seek "for truth with the utmost ingenuity" and to follow the "truth" only where the processes of reason would lead was the ideal. Thomson's statement, along with his early associations and his known devotion to reason and the advancement of science all indicate that he had become a religiously radical product of the Enlightenment.

But the facts indicate otherwise. Thomson was trained and educated under Dr. Francis Alison who was a strict Presbyterian and one of the religious leaders of his day. Although according to stories told in later days Thomson failed to follow the strict Presbyterianism of the Alison home, he had great respect for his schoolmaster friend and for his religious beliefs. Thomson objected to such matters as learning his catechism and studying the biblical interpretations of others, but he did this in order that he might study on his own and develop his own beliefs from his study of the scriptures. As time passed, Thomson became more conventional in his religious views and by 1761 he held one-half of a pew in the First Presbyterian Church of Philadelphia. He became secretary and treasurer to the congregation in 1762 and remained in that office until 1770 when he moved away from the city. At some time during his association with the church, Thomson was an elder, which suggests a rather strict adherence by him to Presbyterianism. In later years Thomson allowed his interest in the Presbyterian Church to slacken and he attended instead the Lower Merion Baptist Church located on a plot of land from the "Harriton Estate," but this was probably more a matter of convenience rather than conviction.[9]

Thomson was an enlightened and a religious man. A man of thought and reason, he was indeed "Attached to no system, no peculiar tenets of any sect or party . . ." and he could also say "I have sought for truth with the utmost ingenuity. . . ." Many Americans of the Enlightenment related their application of reason in all fields, including religion, to a religious belief that was orthodox enough to enable them to continue as members and active leaders in the established American churches.[10]

As a churchman as well as a scholar, Thomson, "Late Secretary to the Congress of the United States," published his translation of "The Old and New Covenant, Commonly called the Old and the New Testament." It comprised four volumes, three for the Old Testament and one for the New, and was printed in Philadelphia in 1808 by Jane Aitken.[11] One of the few women printers in America, and certainly the first woman to print any part of the Scriptures, Miss Aitken did an excellent job. The volumes available today have very clear and sharply printed pages that are quite free of typographical errors and defacements. Jane Aitken took over the business of her father, Robert Aitken, after his death in 1802, and achieved some note as a printer. Since her father printed the first complete English Bible produced in America in 1782, it was fitting that the first English translation of the entire Bible from the Greek should be printed in America by his daughter.[12]

The first "proposals" for the Thomson Bible appeared in the Philadelphia *Aurora* on November 30, 1807. The work as there described would consist of four volumes quarto (approximately twenty-five to thirty centimeters high), and would be sold on a subscription basis. The change in the size of the volumes came as a result of a suggestion by Thomas Jefferson, who was then president of the United States. From the new Capitol in Washington, Jefferson wrote to Thomson:

> I see by the newspapers your translation of the Septuagist [sic] is now to be printed, and I write this to pray to be admitted as a subscriber. I wish it may not be too late for you to reconsider the size in which it is to be published.

Folios and quartos are now laid aside because of their inconvenience. ... Johnson, of Philadelphia, set the example of printing a handsome edition of the Bible in 4v., 8vo. I wish yours were in the same form.[13]

Thomson respected the advice of Jefferson and replied thanking him for his suggestion:

On receiving it I went to Philadelphia and altered the size proposed for my translation from a quarto to an octavo and I have ordered new proposals to be issued accordingly. It will be printed on a good medium paper with a new type in pica and will I hope be begun in May & finished in the course of the summer.[14]

The final octavo form of the volumes (about twenty centimeters high) made attractive and more easily handled books of a size that was more acceptable to modern tastes.

During the printing of his translation, Thomson availed himself of the services of a friend, Ebenezer Hazard. Hazard had been Postmaster General for the United States under the Confederation and had worked for years compiling documents and manuscripts, portions of which he would ultimately print in two volumes entitled *Historical Collections: Consisting of State Papers and Other Authentic Documents; Intended as Materials for An History of the United States of America* (Philadelphia, 1792-1794). A scholar with a sense of history that was unique for his time, Hazard recognized the value of a work such as Thomson's. In addition, Hazard was an excellent Greek scholar.[15]

Their correspondence reveals that Hazard made many suggestions that Thomson incorporated into the text of his Bible. Hazard, in addition to his duties as critic and advisor, served as overseer of the actual printing procedure. He lived in Philadelphia and could more easily attend to necessary corrections to the proof and to other needed changes than Thomson who would have had to travel into the city to attend to such matters for himself.

A series of letters from Thomson to Hazard extending from May 1808 to March 1809 reveal that Thomson made many numerous slight modifications in the text following suggestions by Hazard.[16] In several instances, however, Thomson rejected his friend's suggestions, stating that he believed that his translation more faithfully rendered the sense of the passage in question. These letters also reveal Thomson's concern that the finsihed product be both accurate and pleasing to the eye. On one occasion, he ordered the already printed book of Proverbs reprinted so as to express the individuality of each saying, even though it meant discarding previously printed material.[17]

The correspondence with Hazard reveals that Thomson still had an extremely agile mind although he was then entering his eightieth year. Thomson especially considered the implications on doctrine that his modifications in the readings would make. He desired that the fruits of his labor be accurate in as many respects as possible. And he asserted his opinion when he believed himself to be correct, even though contradicted by the best scholars of the time. Finally the letters show a man concerned that his translation be presented to the public on its own worth. From the beginning he refused to have even "Esq." appended to his name on the title page. His work is also notable in that it possesses no preface. Concerning this Thomson wrote:

> Prefaces, Introductions and dedications, I know, are common. But what use are they? Examine them; and what are they but sprouts of fruits of vanity and vain attempts to hide it: Or shy arts to obtain the applause which the author thinks himself intitled to? I therefore think they are as well let alone.[18]

After these many years of labor Thomson wanted his translation read for its scholarship and worth and not because he had occupied a high office during the Revolution.

Though Thomson's translation is highly regarded by biblical scholars today, at the time of its publication the average reader little comprehended its value. Not fully understanding the nature and value of the Septuagint or its greater accuracy than the Biblical texts then in use, prospective purchasers hesitated to buy the Thomson volumes. John F. Watson, one of Thomson's young friends from Philadelphia, believed that the story of the accidental purchase of the two sections of the Septuagint and an indication of its "value in Biblical elucidation" should have been included in a preface in order to increase the sales, but Thomson refused to alter his position.[19]

Without a preface and with their unique character unknown to prospective buyers, very few of the Bibles were sold—so few, in fact, that a Philadelphia printer refused to publish Thomson's projected "Synopsis of the Four Evangelists" on the grounds that the Bible translation had proved so unprofitable.[20] Eventually Ebenezer Hazard bought a great number of unsold volumes and stored them in his garret until his death, when they were sold for waste paper.[21] This explains the relative scarcity of Thomson's translation in recent times.

An indication of the respect in which the Thomson translation is held by Biblical scholars is seen in a statement from an editorial Foreword in the 1954 reprinting of the work.

Thomson's work of translation and scholarship was sound and honest as were his official activities, deserving all the more merit in view of the limited state of ancient discoveries in his day, and also of the fact that he worked practically isolated.[22]

In 1891 a historian and biblical scholar, after examining Thomson's manuscript translation of the New Testament, wrote that "a version of such sterling worth ought not to be left languishing on the shelves of old bookstores... but should be taken up by a good publisher and re-edited with care."[23] A more recent biblical historian speaks of Thomson's translation in this manner: "His revisions are justified by modern scholarship. For clearness, force and felicitous language it would be difficult to surpass Thomson's translation, especially of the New Testament."[24]

Just after the turn of the century an English publisher S. F. Pells, discovered a copy of the Thomson translation in a secondhand bookstore. Pells was so impressed with its worth that he reproduced the Old Testament in facsimile in limited editions in 1904 and 1907. In 1929, Pells did the same for the

Thomson translation of the New Testament, but these editions were so small as to make little contribution toward making the translation known.[25]

Then, in 1954, C. A. Muses edited and revised Thomson's translation of the Septuagint, taking into account corrections that Thomson had made on his personal copy of the volumes, and reprinted the Old Testament part of Thomson's work. It was widely published and sold, and now it only remains for some scholar to provide a companion edition of the New Testament in order to make available, in its complete form, *The Holy Bible*, as translated from the Greek by Charles Thomson, late secretary of the Congress of the United States.

In Thomson's notebook dealing with some of the problems and intricacies of translating, he indicated the standards he had set for his work:

> To translate well is: 1, to give a just representation of the purpose of an author; 2, to convey into the translation the author's spirit and manner; 3, to give it the quality of an original by making it appear natural, a natural copy without applying words improperly, or in a meaning not warranted by use, or combining them in a way which renders the sense obscure, and the construction ungrammatical or harsh.[26]

After twenty years spent in translating, during which he made at least four complete manuscript copies, Thomson at last achieved his goal. The final version as printed has what Thomson's associate Ebenezer Hazard calls a "Hebrew Manner." The style is spare in easy-to-read nineteenth-century English, though it lacks the flowing grace of the Authorized or King James Version. The New Testament is perhaps more polished than the Old Testament, but both make interesting reading. Some familiar passages as rendered by Thomson illustrate the language and the soundness of his translation.

Genesis 1:1-2 reads:
In the beginning God made the heaven and the earth. And the earth was invisible and unfurnished and there was darkness over this abyss, and a breath of God was brought on above the water.

The Twenty-third Psalm deserves reproduction in its entirety:

> The Lord is my shepherd. I shall want nothing. In a verdant pasture he hath fixed by abode. He hath fed me by gently flowing water and restored my soul. He hath led me in paths of righteousness for his name's sake. For though I walk amidst the shades of death: I will fear no ills, because thou art with me; thy rod and thy staff have been my comfort. Thou hast spread a table before me; in the presence of them who afflict me. With oil thou hast anointed my head; and thine exhilarating cup is the very best. Thy mercy will surely follow me all the days of my life; and my dwelling shall be in the house of the Lord to the length of days.

And the Hundreth Psalm as well:

> Shout triumphantly for the Lord, all ye of the land. Serve the Lord with gladness. Come before him with the sound joy. Know that the Lord is very God: he made us and not we ourselves: we are his people and the sheep of his pasture. O enter his gates with thanksgiving—his courts with songs of praise: give thanks to Him and praise His name: for the Lord is good; His mercy endureth forever—and His truth to all generations.

The New Testament passages read with even more clarity. The Christmas story as given in Luke 2:8-14 is especially well done:

> Now in that country there were shepherds in the open fields tending their flocks by turns, during the night watches. And lo! an angel of the Lord stood by them; and a glory of the Lord shone around them; at which they were greatly affrighted. Whereupon the angel said to them, Be not afraid; for lo! I bring you glad tidings—matter of great joy, which will be to all the people—That to you there is born this day, in the city of David, a Saviour, who is Christ the Lord. And this will be the sign for you. You will find a babe swathed, lying in the manger. Then suddenly there was with the angel a multitude of heavenly host, praising God and saying, Glory to God in the highest heaven! And on earth, peace! good will among men!

The Model or Lord's Prayer is presented in Luke 11:2-4 in this way:

> When you pray, say, Our Father, who are in heaven; hallowed be thy name; thy reign come; thy will be done on earth, as it is in heaven; give us day by day our daily bread,* and forgive us our sins for we indeed do forgive every one who offendeth us: and bring us not into temptations; but deliver us from the evil one.

The asterisk indicates a second reading given by Thomson for "our daily bread" as the "bread sufficient for our subsistence." In the prayer as given in Matthew 6:10-14 the words "for thine is the kingdom and the power and the glory for the ages, amen." are appended to the end of the prayer with the "The words thus inclosed are not in many ancient manuscripts."

In the thirteenth chapter of First Corinthians, Thomson used "love" instead of the King James' "charity," and in John 1:14, an interesting piece of imagery from the Greek is given by "Now the *Word* became incarnate, and dwelt as in a tent among us." Other passages might be given but these show the language, the force, and the style of Thomson's translation.

In 1815, Thomson printed a *Synopsis of the Four Evangelists* in the words of his translation.[27] Of the one thousand copies printed, Thomson gave most to local church groups and schools, as is evidenced by the many letters of thanks and appreciation among Thomson's correspondence. In the *Synopsis*, Thomson arranged the similar passages of the four Gospels side by side in order that an easy comparison might be made. Jefferson said of the book: "This work bears the stamp of that accuracy which marks everything from you, and will be useful to those who, not taking things on trust, recur for themselves to the fountain of pure morals."[28] It was deserved praise for an old man of eighty-six who with his *Synopsis* contributed to the ease with which his readers might consult and understand the Bible.

The actual public influence of Thomson's translation of the Bible was small. It is of interest primarily to biblical scholars and historians as an example of the work done along these lines in early nineteenth-century America. It ranks highly for its day and deserves great respect. Though not widely known, it was a great contribution to biblical knowledge and as such cannot be passed over lightly. Like much of his other work, Thomson's translation reflects a continuing effort to develop an American language. In the same sense that Noah Webster contributed his dictionary, Thomson contributed his biblical translation to advance his nation's culture.

Thomson wisely chose the edition that he translated. Though he may have first discovered the Greek Septuagint at an auction, before proceeding to his task he consulted contemporary translations and references, and probably other Greek texts as well. He chose the best text available by intent not by accident. His presentation of most passages does not differ greatly with the King James Version, which was most popular at that time, but the differences are meaningful. Often the changes in wording reflect changes in language that had taken place in the United States. The language in use in King James' England was no longer the language of Americans in the nineteenth century. Thomson realized this and he devoted a great amount of time to making sure that his translation used the language of the people.

But the greatest contribution of the work lies in the fact that it represents a striving for an American culture. The United States was a young country and was prone to suffer by comparison with European nations in matters of culture and learning. Writers in many American magazines and newspapers lamented the lack of American scholars, artists, writers, inventors, and even highly successful industrialists. As the political development of the nation began, the movement to develop an American culture also began. In this movement Thomson and his work with the Bible have a prominent place. It was propitious to be able to say that an American scholar had translated the entire Bible from the Greek; it was satisfying to indicate that the American public was ready for such scholarly advancements by publishing such a work. Though the publication proved not to be profitable, at least it was published and made available both to other scholars and to the people of the new nation.

These stirrings, these desires, and the fruit that came from them in the form of Thomson's Bible illustrate that the Enlightenment in America was not wholly confined to the advancement of useful knowledge toward material ends. The Thomson translation of the Bible was an excellent contribution to American culture and a fine example of American scholarship.

NOTES

1. For a good, brief discussion of the origin and value of the Septuagint, see Madeleine S. Miller and J. Lane Miller, eds., *Harper's Bible Dictionary* (New York, 1952), articles on "Septuagint," and "Texts, versions" pp. 662, 743-50.

2. John F. Lyons, "Thomson's Bible," *Journal of the Presbyterian Historical Society* 18 (1938-1939): 212.

3. Watson, *Annals of Philadelphia and Pennsylvania in the Olden Time* (Philadelphia, 1850), 1: 568; and Benjamin Rush, *Autobiography of Benjamin Rush*, ed. George W. Corner (Princeton, 1948), p. 290.

4. The passage is found in the manuscript collections of the Pennsylvania Historical Society and is printed in an article by Albert J. Edmunds, "Charles Thomson's New Testament," *PMHB* 15 (1891): 329.

5. Rush, *Autobiography*, p. 290.

6. Thomson to Jefferson, Febraury 24, 1808, Thomson Papers, Library of Congress.

7. Lewis R. Harley, *Life of Charles Thomson*, (Philadelphia, 1900), p. 202.

8. Thomson to Reverend Samuel Miller, January 6, 1801, cited by Paul Odell Clark, "Letters of Charles Thomson on the translation of the Bible," *Journal of the Presbyterian Historical Society* 33 (1955): 242.

9. Editorial note Ibid., and note by "T. S." in "Notes and Queries," *PMHB* 15 (1891): 499.

10. The best example of such a combination of orthodox Calvinism and enlightened thought is Edmund S. Morgan, *The Gentle Puritan, A Life of Ezra Stiles, 1727-1795* (New Haven, 1962).

11. *The Holy Bible Containing the Old and New Covenant, Commonly Called the Old and New Testament*: translated from the Greek by Charles Thomson, Late Secretary to the Congress of the United States, 4 vols. (Philadelphia, printed by Jane Aitken, 1808).

12. Lyons, "Thomson's Bible," pp. 215-16.

13. Jefferson to Thomson, January 11, 1808, Charles Thomson Papers, Library of Congress.

14. Thomson to Jefferson, February 24, 1808, Ibid.

15. Fred Shelley, "Ebenezer Hazard: America's First Historical Editor," *William and Mary Quarterly* 3d ser. 22 (1955): 44-73. Hazard and Thomson became close associates in the period from 1785 to 1789 when both were in New York serving the government. Both felt that they had been unfairly prevented from continuing in their positions.

16. "Letters of Charles Thomson," *Journal of the Presbyterian Historical Society* 33 (1955): 239-56; 34 (1956): 112-23.

17. Thomson to Hazard, October 31, 1808, ibid. 33 (1955): 254.

18. Thomson to Hazard, May 10, 1808, ibid., p. 247.

19. Watson, *Annals of Philadelphia*, 1: 569.

20. Though praising the translation and the projected *Synopsis*, the printer indicated that the intrinsic merit of the books would not "ensure extensive circulation" for either of them. Thomas Dobson to Thomson, August 10[ca. 1810], Thomson Papers, Pennsylvania Historical Society.

21. So indicates his grandson Willis Hazard in John F. Watson, *Annals of Philadelphia and Pennsylvania in the Olden Time*, 3 vols., Enlarged with many revisions and additions by Willis P. Hazard (Philadelphia, 1900), 3: 443.

22. Charles Thomson, *The Septuagint Bible*, as edited, revised, and enlarged by C. A. Muses (Indian Hills, Colo., 1954), p. x.

23. Edmunds, "Charles Thomson's New Testament," p. 335.

24. P. Marion Simms, *The Bible in America* (New York, 1936), p. 145.

25. Lyons, "Thomson's Bible," p. 212.

26. Quoted in Thomson, *The Septuagint Bible*, ed. C. A. Muses, p. xii. Cf. Thomson to Rev. Samuel Miller, January 6, 1801, Thomson Papers, Library of Congress, which is essentially the same.

27. Charles Thomson, *A Synopsis of the Four Evangelists* (Philadelphia: Published for the author by William McCullock, Printer, 1815).

28. Jefferson to Thomson, January 9 [1816], Thomson Papers, Library of Congress.

10

Master of "Harriton"

At the end of Charles Thomson's service as secretary to Congress, he returned to Pennsylvania and moved to "Harriton." The house that the Thomsons occupied was a substantial one, built of native stone, including two full stories, a cellar, and an attic lighted by dormer windows. The main house was erected in 1704 by a Welshman, Rowland Ellis, who called the house and the seven hundred acre estate which surrounded it, "Bryn-Mawr," after his birthplace in Wales. So it remained until 1719 when Richard Harrison, a Maryland planter, acquired the property and renamed it "Harriton." Harrison's choice of a name followed the lead of his second wife Hannah Norris' family—her father Isaac Norris had call his Merion estate "Norriton." After Richard Harrison's death in 1747 the Harrison family remained at "Harriton" until 1759 when, following the death of the elder son, Thomas, the widow Harrison moved her family to Summerville, another family possession nearer Philadelphia. When Hannah Harrison died in 1775, she was survived by her daughter Hannah who had married Charles Thomson in 1774 and who had assisted her mother in educating her only close relatives—her brother Thomas' three daughters. Since there would be no Thomson children, the "Harriton" estate ultimately reverted to the family of Amelia Sophia Harrison McClenachan—the only member of the Harrison family to produce offspring.[1]

Even prior to moving to "Harriton" in 1789 or 1790, Thomson had begun to prepare the place as his residence. His trip to Philadelphia in 1787, "on private business" while the

184

Constitutional Convention was in session, may in part have been made to permit him to see about work being done at "Harriton." At this time Thomson was having streams cleared, dams rebuilt, and other repairs made to the farmland that had deteriorated in the decades since Richard Harrison had profitably grown tobacco and other crops on the estate. The Revolutionary War had been especially hard on the Lower Merion region, and "Harriton" was no exception. Thomson's tenants seem to have been no better or worse than usual but they had not maintained the farm as he would have liked.[2]

Shortly after his move Thomson sketched a diagram showing just how he wanted the house and grounds to appear.[3] "Harriton" sits upon a knoll and Thomson's sketch shows the stone-walled "Courtyard" that extends in front of the house. The house stands far back from the road (the "great road" on Thomson's sketch—presently known as Old Gulph Road) and Thomson envisioned the area in between as a grassy meadow. Connecting the house to the road, a 140-foot land would cross the "fine purling stream" on "a bridge to be built." Behind the house to the west was to be an orchard and truck garden, and to the east, a large courtyard. Beyond the courtyard was to be a "grove of stately oaks for ornament." A stream of water would flow through the courtyard "to supply a pool" near the house and to "water the meadows below the house." To the east front of the mansion was sketched a building which must have been "Harrison's schoolhouse" actually some distance from "Harriton," in which Quaker services had been held during Richard Harrison's lifetime. Whether "Harriton" ever looked precisely as Thomson sketched it in 1791 is not known. But his plan does show Thomson's pride in his estate, the relative wealth of his position, and the scope of his dreams. His vanity was further exercised in his having several engravings made of "Harriton" and having these placed atop stationary that he used in his correspondence. "Harriton" was an estate to be proud of, and Thomson felt it enhanced his station in life.[4]

In 1792, Thomson heard from his brother Alexander. He responded quickly:

I wished to hear from you as we are both considerably advanced in years & cannot count on many more. I was born on Nov. 1729 & am now near 63 compleat. How much older you are possibly you may know. About this time three years I took leave of public affairs and retired to this farm about 11 miles from Philadelphia, where I should be glad to see you if you can venture to ride so far. I have enjoyed a great share of health since I quit public business and what is still more a great deal of tranquility & peace of mind. My farm I let out on shares & consequently have not much trouble from it. My study & amusement has been a translation of the bible or old testament which I have just compleated and which I may possibly give to the public. It has been an agreeable & useful employment to my mind and gives me a fuller & clearer view of that sacred book. I wish you had informed me whether our other brothers are still alive & in what circumstances.[5]

Thomson's account to his brother agrees with a record left by Benjamin Rush, Philadelphia physician who visited Thomson in 1790 and noted that Thomson "said 'that he had enjoyed more health, peace and happiness within nine months on his farm than he had enjoyed in the last 20 years of his life.' "[6] Despite his reluctance to leave government service, Thomson enjoyed the return to private life and his estate, family, and friends.

The management of the Thomson home was, of course, the responsibility of Hannah Thomson. A household memorandum book that she kept for the years 1792-1793 reveals much about the running of the house and the style of living the Thomsons enjoyed. There are several inventories of bedding showing a variety of blankets and coverlets—some homespun, some cotton, and some calico.

In December 1793, Mrs. Thomson records weaving twenty-two yards of blanketing "which made 4 blankets." She sent tow (short broken flax or hemp fibers for making coarse thread and cloth) out to be spun and woven; she sent thread out to be dyed; she set servants to spinning and weaving; and she recorded these and other events of the household just as her husband had once chronicled the events of a nation. Pork and beef were salted or smoked and either hung or packed away. Apples were stored in barrels and the opening of a barrel was carefully noted. So many apples were put away in the fall that it was not until mid-May that Hannah wrote: "Cut our last apples." In February 1793 she "sewed radishes in a little box in the window" in anticipation of the coming of warm weather. Periodically she recorded: "burnt chimneys"—a pracitce necessary to keep the chimneys free from soot in a land that had few chimney sweeps. On an October 16 she recorded: "Turkeys in the pen"—presumably for fattening, but she failed to note when they were used. "Bottles of porter" were frequently "brought up"— presumably from the wine cellar—and on at least two occasions a bottle "in the closet bursted." Cows calfed frequently enough to indicate a large herd; occasionally a calf died; and chickens hatched—all events normal for a farm, large or small, but all telling something of the life the Thomsons led and the difficulties of life during that era.[7]

Hannah Thomson acquired full title to "Harriton" in 1781 upon the settlement of the estate of Richard Harrison. Since the Thomsons had no children and since under Pennsylvania law at that time a woman could not dispose of property by will, Charles Thomson and his wife in 1798 provided for the disposition of their property through a series of deeds. After reserving life estates in "Harriton" for themselves, they provided a small life estate for their Negro servant Page Cadorus, gave 100 acres to one nephew, and then settled the rest of the estate on Charles McClenachan, their favorite nephew. He was named for his uncle, and probably assisted Thomson in the translation of the Bible. Hannah Thomson died in 1807 but Charles Thomson's life estate permitted him to remain at "Harriton." In 1811, Charles McClenachan died suddenly, leaving his wife and a six-weeks-old child as his only heirs.[8]

By this time Charles Thomson had been joined at "Harriton" by his spinster sister, Mary, and his nephew John, son of his deceased brother Alexander Thomson. Some of Hannah Thomson's relatives contested the legality of the disposition of the estate to the McClenachan's, and claimed that John Thomson was taking advantage of his uncle's trust and was stripping "Harriton" of valuable timber. Although the suit was ultimately settled in Charles Thomson's favor, it sullied the relationship between Thomson and his wife's relatives and paved the way for future trouble over the proper resting place for Thomson's body.[9]

The years after Thomson's departure from public life were not spent exlcusively in retirement, meditation, and quarreling with relatives. Thomson maintained an active interest in politics and in public affairs. In 1792, he ran for Congress on the Republican (Jeffersonian) ticket. Even though he withdrew from the race as election time neared, Thomson polled a large number of votes in Philadelphia. His withdrawal may have come from a realization that he really was not interested in returning to public life, or it may have come from a recognition of the fact that a politician cannot remove himself from his electorate for many years and expect his political following to remain loyal. Shortly afterward, Thomson refused an offer from George Washington of an appointment as an emissary to several western Indian tribes. Indeed he may have decided that his time of public political service was over. Nonetheless he served as a Jeffersonian presidential elector in 1800 and again in 1804. Thomson was considered as an anti-Madison elector in 1816, but he refused to serve in this capacity. His letters of this period show little involvement in political affairs but do reflect an awareness of national problems, a generally Jeffersonian approach to their solution, and an apparent willingness to let the younger generation handle political life.[10]

Thomson's income during this period seems to have been adequate but not overly affluent. Rents from his property and interest on investments formed his chief income and made it necessary for someone to manage his investments. Joseph Norris, a young relative living in Philadelphia, was Thomson's attorney and managed his property quite well. Thomson owned government securities as well as stock in banks and public utilities. Because of his constant interest in internal improvement, it is no surprise to find Thomson ordering Norris to purchase stock in the Philadelphia waterworks, the Schuykill River Bridge, and other similar projects.[11]

Throughout his retirement Thomson steadfastly refused to write a history of the Revolution. Many of his contemporaries urged him to do so, but Thomson remained adamant in his refusal. Benjamin Rush recorded Thomson's comments on one occasion, when someone suggested that Thomson ought to write such a history.

'No' said he, 'I ought not, for I should contradict all the histories of the great events of the Revolution, and shew by my account of men, motives and measures, that we are wholly indebted to the agency of providence for its successful issue. Let the world admire the supposed wisdom and valor of our great men. Perhaps they may adopt the qualities that have been ascribed to them, and thus good may be done. I shall not undeceive future generations.'[12]

Later during his retirement Thomson even destroyed most of his papers. He commented that he did so because, if the truth were known, many careers would be tarnished and the leadership of the nation would be weakened. Just what disgraceful deeds Thomson referred to will never be known, since the records his papers contained are lost forever.[13]

It is possible that Thomson destroyed his papers while he was under the influence of a "paralytic stroke," which he suffered in 1816. For more than a year Thomson lived with a memory "like a riddle" and with little comprehension or intelligence. After some months in such a state, he gradually began to recover his powers and finally regained everything except his hearing which remained poor for the rest of his life.[14]

Thomson's last years were not without honor from the land which he had helped form. Testimonials to his greatness came from Washington, Jefferson, and other national leaders. Until his death Thomson was addressed as the "late secretary to Congress" and spoken of as the "venerable Charles Thomson." In 1780, while the Revolution was still in progress, Princeton awarded Thomson an honorary M.A. degree for his services as a founder of the College of New Jersey and his work for his country. In 1784, the University of Pennsylvania presented him with an LL.D., and Princeton awarded him the same degree in 1824, just months before his death. Thomson was painted by the principal portrait painters of the day, and collections of engravings of revolutionary heroes contained his likeness along with the more familiar "Founding Fathers." Renderings of the signing of the Declaration of Independence placed Thomson in his accustomed prominent position. In September 1824, just a month after his death, Independence Hall was redecorated and a portrait of Thomson was placed alongside portraits of Jefferson, Hancock, and Adams.[15]

Thomson died at "Harriton" on August 16, 1824. Funeral services were held at the Lower Merion Baptist Church near the "Harriton" family burying ground. His will provided that the remainder of his estate, consisting of stocks, bonds, and other property, and Thomson's library and remaining papers, was to go to John Thomson, the nephew who had cared for him for many years.[16]

John Thomson remains somewhat of an enigma. Apparently he took good care of his uncle during his later years. Thomson's friends who stopped by to see him found Thomson in good spirits, well fed, and well clothed, despite the fact that Thomson's mind began to wander well before he approached his ninety-fifth year. But even before Thomson's death there were charges that John was dissipating the "Harriton" estate which ultimately would pass into the hands of the McClenachans. Many Philadelphians believed that John Thomson did not honor his deceased uncle properly, even though he contributed parts of the Thomson library to the newly founded Allegheny College and made other memorial gifts in Charles Thomson's memory.[17]

In 1838, it was proposed that Charles Thomson's body be moved to Laurel Hill, a newly opened public cemetery. The owners of the new cemetery apparently sought to honor the deceased Thomson and obtain publicity by having Thomson's body moved to their location and a monument erected to mark the grave. The Harrison relatives were consulted and refused to grant permission for Thomson's body to be moved because the terms of his will specified that he should be buried beside his wife in the burying ground of her ancestors. Some days later John Thomson authorized the removal of his uncle's remains, and a nighttime expedition removed two bodies from the "Harriton" cemetery. The bodies were reinterred at Laurel Hill, and a monument was erected over what was proclaimed to be the bodies of Charles and Hannah Thomson. The "Harriton" burying ground was inadequatley marked, however, and considerable doubt exists as to whether the graves opened were actually those of Charles and Hannah Harrison Thomson. It may well be that Thomson's body still rests, as he requested in his will, in the Harrison family plot by his wife's side.[18]

NOTES

1. George Vaux, "Settlers in Merion—The Harrison Family and Harriton Plantation," *PMHB* 13 (1889): 47-459. The Harriton Association, Bryn Mawr, Pennsylvania, is presently restoring "Harriton" for use as a house museum.

2. Receipted bills from Philadelphia builders and craftsmen for some of the work being done at "Harriton" are in the bill folder for 1787, Thomson Papers, Historical Society of Pennsylvania.

3. Charles Thomson, "a letter to the governor," July 22, 1791. The sketch is drawn on the back of this letter or the rough draft of the letter may have been written on the back of the sketch. It seems safe to assume that the sketch and letter are of approximately the same date. Thomson Papers, Historical Society of Pennsylvania.

4. Thomson to George Washington, July 23, 1789, and Thomson to John Montgomery, August 22, 1784. Manuscript Division, New York Public Library.

5. Charles Thomson to Alexander Thomson, July 26, 1792. Thomson Papers, Historical Society of Pennsylvania.

6. Benjamin Rush, *Autobiography of Benjamin Rush*, ed. George W. Corner (Princeton, 1948), p. 183.

7. Hannah Thomson, "Household Memorandum Book," Thomson Papers, Historical Society of Pennsylvania. George Vaux, "Settlers in Merion," *PMHB* 13 (1889): 458. Perhaps the most telling entries have to do with Page Cadorus, apparently a favorite servant. He was provided with bedding equal to that of the family, he was sent to school, and his coming and going were noted with such care that he might have been a member of the family. When they disposed of their property, the Thomsons provided Cadorus with a life estate in a small piece of land.

8. George Vaux, "Settlers in Merion," *PMHB* 13 (1889): 458-59.

9. Correspondence and depositions regarding the suit are in the Thomson Papers, Historical Society of Pennsylvania. See also George Vaux, "Settlers in Merion," *PMHB* 13 (1889): 459.

10. Harry M. Tinkcom, *The Republicans and Federalists in Pennsylvania, 1790-1801* (Harrisburg, 1950), pp. 49, 61, 62, 149, 284; and Sanford W. Higginbotham, *The Keystone in the Democratic Arch: Pennsylvania Politics, 1800-1816* (Harrisburg, 1952), p. 317. Marginal notes to these books by D. H. Gilpatrick, author of

Jeffersonian Democracy in North Carolina (New York, 1931). Notes in possession of the author.

11. Several letters between Thomson and Norris are in the Thomson Papers, Historical Society of Pennsylvania. See also Harry Lane Kneedler, "Charles Thomson" M.A. thesis, Temple University, 1940), pp. 75-86.

12. Rush, *Autobiography*, p. 155.

13. Deborah Logan, *Diary*, 1, 253, Historical Society of Pennsylvania. See also Tolles, *George Logan of Philadelphia*, pp. 307-11. Persistent rumors that the Thomson papers are in the Pennsylvania Masonic records seem to have no basis in fact. There is no evidence that Thomson was ever a Mason. Bowling, "Good-by 'Charlie'," pp. 314-15, concludes that Thomson had indeed prepared a lengthy history of the Revolution, which he subsequently destroyed. That such a document existed is not firmly established.

14. Thomson to Jefferson, May 16, 1816, "Thomson Papers," New York Historical Society *Collections* 11 (1878): 266-67.

15. Lewis R. Harley, *Life of Charles Thomson*, (Philadelphia, 1900), p. 154; Watson, *Annals of Philadelphia*, 1, 567-72; Luther P. Eisenhart, ed. *Historic Philadelphia, Transactions* of the American Philosophical Society, vol. 43, pt. 1 (Philadelphia, 1953), p. 33.

16. George Vaux, "Settlers in Merion," *PMHB* 13 (1889): 459. "Will of Charles Thomson," *PMHB* 14 (1890): 322-23.

17. Charles Thomson was a friend of Timothy Alden, founder of Allegheny College. Correspondence between John Thomson and Alden indicates a reluctance on the part of John Thomson to part with anything that might be of real value. Thomson Papers, Historical Society of Pennsylvania.

18. George Vaux, "Were Charles Thomson's Remains Disturbed?" paper presented before the Lower Merion Historical Society, October 29, 1956. Mr. Vaux, grandson of the author of "Settlers in Merion," expressed doubt that the proper graves were located and opened. For another account and for the inscription that was composed for the monument in the Laurel Hill Cemetery, see Watson, *Annals of Philadelphia and Pennsylvania in the Olden Time*, 3 vols. (Philadelphia, 1850), 1: 571-72.

Conclusion

By the time of Charles Thomson's death in 1824, the United States had become a well-established nation. Thomson and a host of other American nation builders had done their job well. Thomson, unlike many of his revolutionary colleagues, had lived to see evidence of the quality of their labors. Many of the nation makers had made more spectacular contributions than Thomson and they have deservedly received homage as the Founding Fathers. Thomson was, however, of the stuff of which nations are made. He served where he could, he made paths where there were none, he improved his own life and that of those about him. He was educator, Greek and Latin scholar, friend to the Indians, businessman, rum merchant and distiller, learned society founder, provincial politician, agitator, propagandist, leader of radicals, secretary and quasi-executive to Congress, agricultural experimenter and author, scientific dilettante, Bible translator, and revered elder statesman. And through it all he sought and obtained little glory for himself. The nature of Thomson's work left little public record and he added to his own anonymity by refusing to write a history of the Revolution and by destroying his own papers.

Thomson's involvement in the process that forged a new nation is written in the records of the Continental Congress, the correspondence of the Founding Fathers, the newspapers, and the public and private records of the era. He served with ability, dignity, and integrity. The story of his remarkable life is adequate justification for a study of Charles Thomson and the making of a nation.

Bibliography

Manuscripts

New York. New York Public Library. Charles Thomson Papers.

Philadelphia. American Philosophical Society. Miscellaneous Collection.

Philadelphia. Historical Society of Pennsylvania. Gratz Collection, Logan Collection, Miscellaneous Collection, and Charles Thomson Papers.

Philadelphia. Library Company of Philadelphia. Manuscripts Collections.

Philadelphia. University of Pennsylvania Veterinary School Library. Minutes of the Philadelphia Society for Promoting Agriculture.

Washington, D. C. Library of Congress. George Morgan Papers. Charles Thomson Papers.

Washington, D. C. National Archives. Papers of the Continental Congress. Microcopy no. 247.

Published Writings

Adams, John. *The Adams Papers*. Edited by L. H. Butterfield. Cambridge, Mass., 1961-.

_____. *The Works of John Adams*. Edited by Charles Francis Adams. 10 vols. Boston, 1850-56.

Adams, Samuel. *The Writings of Samuel Adams*. Edited by H. A. Cushing. 4 vols. New York, 1904-8.

Dickinson, John. *The Writings of John Dickinson, 1764-1774*. Memoirs of the Historical Society of Pennsylvania, vol. 14. Edited by P. L. Ford. Philadelphia, 1895.

Drinker, Mrs. Henry. "Extracts from the Journal of Mrs. Henry Drinker." *Pennsylvania Magazine of History and Biography* 13 (1889):298-308.

Franklin, Benjamin. *The Papers of Benjamin Franklin.* Edited by Leonard W. Labaree et al. New Haven and London, 1959-.

———. *The Writings of Benjamin Franklin.* Edited by A. H. Smyth. 10 vols. Princeton, N.J., 1905.

Galloway, Grace G. "Diary of Grace G. Galloway." *Pennsylvania Magazine of History and Biography* 55 (1931):35-94.

Hiltzheimer, Jacob. *Extracts from the Diary of Jacob Hiltzheimer of Philadelphia.* Philadelphia, 1893.

Jefferson, Thomas. *The Papers of Thomas Jefferson.* Edited by Julian P. Boyd. Princeton, N.J., 1950-.

MacLay, William. *The Journal of William MacLay.* New York, 1927.

Rush, Benjamin. *The Autobiography of Benjamin Rush.* Edited by George W. Corner. Princeton, N.J., 1948.

Thomson, Charles. "Letters of Charles Thomson on the Translation of the Bible." *Journal of the Presbyterian Historical Society* 33 (1955):239-56; 34 (1956):112-23.

———. "Thomson Papers." New York Historical Society *Collections* 11 (1878):3-286.

Thomson, Hannah. "Letters of Hannah Thomson." *Pennsylvania Magazine of History and Biography* 14 (1890):28-40.

Washington, George. *The Writings of George Washington.* Edited by John C. Fitzpatrick. 39 vols. Washington, D. C., 1931-44.

Public Documents

Burnett, Edmund C., ed. *Letters of Members of the Continental Congress.* 8 vols. Washington, D. C., 1921-36.

Force, Peter, ed. *American Archives.* Fourth Series. 6 vols. Washington, D. C., 1837-46.

Ford, Worthington C. et al., eds. *Journals of the Continental Congress, 1774-1789.* 34 vols. Washington, D. C., 1904-47.

New Jersey Archives. First Series. 25 vols. Newark, N.J., 1880-86.

Pennsylvania Archives. Colonial Records. 16 vols. Philadelphia and Harrisburg, 1851-53.

———. First Series. 12 vols. Philadelphia, 1852-56.

———. Third Series. 30 vols. Harrisburg, Pa., 1894-98.

———. Eighth Series. 8 vols. Harrisburg, Pa., 1931-35.

Smith, Paul H. et al., eds. *Letters of Delegates to Congress, 1774-1789.* Washington, D. C. 1976-.

Newspapers

Philadelphia, Pennsylvania. *Pennsylvania Gazette.* 1728-1815.

196   BIBLIOGRAPHY

Philadelphia, Pennsylvania. *Pennsylvania Journal.* 1742-93.

Richmond, Virginia. *Richmond Enquirer.* 1804-77.

Books

Bailyn, Bernard. *Education in the Forming of American Society.* Chapel Hill, N.C., 1960.

Bauman, Richard. *For the Reputation of Truth: Politics, Religion and Conflict Among the Pennsylvania Quakers, 1750-1800.* Baltimore, Md., 1972.

Bell, Whitfield, J., Jr. *John Morgan: Continental Doctor.* Philadelphia, 1965.

Boyd, Julian P. *Anglo-American Union.* Philadelphia, 1941.

Boyer, Charles S. *Early Forges and Furnaces in New Jersey.* 1931. Reprint. Philadelphia, 1963.

Bridenbaugh, Carl. *The Spirit of '76.* New York, 1975.

Bridenbaugh, Carl, and Bridenbaugh, Jessica. *Rebels and Gentlemen: Philadelphia in the Age of Franklin.* New York, 1942.

Burnett, Edmund C. *The Continental Congress.* New York, 1941.

Cheyney, Edward Potts. *History of the University of Pennsylvania.* Philadelphia, 1940.

Commager, Henry Steele. *The Empire of Reason, How Europe Imagined and America Realized the Enlightenment.* Garden City, N.Y., 1977.

Crane, Verner W. *Benjamin Franklin's Letters to the Press, 1758-1775.* Chapel Hill, N.C., 1950.

Curti, Merle. *The Growth of American Thought.* New York, 1943.

Davidson, Philip. *Propaganda and the American Revolution, 1763-1783.* Chapel Hill, N.C., 1941.

Davidson, Robert L. *War Comes to Quaker Pennsylvania, 1682-1756.* New York, 1957.

Department of State. *The Seal of the United States.* Washington, D. C., 1957.

Dumond, Dwight L. *Antislavery.* Ann Arbor, Mich., 1961.

Dunaway, Wayland S. *The Scotch-Irish of Colonial Pennsylvania.* Chapel Hill, N.C., 1944.

[Du Ponceau, Peter S.] *An Historical Account of the Origin and Formation of the American Philosophical Society.* Philadelphia, 1914.

Early Transactions of the American Philosophical Society. American Philosophical Society Memoirs, no. 77. Philadelphia, 1969.

Eisenhart, Luther P., ed. *Historic Philadelphia*. Transactions of the American Philosophical Society, vol. 43, pt. 1. Philadelphia, 1953.

Ernst, Joseph A. *Money and Politics in America, 1755-1775*. Chapel Hill, N.C., 1973.

Fehrenbach, T. R. *Greatness to Spare: The Heroic Sacrifices of the Men Who Signed the Declaration of Independence*. Princeton, N.J., 1968.

Ferguson, E. James. *The Power of the Purse*. Chapel Hill, N.C., 1961.

Filler, Louis. *The Crusade Against Slavery, 1830-1860*. New York, 1960.

Fiske, John. *The Critical Period of American History*. New York, 1888.

Gipson, Lawrence H. *The British Empire Before the American Revolution*. 15 vols. Caldwell and New York, 1936-70.

_____. *The Coming of the Revolution, 1763-1775*. New York, 1954.

Gummere, Richard M. *The American Colonial Mind and the Classical Tradition*. Cambridge, Mass., 1963.

Hanna, William S. *Benjamin Franklin and Pennsylvania Politics*. Stanford, Calif., 1964.

Harley, Lewis R. *Life of Charles Thomson*. Philadelphia, 1900.

Hawke, David. *In the Midst of a Revolution*. Philadelphia, 1961.

Hazelton, John H. *The Declaration of Independence, Its History*. New York, 1906.

Henderson, H. James. *Party Politics in the Continental Congress*. New York, 1974.

Higginbotham, Sanford W. *The Keystone in the Democratic Arch*: *Pennsylvania Politics, 1800-1816*. Harrisburg, Pa., 1952.

Hindle, Brooke. *The Pursuit of Science in Revolutionary America, 1735-1789*. Chapel Hill, N.C., 1956.

Huston, James H. *Pennsylvania Politics, 1746-1770: The Movement for Royal Government and Its Consequences*. Princeton, N.J., 1972.

Jacobson, David L. *John Dickinson and the Revolution in Pennsylvania 1764-1776*. Berkeley and Los Angeles, Calif., 1965.

James, Sidney V. *A People Among Peoples*: *Quaker Benevolence in Eighteenth-Century America*. Cambridge, Mass., 1963.

Jefferson, Thomas. *Notes on the State of Virginia*. Edited with notes by William Peden. Chapel Hill, N.C., 1955.

Jensen, Arthur L. *The Maritime Commerce of Colonial Philadelphia*. Madison, Wis., 1963.

Jensen, Merrill. *The Founding of a Nation*. New York, 1968.

_____. *The New Nation: A History of the United States During the Confederation, 1781-1789*. New York, 1950.

Jones, Joseph H. *The Life of Ashbel Green*. New York, 1849.

Ketchum, Alton. *Uncle Sam: The Man and the Legend*. New York, 1959.

Klein, Philip S., and Hoogenboom, Ari. *A History of Pennsylvania*. New York, 1973.

Knollenberg, Bernard. *Origin of the American Revolution: 1759-1766*. New York, 1960.

Koch, Adrienne. *The American Enlightenment*. New York, 1965.

_____. *The Philosophy of Thomas Jefferson*. Chicago, 1964.

Labaree, Benjamin Woods. *The Boston Tea Party*. London, 1964.

Lincoln, Charles H. *The Revolutionary Movement in Pennsylvania, 1760-1776*. Philadelphia, 1901.

Leyburn, James G. *The Scotch-Irish, A Social History*. Chapel Hill, N.C., 1962.

Maier, Pauline. *From Resistance to Revolution*. New York, 1972.

May, Henry F. *The Enlightenment in America*. New York, 1978.

Miller, John C. *Sam Adams: Pioneer in Propaganda*. Stanford, Calif., 1936.

Miller, Madlein S., and Miller, J. Lane, eds. *Harper's Bible Dictionary*. New York, 1952.

Mintx, Max M. *Gouverneur Morris and the American Revolution*. Norman, Okla., 1970.

Montgomery, Thomas H. *A History of the University of Pennsylvania to A. D. 1770*. Philadelphia, 1900.

Montross, Lynn. *The Reluctant Rebels: The Story of the Continental Congress*. 1950. Reprint. New York, 1970.

Morgan, Edmund S. *The Gentle Puritan, A Life of Ezra Stiles, 1727-1795*. New Haven, Conn., 1962.

Morgan, Edmund S., and Morgan, Helen M. *The Stamp Act Crisis*. Chapel Hill, N.C., 1953.

Mosier, Richard D. *The American Temper*. Berkeley and Los Angeles, Calif., 1952.

Nash, Gary B. *Quakers and Politics: Pennsylvania, 1681-1726*. Princeton, N.J., 1968.

Newcomb, Benjamin H. *Franklin and Galloway: A Political Partnership*. New Haven, Conn., 1972.

Nye, Russel B. *The Cultural Life of the New Nation, 1776-1830.* New York, 1960.

Pickering, O., and Upham, C. *Life of Timothy Pickering.* Boston, 1927.

Reed, William B. *Life of Joseph Reed.* 2 vols. Philadelphia, 1847.

Roche, John F. *Joseph Reed.* New York, 1957.

Rossman, Kenneth R. *Thomas Mifflin and the Politics of the American Revolution.* Chapel Hill, N.C., 1952.

Sanders, Jennings B. *Evolution of the Executive Departments of the Continental Congress, 1774-1789.* Chapel Hill, N.C., 1935.

Savelle, Max. *George Morgan: Colony Builder.* New York, 1932.

Scharf, J. Thomas, and Wescott, Thomas. *History of Philadelphia; 1609-1884.* 3 vols. Philadelphia, 1884.

Schlesinger, A. M. *The Colonial Merchants and the American Revolution.* New York, 1918.

_____. *Prelude to Independence: The Newspaper War on Britain, 1764-1776.* New York, 1957.

Selsam, J. Paul. *The Pennsylvania Constitution of 1776.* Philadelphia, 1936.

Simms, P. Marion. *The Bible in America.* New York, 1936.

Sloan, Douglas. *The Scottish Enlightenment and the American College Ideal.* New York, 1971.

Steiner, Bernard C. *The Life and Correspondence of James McHenry.* Cleveland, 1907.

Stille, Charles J. *Life and Times of John Dickinson.* Philadelphia, 1891.

Street, James. *The Revolutionary War.* New York, 1954.

Thayer, Theodore. *Pennsylvania Politics and the Growth of Democracy, 1740-1776.* Harrisburg, Pa., 1953.

Thomson, Charles. *Causes of the Alienation of the Deleware and Shawnese Indians from the British Interest.* Facsimile edition. Philadelphia, 1867.

_____. *An Enquiry into the Causes of the Alienation of the Delaware and the Shawanese Indians from the British Interest, and into the Measures Taken for Recovering Their Friendship.* London, 1759. Reprint. St. Clair Shores, Mich., 1970.

_____. *The Holy Bible Containing the Old and New Covenant, Commonly Called the Old and New Testament.* 4 vols. Philadelphia, 1808.

_____. *Notes on Farming.* New York, 1787.

_____. *The Septuagint Bible.* Edited, revised, and enlarged by C. A. Muses. Indian Hills, Col., 1954.

_____. *A Synopsis of the Four Evangelists.* Philadelphia, 1815.

Tinkcom, Harry M. *The Republicans and Federalists in Pennsylvania, 1790-1801.* Harrisburg, Pa., 1950.

Tolles, Frederick P. *George Logan of Philadelphia.* New York, 1953.

Van Doren, Carl. *Benjamin Franklin.* New York, 1938.

Wainwright, Nicholas B. *George Croghan, Wilderness Diplomat.* Chapel Hill, N.C., 1959.

Wallace, Anthony F. C. *King of the Delawares: Teedyuscung, 1700-1763.* Philadelphia, 1949.

Wallace, Paul A. W. *Conrad Weiser, 1696-1760.* Philadelphia, 1945.

_____. *Indians in Pennsylvania.* Harrisburg, Pa., 1961.

Watson, John F. *Annals of Philadelphia and Pennsylvania.* 2 vols. Philadelphia, 1850.

_____. *Annals of Philadelphia and Pennsylvania.* 3 vols. Enlarged with many revisions and additions by Willis P. Hazard. Philadelphia, 1900.

Wish, Harvey. *Society and Thought in America.* 2 vols. New York, 1950-52.

Wolf, Harry. *The Transits of Venus: A Study of Eighteenth-Century Science.* Princeton, N.J., 1956.

Wood, Gordon. *The Creation of the American Republic, 1776-1787.* Chapel Hill, N.C., 1969.

Woody, Thomas. *Early Quaker Education in Pennsylvania.* New York, 1920.

Wroth, Lawrence C. *An American Bookshelf, 1755.* Philadelphia, 1934.

Zobel, Hiller B. *The Boston Massacre.* New York, 1970.

Articles

"American Biography." *The American Quarterly Review* 1 (1827): 2-38.

Becker, Carl L. "Samuel Adams." *Dictionary of American Biography.* Edited by Allen Johnson and Dumas Malone. 20 vols. New York, 1928-36, 1:95-101.

Boling, Kenneth R. "Good-by 'Charle': The Lee-Adams Interest and the Political Demise of Charles Thomson, Secretary of Congress, 1774-1789" *Pennsylvania Magazine of History and Biography* 100 (1976):314-35.

Burnett, Edmund C. "Charles Thomson." *Dictionary of American Biography*. Edited by Allen Johnson and Dumas Malone. 20 vols. New York, 1928-36, 18:481-82.

Cary, Catherine Snell. "The Double Life of the Tory and the Spy; James Rivington." *William and Mary Quarterly*, 3d ser. 16 (1959):61-72.

Chappin, Robert J. "The Townshend Acts of 1767." *William and Mary Quarterly*, 3d ser. 29 (1970):90-121.

Commetti, Elizabeth. "The Civil Servants of the Revolutionary Period." *Pennsylvania Magazine of History and Biography* 75 (1951):159-69.

Dercum, Francis X. "The Origin and Activities of the American Philosophical Society." *American Philosophical Society Proceedings* 66 (1927):19-45.

Edmunds, Albert J. "Charles Thomson's New Testament." *Pennsylvania Magazine of History and Biography* 15 (1891):327-35.

Friedenwald, Herbert. "The Journals and Papers of the Continental Congress." *American Historical Association, Annual Report* 1 (1896):85-135.

Gambrill, Olive Moore. "John Beale Bordley and the Early Years of the Philadelphia Agricultural Society." *Pennsylvania Magazine of History and Biography* 65 (1942):419-39.

Griffiths, Ralph. Review of *An Enquiry into the Causes of the Alienation of the Delaware and the Shawanese Indians* by Charles Thomson. *Monthly Review*, June 1759, pp. 545-48.

Hendricks, J. Edwin. "Charles Thomson and the Creation of 'A New Order of the Ages.' " In *America the Middle Period; Essays in Honor of Bernard Mayo*, edited by John Boles. Charlottesville, Va., 1973.

————. "Charles Tomson's Philadelphia Rum." *Pennsylvania Magazine of History and Biography* 89 (1965):151.

————. "The 'Signer' Who Didn't Get to Sign." Furman Studies, June 1978, pp. 3-9.

Hunter, William A. "The Walking Purchase." *Historic Pennsylvania Leaflet No. 24*. Pennsylvania Historical and Museum Commission. Harrisburg, Pa.

Hutson, James H. "The Campaign to Make Pennsylvania a Royal Province, 1764-1770." *Pennsylvania Magazine of History and Biography* 94 (1970): 427-63; 95 (1971):28-49.

Hutson, James H. "Benjamin Franklin and Pennsylvania Politics, 1751-1755: A Reappraisal." *Pennsylvania Magazine of History and Biography* 93 (1969):303-71.

———. "An Investigation of the Inarticulate: Philadelphia's White Oaks." *William and Mary Quarterly*, 3d ser. 29 (1972): 109-42.

Ketcham, Ralph H. "Conscience, War, and Politics in Pennsylvania, 1755-1757." *William and Mary Quarterly*, 3d ser. 20 (1963): 416-39.

Lyons, John F. "Thomson's Bible." *Journal of the Presbyterian Historical Society* 15 (1938-39):211-20.

Mood, Fulmer. "The Continental Congress and the Plan for a Library of Congress in 1782-1783." *Pennsylvania Magazine of History and Biography* 72 (1948):3-24.

Morgan, George. "The Colonial Origin of Newark Academy." *Delaware Notes*, 8th ser. (1934), pp. 7-30.

Newcomb, Benjamin H. "Effects of the Stamp Act on Colonial Pennsylvania Politics." *William and Mary Quarterly*, 3d ser. 23 (1966):257-72.

Pears, Thomas Clinton. "Francis Alison, Colonial Educator." *Delaware Notes*, 17th ser. (1944), pp. 9-22.

Phillips, Henry, Jr. "Early Proceedings of the American Philosophical Society." *American Philosophical Society Proceedings* 22 (1885):1-711.

Rawle, William B. "Laurel Hill, and Some Colonial Dames Who Once Lived There." *Pennsylvania Magazine of History and Biography* 35 (1911):385-414.

Roach, Hannah Benner, "Benjamin Franklin Slept Here." *Pennsylvania Magazine of History and Biography* 84 (1960):127-74.

Ryerson, R. A. "Political Mobilization and the American Revolution: The Resistance Movement in Philadelphia, 1765 to 1776." *William and Mary Quarterly*, 3d ser. 31 (1974):565-88.

Shelley, Fred. "Ebenezer Hazard: America's First Historical Editor." *William and Mary Quarterly*, 3d ser. 22 (1955):44-73.

Smith, Paul H. "Charles Thomson on Unity in the American Revolution." *The Quarterly Journal of the Library of Congress* 28 (1971):158-72.

Stone, Frederick D. "The Ordinances of 1787." *Pennsylvania Magazine of History and Biography* 8 (1889):309-40.

Straub, Jean S. "Teaching in the Friends' Latin School of Philadelphia in the Eighteenth Century." *Pennsylvania Magazine of History and Biography* 95 (1967):434-56.

Thayer, Theodore. "The Friendly Association." *Pennsylvania Magazine of History and Biography* 67 (1943):356-76.

Thomson, Charles. "An Essay on Indian Affairs." *Collections of the Historical Society of Pennsylvania* 1 (1853):80-85.

Vaux, George. "Settlers in Merion—The Harrison Family and Harriton Plantation." *Pennsylvania Magazine of History and Biography* 13 (1889):447-59.

Wainwright, Nicholas B. "Governor William Denny in Pennsylvania." *Pennsylvania Magazine of History and Biography* 81 (1957):170-98.

Zimmerman, John J. "Charles Thomson, 'The Sam Adams of Philadelphia.' " *The Mississippi Valley Historical Review* 45 (1958):464-80.

Dissertations, Theses, and Addresses

Hindle, Brooke. "The Rise of the American Philosophical Society, 1766-1787." Ph.D. dissertation, University of Pennsylvania, 1949.

Kneedler, Harry Lane. "Charles Thomson." Master's thesis, Temple University, 1940.

Lightfoot, Bill B. "A Time to Cast Away: The End of the Public Career of Charles Thomson." Read to the Missouri State Conference on History, 1968.

Lowrie, Sarah D. "Lest We Forget: A Study of the Life and Service of the Patriot Charles Thomson." An address to the Philadelphia Athanaeum, 1953.

Rolater, Frederick S. "Charles Thomson, Secretary of the Continental Congress." Master's thesis, University of Southern California, 1965.

———. "The Continental Congress: A Study in the Origin of American Public Administration, 1774-1781," Ph.D. dissertation, University of Southern California, 1970.

Vaux, George. "Were Charles Thomson's Remains Disturbed?" Paper presented to the Lower Merion Historical Society, 29 October 1956, in Ardmore, Pa.

Index